Latin America during World War II

Jaguar Books on Latin America Series
William Beezley and Colin MacLachlan, Series Editors

Latin America during World War II

Edited by
Thomas M. Leonard
and
John F. Bratzel

ROWMAN & LITTLEFIELD PUBLISHERS, INC.
Lanham • Boulder • New York • Toronto • Plymouth, UK

ROWMAN & LITTLEFIELD PUBLISHERS, INC.

Published in the United States of America
by Rowman & Littlefield Publishers, Inc.
A wholly owned subsidary of The Rowman & Littlefield Publishing Group, Inc.
4501 Forbes Boulevard, Suite 200, Lanham, Maryland 20706
www.rowmanlittlefield.com

Estover Road, Plymouth PL6 7PY, United Kingdom

British Library Cataloguing in Publication Information Available

Library of Congress Cataloging-in-Publication Data

Latin America during World War II / edited by Thomas M. Leonard and
John F. Bratzel.
    p.   cm.—(Jaguar books on Latin America series)
Includes bibliographical references and index.
ISBN-13: 978-0-7425-3740-8 (cloth : alk. paper)
ISBN-10: 0-7425-3740-4 (cloth : alk. paper)
ISBN-13: 978-0-7425-3741-5 (pbk. : alk. paper)
ISBN-10: 0-7425-3741-2 (pbk. : alk. paper)
    1. World War, 1939-1945—Latin America.   2. Latin America—History—
1898–1948.   I. Leonard, Thomas M., 1937–   II. Bratzel, John F.   III. Series:
Jaguar books on Latin America.
D768.18.L38   2007
940.53'8—dc22

                                                                    2006010909

Printed in the United States of America

♾ ™ The paper used in this publication meets the minimum requirements of
American National Standard for Information Sciences—Permanence of Paper for
Printed Library Materials, ANSI/NISO Z39.48-1992.

Contents

Preface

Despite the significant impact that World War II had upon Latin America, the story has yet to be fully told. The availability of new archival materials, personal papers, oral histories, and the like during the last generation has not yet brought about a scholarly and comprehensive study to update R. A. Humphries's fine two-volume 1981–1982 work, *Latin America and the Second World War*. Nor have scholars updated the two-generation-old texts by Conn, Engelman, and Fairchild on the U.S. Army's Latin American wartime strategies. Yet, using the new materials, scholars *have* produced an abundance of literature that focuses on Latin American political leaders at that time, their turn to the import substitution industrialization economic model, and, more recently, Nazi influence throughout the Western Hemisphere.

This volume addresses the void in the historical literature by drawing upon the expertise of those who have examined various facets of World War II in selected Latin American countries. In so doing, this volume provides the reader with a greater appreciation of the total impact the war had upon Latin America.

The studies in this volume examine seven individual countries (Argentina, Brazil, Chile, the Dominican Republic, Mexico, Panama, and Peru); two regions (Central America—Costa Rica, El Salvador, Guatemala, Honduras, and Nicaragua—and the Bolivarian nations of Colombia, Ecuador, and Venezuela); and one territory (Puerto Rico). The breadth of coverage provides for an understanding of the war's impact upon the different societies of Latin America.

As originally conceived, the contributors were asked to focus upon a common set of questions for each polity:

- How did the country, region, or territory respond to the outbreak of war in Europe in 1939 and the events leading to the global conflict that erupted in December 1941?

- After that date, what were its policies toward the Axis?
- How did it deal with the internal Axis threat?
- Did it cooperate with the Allies in a particular fashion?
- What were the responses to the economic and social dislocations caused by the war?

In an effort to avoid placing constraints upon the contributors, the United States was deliberately left out of this equation.

As John Bratzel explains in the introduction and the reader will experience throughout the volume, the answers to these questions vary significantly for each country. The reader will also discover that U.S. policies contributed to the war's impact upon each Latin American nation.

For readers wanting to explore Latin America's World War II experience further, the bibliography at the conclusion of this volume presents the most salient literature on the subject. For those who wish to conduct further research on the Latin American experience, the same bibliography provides notations on the availability and extent of archival materials, and the constraints placed upon them, across Latin America and elsewhere.

Many individuals made this volume possible. William Beezley and Richard Hopper, originally at Scholarly Resources, accepted the proposal for this work. Following Rowman and Littlefield Publishers' acquisition of Scholarly Resources, the editorial director for history, area studies, and geography, Ms. Susan McEachern, and her staff brought the project to its completion. Importantly, the historical value of the volume rests with the expertise of each contributing author who took time from their own work to prepare these essays.

1

Introduction

John F. Bratzel

World War II is aptly named because it was truly a global event. The war affected the whole world. Even citizens and countries in regions where no fighting took place or that were not central to the actual war had their society and their history significantly altered. The Latin American states are in this group. Each nation had to respond in its own way to World War II. Some nations that were notably more successful than others took advantage of their unique positions and made good decisions. When the war ended, some of these nations had improved themselves economically, some militarily; some had developed a new sense of nationhood, and some had new, more democratic governments. Other states, however, squandered the opportunity the war provided. Domestic discord was often the problem, but other factors such as location, economy, politics, and social structure left these Latin American states in a difficult position.

To comprehend events in Latin America during the war, an understanding of the U.S. role and view of the war is essential. Fundamentally, the United States saw World War II as a battle between good and evil. If a nation was not demonstrably supportive of the United States, then that nation was deemed by most U.S. policy makers to be in league with the Axis powers. This way of thinking was particularly true in the case of Latin America. For that region, uncooperative nations were seen not as opponents with their own interests, but almost as traitors.

This vision of Latin America comes out of a long history of U.S.–Latin American relationships that saw the region as similar and kindred, yet also strange, exotic, and different. The United States wanted to help Latin America, but could not quite figure out how to do it. At one moment, the

United States wanted to lead the hemisphere, while at others, isolationism and fear of the unknown caused the United States to shrink from seriously confronting the realities of the region.

THE UNITED STATES BACKDROP

The Good Neighbor Policy, 1932–1935: Nonintervention and Reciprocal Trade

The history of U.S. intervention in Latin America had been both extensive and generally unsuccessful. Latin American resentment against U.S. economic control and power was high, but it was the military interventions in Latin America that, more than anything else, crystallized widespread anti-U.S. feeling. The image of the U.S. military patrolling the streets of Latin American states created considerable ill will. While it is true that the invading Marines brought temporary stability, national elements quickly insisted that the Yankees must go home. Eventually, this is exactly what did happen. In most cases, the United States left relatively well established—even if not totally representative—governments, but subsequent political wrangling mixed with corruption inevitably obviated any long-term success. Nevertheless, despite continual failures, Charles Evans Hughes, the leader of the U.S. delegation at the 1928 Inter-American meeting held in Havana, defended intervention. Hughes claimed that "a government is fully justified in taking action . . . for the purpose of protecting the lives and property of its nationals."

During the administration of President Herbert Hoover, the Department of State retreated from Hughes's blunt assertion. It was not, however, until Franklin Roosevelt took office and proclaimed the "Good Neighbor Policy" that the United States—at least for a while—agreed to retreat from intervention. At Montevideo in December 1933 during the Seventh International Conference of American States, Secretary of State Cordell Hull publicly agreed to abandon direct intervention in the Americas. Hull also indicated that he was willing to begin negotiations on reciprocal trade agreements.

The United States' willingness to adopt nonintervention was based on a history of failed interventions such as in Nicaragua, a growing sense that interference was morally wrong, and most importantly, the domestic demands of the Great Depression. Moreover, when the Good Neighbor Policy was promulgated, the U.S. economy was in shambles, unemployment was extremely high, and there was no social safety net to ameliorate the crushing effects of the economic downturn. The Roosevelt administration had neither the readily available resources nor the inclination to deal with problems in Latin America. FDR made the best of his reluctance to become involved in interventionist adventures and offered a positive cast to the policy he wanted to follow anyway. In the process, he gained at least temporary plaudits from Latin American leaders.

Certainly Latin Americans wanted a noninterventionist United States, but they also wanted easy access to U.S. markets. Latin America applauded Cordell Hull's offer to begin negotiating reciprocal trade agreements. Shortly thereafter, the U.S. Congress passed laws under which these agreements could be structured. Many Latin Americans believed that access to U.S. markets had finally been achieved. The reciprocal trade agreements, as finally delineated by the United States, however, were not what most of the Latin American nations wanted. Hull insisted on nondiscrimination in tariffs and in the regulation of foreign exchange, while most of the Latin American nations wanted bilateral agreements that would allow them to maintain an equal balance of payments with the United States. Moreover, Hull did not have a free hand to negotiate. Powerful domestic interests were adamant about maintaining protectionist duties and rules against competing Latin American products. Ultimately, the reciprocal trade plan of the United States did not meet the desires of most Latin American states.

Nations that failed to reach an accord with the United States, such as Argentina and Chile, found the negotiations to be difficult and ultimately unrewarding. The strident protectionist objections voiced in the U.S. Congress were reported in great detail in Latin America and not only did most countries in the region not gain access to U.S. markets but they felt insulted as well. Indeed, it can reasonably be argued that the reciprocal trade program did considerable damage to the standing of the United States in Latin America.

The Good Neighbor Policy, 1935–1942: Unifying the New World against the Axis

Diplomacy

Anger over the reciprocal trade program would take a few years to develop, but even without the ill will that was growing over trade, international events would cause the United States to redefine the Good Neighbor Policy. By 1935–36, fascism was growing in Europe, and Japan was becoming increasingly aggressive. The United States therefore redefined the new Good Neighbor Policy; it would now be based on the principle of unifying the New World against foreign foes under the leadership of the United States.

Not all of Latin America, however, was amenable to such a change. Argentina, in particular, saw its future with Europe. Moreover, the United States was unwilling to sign trade agreements with Argentina for its beef and grain. At the 1936 Buenos Aires meeting, Argentina challenged U.S. leadership and insisted that Latin America not be controlled by the agenda of the United States.

The tension revealed in Buenos Aires would continue through a series of meetings of the American states aimed at dealing with the increasingly tense situation in Europe and the Far East, and ultimately with the start of hostilities in Europe. When Germany invaded Poland and war broke out in Europe in September 1939, the United States called for a neutrality cordon around itself and Latin America, and this was adopted at Panama in 1939. Then, after France and the Netherlands fell to the Germans, the United States, at Havana in 1940, promoted a general agreement among the Latin American states that French and Dutch holdings in the New World would not fall under Nazi control. Argentina opposed the United States on this and raised the possibility that these territories would become U.S. colonies.

U.S. anger with Argentina was further exacerbated following the Japanese attack on Pearl Harbor. Washington wanted all the nations of the New World that had not already done so to break relations with the Axis. At the 1942 Foreign Ministers Conference held in Rio de Janeiro, Argentina and Chile refused. They insisted upon, and ultimately achieved, a watered-down final communiqué in which the foreign ministers only recommended breaking relations with the Axis nations. Argentina did not withdraw its ambassador from Germany, Italy, or Japan.

Economics and Politics

The United States was also intent on blunting the Axis economic penetration. Before the war, the Germans used bilateral trade agreements to insure that the balance of payments between themselves and any Latin American nation would be equal. Latin America looked positively toward this policy, and German trade with nations such as Mexico, Argentina, and Brazil soared. Given the domestic politics of the day, there was little the United States could do, but with the beginning of hostilities in Europe in September 1939, German ships could no longer get to Latin America, and trade collapsed.

The United States was also intent on ending the various airlines that were dominated by the Germans or Italians in Latin America. The United States saw these airlines as courier planes bringing information, spies, and essential war products back and forth to Latin America. Eventually, these airlines were pushed out by the United States (their fates are detailed in the various chapters) and replaced for the most part by Pan American World Airways.

Border conflicts were also a source of distress for the United States. To gain a unified New World, squabbles and problems would have to be solved quickly. One concern was the Chaco Peace Conference aimed at ending the Chaco War between Paraguay and Bolivia. Argentina's foreign minister,

Carlos Saavedra Lamas, effectively stymied the negotiations while the United States argued strongly that they should move expeditiously to end the conflict. It was not until 1938 that a final peace accord was reached. There was also considerable discord between Peru and Ecuador over their unclear boundaries. In July 1941, Peruvian and Ecuadorian troops clashed in the disputed territory. Peru subsequently used the U.S. desire for calm and unity in Latin America to pressure Ecuador into signing a boundary agreement.

Another vexing problem was the seizure of the oil industries by Bolivia in 1937 and Mexico in 1938. In the case of Mexico, in particular, there were calls for a U.S. invasion to take back the oil and to deal with the anticlerical attitude of the Mexican government. The United States never seriously considered such an invasion, but tensions were nevertheless very high between the two nations. What the oil companies demanded in compensation for their seized oil property was far in excess of what Mexico offered. With war likely—and, in the case of Mexico, growing trade with Germany—the U.S. government insisted the issue be solved expeditiously. A few weeks after the Japanese attack on Pearl Harbor, the two sides reached an agreement. Much the same thing happened in Bolivia; the war created the urgency that led to a final settlement.

Creating an Espionage and Counterespionage Establishment

Besides aiding the British, Roosevelt also started preparing the United States for war. Whether Latin America would be the scene of actual fighting was not clear, but what was certain was that there would be at the very least a shadow war, a battle between espionage services of the Allies and Axis for information and influence with the Latin American states.

The problem was that the United States did not have a well-developed espionage or counterespionage service. The lack of training and experience of U.S. counterespionage forces had their roots in the 1920s. Following World War I, Secretary of State Henry Stimson ended U.S. intelligence efforts with the oft-quoted statement: "Gentlemen do not read each other's mail."[1] The "no espionage" dictum was sustainable in the 1920s and early 1930s, but by the mid-1930s, U.S. concern about the threat of German influence caused a rethinking of the previous "no-eavesdropping" policy.

In 1936, the number of military attachés in Latin America was increased and the Office of Naval Intelligence (ONI) was given the task of "protection against subversive activities inimical to the national defense." Moreover, naval attachés were given permission to disperse money for intelligence information. Typical of the confusion that marked early U.S. intelligence efforts, Army intelligence was not allowed to buy information.[2]

Overcoming inexperience is difficult, but the bureaucratic contest that developed, especially after 1939, to control intelligence aggravated an already complicated situation. Clearly, control of counterintelligence for the U.S. government would be critical to the status and budget of the agency gaining dominance. Moreover, the people in these agencies wanted to contribute and believed that they could succeed. Roosevelt realized this, and ordered George Messersmith to establish some sort of system to delineate and regulate activities. As Messersmith relates it, Roosevelt was concerned that ONI, the Military Intelligence Division (MID), and the Federal Bureau of Investigation (FBI) "were often following the same matter at the same time and constantly crossing each other's tracks." He also noted that the Secret Service, Treasury agents, and the Department of State were also becoming involved.[3]

Messersmith suspected the task was hopeless, commenting that investigation agencies were "more zealous" in protecting their agencies than in rooting out spies and that "no one trusted the other"—but he nevertheless tried. By early 1940, Messersmith reported that the situation was well in hand.[4] This assertion, however, is fanciful because the various agencies and departments were still building separate, competing, and generally uncooperative counterespionage organizations.

The consequence of the uncoordinated U.S. counterespionage network was a great many inaccurate reports. Ambassador to Argentina Norman Armour, for example, forwarded to Washington in January 1941 a list of Nazi agents he had purchased from an unimpeachable source for four hundred pesos. In his transmittal letter, Armour told Washington that the informant was "so certain of his source that he gave an unconditional money-back guarantee in case they [the names] prove to be false." It is not clear whether Armour ever followed up on the guarantee, but he should have. According to postwar records, not a single name listed was ever an espionage agent for the Germans.[5]

A lengthy MID missive, this one sent in March 1941, detailed the "Nazi organization in Argentina." The memo talked about the "Assault Troops" and "Storm Troops." It also lists the chief of the cavalry, infantry, and aviation sections. The document is quite detailed, but all the information is wrong except for one piece: it states that German military attaché Gunter Niedenfuhr was acting as an agent for Germany.[6] Of course, discovering that a military attaché is gathering information for his country is hardly an espionage coup.

Obviously, not every report sent to Washington was inaccurate. In fact, the FBI in particular did a good job of tracking down actual German spies after the Federal Communications Commission identified transmitter locations through triangulation. The FBI's problem was not catching Nazi agents but rather the incredible overstatements and puffery contained in its reports and analysis.

While it is true that intelligence materials are often in error, the level of inaccuracy in these dispatches—particularly since in almost every case each message indicates that the information is entirely reliable—points to a mixture of overzealousness to stop the Axis with inexperience and ambition. Missing from these messages were any cautious statements suggesting that only portions or elements of the society and government supported the Germans or had fascist sympathies. Worse, distinctions were seldom drawn between being pro-Axis and being anti-U.S.—or, more probably, nationalistic.

FDR Uses Concern about Latin America to Aid the United Kingdom

As it turned out, Latin America was not central to the U.S. war effort. With the England's victory in the Battle of Britain, the ability of the Germans to project their power and threaten Latin America diminished. But in the first years of the war, Latin America seemed vulnerable to Axis efforts, and FDR used this concern as the basis for policies intended to buttress Great Britain against Germany.

Despite the tension between some of the Latin American nations and the United States, the majority of people in the United States believed that Latin America must be defended. Culturally, Pan-Americanism was growing, and moreover, the American people believed that U.S. security and the U.S. economy were tied to control of the Panama Canal. Military leaders also saw the "bulge" of Brazil, the Brazilian Northeast, as critical to hemispheric defense to stop an imagined German invasion from North Africa.

Following the declaration of war in Europe in September 1939, for example, a mere 5 percent of the U.S. people was agreeable to sending the U.S. Army and Navy to fight Germany. When asked about Cuba, however, fully 72 percent indicated that the United States should fight to protect that neighboring island. Indeed, fully 53 percent of the U.S. populace was willing to send troops to help defend "Brazil or Chile or any other South American country." By June 1940, 84 percent of Americans answered affirmatively to the question, "If Germany defeats the Allies, should the United States fight if necessary to keep Germany out of the British, French, and Dutch possessions located in the area of the Panama Canal?" In subsequent surveys, the percentage of yes answers increased. By comparison, at about the same time, only 17 percent of respondents in the United States were willing to aid the British against Germany.[7]

President Roosevelt used the willingness of the American people to protect Latin America to his advantage. In August 1940, Great Britain was standing by itself against Germany and the survival of that country was not a surety. In order to help the British, Roosevelt decided to sell England fifty old destroyers, and at about the same time, England agreed to lease bases to the United States that appeared to be useful in protecting the Panama Canal. FDR claimed that there was no relationship between the sale of the destroyers and the willingness of Great Britain to lease the bases. Nevertheless, the juxtaposition of the two developments suggests that FDR knew what would mollify U.S. critics.

The same situation occurred again in the summer of 1941. The hard-pressed British could not afford to garrison Iceland, and the United States agreed to replace them. That this should occur is not strange, but what is strange is the claim that Iceland was supposedly being occupied to protect the Panama Canal. As *Time* magazine put it, "The Western Hemisphere had stretched once more."[8]

FDR made this ludicrous statement because he knew that protecting the canal was popular. At least a few people got a laugh out of FDR's sense of geography. The acting head of the Panamanian Consulate in San Francisco, Guillermo Benedetti, wrote rather incredulously to President Arnulfo Arias, "Yesterday came in the news of the invasion of Iceland by US troops and today they [the Roosevelt Administration] found a geography professor who says that Iceland is part of the Americas."[9]

The British also knew that the FDR wanted to emphasize the threat to Latin America, and so they put their forgers to work supplying him with material to make his case with the U.S. people. It is not strange then that a map detailing the countries of South America following a Nazi victory should magically fall into Roosevelt's hands. FDR talked about it with reporters, but never let them see it. He claimed it would have revealed secret sources, but one wonders if he had doubts about whether the map would stand up to serious scrutiny.[10]

The United States viewed the war as a battle between good and evil. If a person or a country opposed the agenda of the United States, their reasons were not important; the only important factor was their opposition to the United States in its crusade against the Axis. Nations had to demonstrate that they actively supported the United States; anything less was unacceptable. This type of thinking colored all aspects of U.S. policy and resulted in many misunderstandings with Latin American nations.

LATIN AMERICA RESPONDS
TO WORLD WAR II

How the nations of Latin America responded to World War II was determined by geography, internal politics, intra–Latin American relations, economic factors, history, and a host of other variables. While each nation responded differently, it is still possible to see patterns in their responses.

Geography

Geography was a determining factor in what happened in the various Latin American states. Brazil gained economic and military benefits from the United States because northeastern Brazil was strategically placed to allow for patrolling between Brazil and Africa and as a ferry point for U.S.-made airplanes bound for the fighting. It was also seen as a possible German invasion route that needed to be garrisoned. Rio de Janeiro was able to broker highly favorable treaties with the United States in exchange for granting U.S. landing rights in Natal and Fortaleza.

Geography also privileged those nations near the Panama Canal, including Colombia, Peru, the Dominican Republic, Ecuador (and the Galapagos Islands), the U.S. territory of Puerto Rico, and, of course, Panama itself. It was considerably easier to convince the U.S. government to supply aid to nations the United States might need in the future for the defense of the canal. All made use of their strategic position to insist upon concessions from the United States.

The Axis Establishment in Latin America

At the beginning of World War II, fascism was seen as a positive alternative by some Latin American leaders and groups that were profoundly impressed by the governments of Adolf Hitler and Benito Mussolini. Rafael Trujillo, for example, the dictator of the Dominican Republic, admired Hitler for his style and his militaristic rallies. Similar views were held by Jorge Ubico in Guatemala and Maximiliano Hernández Martínez in El Salvador. In Brazil, Argentina, Chile, and elsewhere, the strong sense of unity and purpose created by fascism was quite attractive. Each of these nations had an influential fascist political party. Brazil's *Integralistas* dressed in jackboots and green, military-style shirts and were open admirers of Mussolini's Italy.

Not only were the politics of fascism attractive, but the Germans also enjoyed growing economic penetration using strict binational trade agreements to ensure that the economic relationship with various Latin American nations would be equal. Brazil, Mexico, Guatemala, Costa Rica, and the Dominican Republic all had trade agreements with Germany. Brazil's trade with Germany, for example, doubled from 1933 to 1938. With the start of the war, however, Axis ships could no longer cross the Atlantic, and trade with Germany and Italy effectively ended. Losing a major trading partner obviously hurt some of the Latin American states. In most cases, the only nation that could replace the Axis trade was the United States.

Wartime Trade between Latin America and the United States

As a result, most nations suddenly found that they were dependent on the United States for trade. This was true of the Dominican Republic, Mexico,

Chile, Brazil, Peru, Argentina, Venezuela, and all the Central American nations. Moreover, the U.S. need for particular products during the war further distorted trade. The United States, for example, wanted all of Colombia's production of platinum, all of Peru's cotton, and all of Chile's copper. Set prices were agreed upon, often with a high premium, but these nations also lost their ability to bargain and trade in the open market. Shortages of consumer goods and other products was also a problem. The demands of war production in the United States and a shortage of shipping meant goods were simply not available and prices for what did exist increased. Central America, in particular, suffered as a result of this shortage. Gasoline and oil products were difficult to find and very expensive, and food shortages appeared in the cities. Ultimately, this resulted in inflation in Latin America during World War II.

One of the nations that did not use the war to its long-term benefit was Peru. That country placed price controls on products, which meant that its foreign reserves did not increase as much as those of other nations, and Peru lost badly needed capital. Argentina, despite its contentious relationship with the United States, did very well as trade increased rapidly. Panama also benefited economically and prospered because of increased traffic through the canal and the concomitant demand for goods from ships transiting the isthmus. Puerto Rico was aided by Europe's inability to supply liquor. Puerto Rican rum now had few competitors.

Mexico and Venezuela both were aided by the high price of oil. Mexico used this commodity to force a deal on its terms to settle its dispute with U.S. and European oil producers for its seizure of oil in 1938. Moreover, during the war, President Manuel Ávila Camacho capitalized on the situation to improve Mexico's bargaining position with the United States.

Military Aid to Latin America

Without doubt, Brazil economically benefited the most of any Latin American nation during World War II. New favorable trade treaties were signed with Washington and the United States offered loans, but of more importance, the drop in competition in manufacturing spurred industry in Brazil.

Brazil's willingness to work in tandem with the United States, and its location, meant that it did well in gaining access to military equipment. Three-quarters of the Lend-Lease arms and support went to Brazil. Ecuador received military aid, but mainly for the building of an air base in the Galapagos. Colombia used the war to modernize its army with the aim of participating in the defense of the Panama Canal. The Dominican Republic also modernized its forces, particularly the air force.

Two nations actually participated in the fighting. Both Mexico and Brazil sent soldiers to fight in the war. Brazil sent a division to Italy, while Mexico contributed a squadron of fighter planes to the war in the Pacific. For both countries, one of the goals of sending forces was to insure a significant place in the peace discussions that would follow the end of the war.

In contrast to the nations noted above, Argentina and Chile received very little military aid, because neither nation would follow the U.S. demand that they cut off dealings at all levels with the Axis. Peru received some aid, but as the war shifted in 1943, it became clear that the west coast of South America had lost any claim to strategic significance, and Peru lost its immediate justification for Lend-Lease weaponry. Central America suffered much the same fate as Peru. By 1943 the Pan-American Highway, which the United States was building for defensive purposes, ceased to be a priority, and work on the road as well as military aid stopped.

Intra–Latin American Relations

In many Latin American nations, World War II rekindled old rivalries and tensions because the shipment of Lend-Lease aid changed the balance of power. Chile, for example, was very concerned about its lack of Lend-Lease weapons, not out of fear of an Axis attack but because it was concerned that Bolivia and Peru might use their newly acquired Lend-Lease aid against Chile to reset boundaries established many years earlier after the War of the Pacific. Ecuador was also very concerned about Peru, because Peru had recently occupied disputed territory and had used the U.S. desire for a calm and secure southern flank to force an unfavorable peace settlement on Ecuador. As a result, Ecuador was very willing to have the United States base troops in the Galapagos because it offered some insurance that the United States would be positively disposed toward Ecuador. Finally, for many years, Argentina had seen itself as the leader of South America, but the war brought new and sophisticated weaponry to its rival, Brazil, while Argentina received nothing. Indeed, Juan Perón came to power partially by claiming that he could redress this change in military status.

The Challenge of Espionage and Axis populations

Almost all Latin American nations had to respond to Axis espionage activity in Central and South America. Mexico, and to a lesser extent Brazil, cooperated with the United States in shutting down Axis cells. Chile and Argentina, however, allowed German espionage activity to continue much longer than the other nations. This was a source of considerable discord between those two nations and the United States.

Many of the Latin American states also had to deal with Axis nationals and individuals of Axis heritage living in their countries. For example, there were more than a million Germans living in Brazil, mostly southern Brazil. Chile also had a large and economically important German population. Peru had a significant number of Japanese residents. Each nation had to respond to the U.S. desire to control these populations, or to at the very least break their power. The reactions of the Latin American nations varied, with resistance to U.S. entreaties often based on the status of the group in the country in question. Some chose to close schools and cultural associations, but others, at the behest of the United States, interned citizens and, in some cases, those interned were sent to the United States. This was true for both Germans and Japanese who had been residing in Central America. The same fate awaited individuals from the Dominican Republic and Peru. In the latter case, Japanese-Peruvians (and lesser numbers from other Latin American nations) were selected in a haphazard manner and shipped off to camps in Texas and other parts of the United States. In most cases, these individuals lost their property, were ultimately deported to Japan, and were not allowed to return to Peru once the war ended.

The Spanish and Italian inhabitants did not elicit as strong a reaction as the Germans and Japanese. Clearly, the FBI was worried about the Spanish residents of Puerto Rico, for example, but it generally ignored a similar population in Chile. Peru, so intent on interning the Japanese, paid almost no attention to its Italian minority.

Governmental Change

Latin America was profoundly affected by World War II governmentally as well. The stresses caused by the war magnified the problems that already existed, while at the same time requiring new ideas and policies to deal with rapidly changing developments. In Mexico and Brazil, this resulted in increased power for the central government. Ávila Camacho in Mexico used the war to expand his agrarian-based political party to include industrial workers. In Brazil, Getúlio Dornelles Vargas was able to increase his power by claiming that the war required him to have emergency powers.

The drumbeat of constant Allied propaganda calling for democracy and an end to fascism and dictators also had an effect. Internal commentary also fostered this ideal. Latin American citizens began to demand that their nations also become democratic, and this led to political changes. In Brazil, Vargas's fascist-style dictatorship lost the support of the citizenry and, more importantly, the army; as a result, elections were held at the end of the war. In Central America, a growing belief among the middle and upper classes that dictators were not acceptable meant that all the governments that existed at the start the war were forced out by 1945. The only exception was Honduras, where the local leader refused military aid so that the army did not gain in power, organization, and prestige.

In Peru, the demand for good government came as a result of the squabbling among the generals who had led troops in the battle with Ecuador. All wished to become president, but they contended with each other in a manner that lost them the support of an army that was trying to become more professional. The military coup that resulted set the stage for other military governments in that country.

A review of the various nations reveals that each dealt with the war differently and that some were much more successful than others. Chilean neutrality cost the country in terms of weapons, finances, and goodwill. Brazil's close cooperation with the United States became the principal characteristic of Brazil's diplomacy and military policy in World War II. Argentina planned to follow the same policy as it had in World War I, but changes in the world and an unwillingness of the part of the United States to understand Argentina's position caused considerable, long-lasting ill will. Colombia, Ecuador, and Venezuela all used their particular assets, geographic and economic, to gain what they wanted out of the war. Colombia wished to remain sovereign in the face of terrific power, Ecuador wanted safety from Peruvian attacks, and Venezuela used its oil to gain royalty concessions.

NOTES

1. See Henry L. Stimson and McGeorge Bundy, *On Active Service in Peace and War* (New York: Harper, 1948), 60–61.

2. National Archives and Record Administration (hereafter referred to as NARA), Record Group 165, War Department, General and Specific Staffs, Decimal file 2610-2-38 (1), #5750, August 26, 1939, 1–2.

3. George E. Messersmith Papers, Special Collections, University of Delaware Library, Newark, Delaware, #2018, 1–6.

4. Messersmith Papers.

5. NARA, Record Group 59, General Records of the Department of State Department (hereafter referred to as RG 59), Decimal file 862.20210/388, January 1, 1941. Armour to Department of State.

6. NARA, RG 59, Decimal File 862.20235/449. *Report on Nazi Organization in Argentina*, March 13, 1941

7. These statistics are found in American Institute of Public Opinion, "Gallup Poll Reports," *Public Opinion Quarterly*, October 6, 1939, 184; June 7, 1940, 227; and July 22, 1941, 233.

8. *Time*, July 14, 1941, 11.

9. Many thanks to Prof. Graeme Mount of Laurentian University and his research assistant Roch Carrier, who were willing to share their research notes from the Arnulfo Arias Papers in the Panamanian National Archives with me. Mount and Carrier indicate that this quote can be found in a letter from Benedetti to Arias dated July 8, 1941 in box 1, file 1, of the Arias papers.

10. Leslie B. Rout and John F. Bratzel, "FDR and World War II: The South American Map Case," *Woodrow Wilson Quarterly* 9, no. 1 (January 1985): 167–73.

I

CENTRAL AMERICA
DURING WORLD WAR II

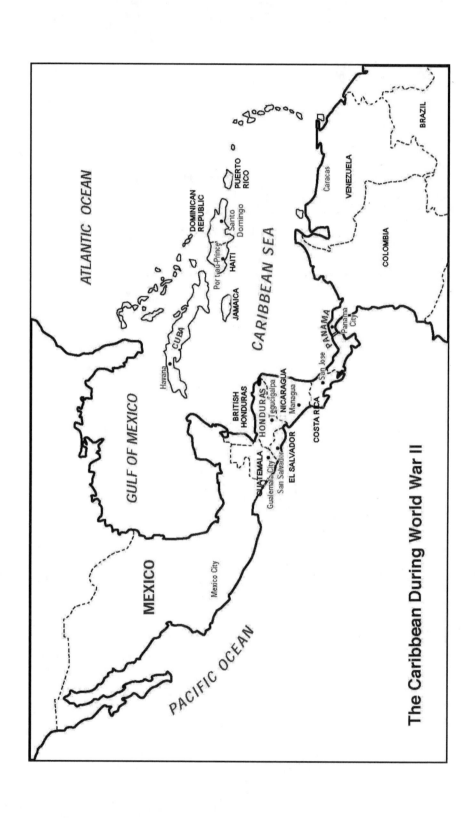

The Caribbean During World War II

2

Mexico: Industrialization through Unity

Monica Rankin

As World War II began, Mexico was finally recovering from decades of revolutionary turmoil. The outbreak of the Revolution in 1910 had plunged the country into a long period of violence and internal division from which it was only beginning to surface in the late 1930s. The world war coincided with an era in which the Mexican government had subdued much of the country's revolutionary fervor and when government officials began to reconsider the direction the Revolution would take. World War II provided the opportunity for the first time since the Revolution for Mexican officials to unify the country and to modernize and industrialize the economy. Through a combination of policy and propaganda, President Manuel Ávila Camacho put together a wartime program that allowed him to unite the country against a common, external enemy and to pursue an aggressive industrialization program. The president also entered into strategic agreements with the United States to facilitate industrial development. By the end of the war, Mexican and U.S. commercial interests diverged, though, as Ávila Camacho implemented protectionist measures and used the industrial foundation established during the war to continue a domestic industrialization program. Most importantly, World War II allowed him to justify an industrialization program in the context of the Mexican Revolution.

Between 1934 and 1940, Mexico entered an era of implementing revolutionary reforms and redefining the nation during Lázaro Cárdenas's administration (1934–40). For Mexicans, the 1930s became a time of recovery and consolidation after decades of internal fighting and continued violence.

17

Between 1910 and 1940, the Revolution had come to have different meanings for different participants.[1] Many sought a way to justify the conflict, while ensuring that their own notions of what the Revolution meant became a part of national identity.

As a result, the Mexican government did not articulate a clear war policy before 1940. The nation had observed the growing hostilities in Europe, but the Cárdenas administration publicly remained officially neutral. Instead, special interest groups dominated the information campaign and the political debate. Responding to international political trends, many Mexicans began to understand Fascism and Communism through the perspective of their national experiences. As the debate between the followers of the two doctrines escalated in Europe, many Mexicans responded by identifying with one or the other. Those ideologies quickly became a part of the nation's political debate.

In Europe, the Spanish Civil War became the first open war between the ideologies that were dividing the continent in the 1930s. The political and social conflict in Spain closely mirrored Mexico's own internal disputes following the 1910 Revolution, and many Mexicans identified with the struggle and began taking sides. As Mexicans learned of the civil war, some recalled the ideological divisions that had emerged in their own revolution and saw the Spanish Civil War as a possible preview of their future. For Mexico's Left, the war in Spain became a symbol of the working-class struggle against Fascism. Leftist leaders such as Vicente Lombardo Toledano associated Mexico's struggle for social justice with the Spanish Republicans' fight against Falangist Fascism. The new national labor union, the Confederación de Trabajadores de México (CTM), raised money and support for the Republicans by asking workers to show their solidarity for Spain's social struggle. Workers identified with "comrade worker militiamen of Spain" fighting against the dictators "who wish to muzzle the liberties of the proletariat."[2]

Mexican conservatives publicly challenged the Left's interpretation of the war. Capitalists, businessmen, Catholics, and middle-class Mexicans who opposed many of the reforms implemented by the revolutionary government sided with the Spanish Falange.[3] The ideological extremes clashed in the Mexican press between 1936 and 1938. Their debate further intensified as thousands of Spanish refugees began arriving in Mexico.[4] Conflict in Spain began to subside in 1938, however, as the spotlight shifted farther east.

Germany's annexation of Austria in the spring of 1938 focused public attention on German and Italian aggression. The invasion and subsequent Nazi belligerence provoked intense debate in Mexico's press. Prior to the annexation, the mainstream Mexican press had paid little attention to Germany's activities in Europe. Throughout 1938, German propagandists began working to manipulate editorials in mainstream newspapers and win support among the Mexican public. German propaganda agent Arthur Dietrich and his staff subsidized Mexican newspapers, and in exchange, editors printed material favorable to the Axis. U.S. military intelligence reports in 1939 indicated that many of the country's most popular newspapers and magazines received large sums of money every month from a bank account that had been traced to the German military attaché in Washington.[5] In particular, the two most widely read Mexico City dailies, *Excelsior* and *El Universal*, were believed to be receiving large subsidies.

The Cárdenas administration remained publicly neutral on the events unfolding in Europe. The president was forced to play a diplomatic balancing act after the government expropriated the oil industry in March 1938. U.S. oil companies that had lost their property in the expropriation pressured U.S. president Franklin D. Roosevelt to force Mexico to pay steep reparations. The companies engaged in a boycott that cut off Mexican oil from its traditional markets. At the same time, the U.S. press initiated an anti-Mexico public relations campaign through editorials.[6] In 1939 Standard Oil Company sponsored the publication of a book by Burt McConnell, *Mexico at the Bar of Public Opinion*, that told the story of the expropriation of U.S. oil properties using editorials from U.S. periodicals. The book offered a scathing critique of Cárdenas, the Revolution, and Mexican national character. It emphasized the socialist inclinations of the Cárdenas government, and at the same time accused Mexico of becoming Fascist because of its economic dealings with Germany.[7]

The U.S. oil boycott forced Cárdenas to look to the Axis for potential markets, and censoring Axis propaganda would have threatened the tenuous economic relationship he was desperately trying to maintain. By 1940, new understandings of Nazi aggression and new opportunities for a resolution with the United States brought with them new concerns, demands, and expectations. U.S. officials wanted assurances that Mexico was not becoming a haven for Axis saboteurs. At the same time, Mexico's mainstream press changed its approach to wartime coverage. Periodicals such as *Excelsior* and *El Universal* were still extremely critical of the United States, but they also had become alarmed by the rapidity with which Germany seemed to be overpowering most of Western Europe—advances that indicated that the Nazis were becoming the new imperialist world power.

Some periodicals also began to express their own concerns about Nazi Fifth Column activities in the Western Hemisphere, and they gradually began to acknowledge the need for Mexico to ally itself formally with the United States in the war. Some reports even expressed concern that Cárdenas was not capable of controlling subversive Fascist elements within Mexico.[8]

The extent of the Axis influence in Mexico is shown in a government report issued in May 1940, which indicated that Nazi agents had been active in Mexico for several years and had established a sophisticated network of propaganda and espionage. Given the extent of U.S. pressure, the German advances in Europe, and the extent of German influence in his own country, on June 11, 1940, Cárdenas declared that Mexico officially supported the U.S. pro-Allied efforts in place at the time, including supplying vital weapons and other materials to the Allied powers. At the same time, Mexico's Ministry of Foreign Affairs declared the German propaganda mastermind Dietrich persona non grata and forced him to leave the country. After Dietrich's expulsion, Axis propaganda faced its first official challenge from the Mexican government. Spanish Falangists quickly stepped in to fulfill Dietrich's mission, but the influence of Axis propaganda received a severe blow.[9] Cárdenas's actions moved Mexico closer to the Allied cause.

PRELUDE TO PEARL HARBOR

While Cárdenas dealt with oil issues and Nazi saboteurs in 1940, the country was also in the middle of a presidential campaign. Cárdenas chose a moderate candidate as his successor, and Manuel Ávila Camacho was inaugurated as Mexico's president in December. The Ávila Camacho administration pushed the country even closer to an official alliance with the United States. As German sedition became more of a threat, and as the government became more directly involved in swaying public opinion, the Mexican public became more sympathetic to the Allies.

The Japanese attack on Pearl Harbor on December 7, 1941, marked the definitive date when Mexico officially declared full support for the Allies, but the hostilities between Mexico and the Axis had escalated throughout 1941. As Hitler's armies enjoyed one military success after another in Europe, Mexicans followed those events in the country's national newspapers. President Ávila Camacho and many ordinary Mexicans became increasingly concerned with what they saw as a war of aggression, with Germany becoming an imperialistic power. By December 1941, Germany had effectively defeated all the major Western European powers with the exception of Great Britain, and defeat of the British seemed imminent. In Asia, China appeared on the verge of falling to the Japanese. World domination by totalitarian powers seemed to be the wave of the future.

Concerned with growing Axis hostility, the Mexican government gradually articulated publicly a pro-U.S. position. In a speech to Congress on March 8, 1941, Foreign Minister Ezequiel Padilla addressed the need for hemispheric cooperation. He connected the U.S. position in the war to Mexican national consciousness by urging Mexicans to embrace their destiny to fight for freedom. He also asserted that the Indian and mestizo populations would be oppressed by German racial policies.[10] Padilla went on to lead Mexico's diplomatic rapprochement with the United States and encouraged the public to mirror his actions with a democratic alliance at the popular level.

In April 1941, the Mexican government took even more aggressive action against Axis interests. Ávila Camacho allowed ten Italian and two German ships to seek asylum in the ports of Tampico and Veracruz. After the crew of one of the Italian ships, the *Atlas*, tried to sink the ship, Mexican officials seized the other eleven for suspicion of Axis subversion, citing the *Atlas* crew's actions as evidence of warlike activity. Hundreds of German and Italian sailors were sent to detention camps in Veracruz. Similar seizures occurred simultaneously in other Western Hemisphere countries, including the United States, Ecuador, Peru, and Venezuela.

The national press, under the considerable influence of a new U.S. propaganda agency (the Office of Inter-American Affairs or OIAA), backed the government's actions fully. The mainstream dailies reported that the actions of the *Atlas*'s crew proved that Axis powers were planning subversive activities in the country.[11] The nation's press also mirrored the government's emphasis on its rights of sovereignty and its responsibility to protect its citizens. Government rhetoric and the position of the press moved the country even closer to an alliance with the United States without presenting it as such. Instead, the government justified its actions in nationalistic terms of sovereignty and security.

On April 13, 1941, the Mexican government announced the signing of an agreement with the United States calling for reciprocal use of air bases in each country in the interest of mutual defense. Since Mexico did not have a significant air force, the agreement amounted to allowing U.S. forces to use Mexican air bases. This agreement augmented one signed earlier by Cárdenas that provided for U.S. assistance in training Mexican aviators.[12] The extreme Right and Fascist sympathizers reeled at this news. Beginning with these April events, Mexican relations with the Axis deteriorated during the rest of 1941.

Ávila Camacho signed the Douglas-Weichers Agreement on June 15, stipulating that Mexico would sell all its strategic mineral output to the United States. The agreement signaled Mexico's move away from trade with the Axis powers. The Douglas-Weichers Agreement became the first in a series of economic pacts between Mexico and the United States during and after the war. It laid the basis for Mexico's wartime economy, which shifted to producing industrial goods and raw materials for wartime consumption.

In July 1941, the United States increased its pressure on Mexico and all of Latin America to sever economic ties with the Axis powers. U.S. investigations concluded that many individuals and businesses throughout Latin America were Axis sympathizers and were involved in subversive activities. Names of 1,800 groups and individuals were compiled on blacklists and distributed throughout Latin America, along with notification that the subjects on the list were to be boycotted by U.S. businesses. The United States expected the other Latin American governments to engage in their own embargo of Axis-affiliated businesses.

At first, the Mexican government did not officially boycott the 181 Mexican persons and businesses included in the blacklists, but Ávila Camacho's administration did nothing to prevent the U.S. boycott. In fact, Foreign Minister Padilla declared that publication of the lists had been a defensive measure for the United States. Most Mexican periodicals gave scant attention to the blacklists. They published the lists, but generally without accompanying commentary. The press's silence ended abruptly, however, when the German consul sent a note of protest to the Ministry of Foreign Relations, urging the government to resist U.S. imperialism and not allow the boycott in Mexico.[13] Most news sources reacted sharply against Germany's attempt to interfere in Mexican–U.S. relations. They reported this protest as an affront to nationalism, and the blacklists quickly became a symbol of resisting German interference. *Excelsior* argued that no self-respecting nation would tolerate foreigners meddling in its internal affairs.

Mexico took additional action against Axis interests and moved closer to the Allies on August 22 by closing all German consulates and expelling its diplomatic corps. At the same time, Ávila Camacho recalled all Mexican diplomatic staff in those European areas occupied by Germany. One month later, the government passed a law to end Axis espionage activity and prevent further Axis strongholds in the country.

The antiespionage legislation in September coincided with German submarine attacks on U.S. civilian ships in the waters of the Western Hemisphere. Influenced by the United States, the Mexican press ignored the fact that the targeted ships had been carrying war materials. Instead, the newspapers reported these incidents as cruel attacks against a pacifist and neutral nation. They emphasized the damage inflicted to U.S. property and the numbers of civilian casualties. The reports elicited sympathy for the United States and enmity toward Germany.[14]

The German submarine attacks had important consequences on official relations between the United States and Mexico. In the early summer of 1941, the United States initiated an oil embargo against Japan, moving those two countries ever closer to open hostilities. As tensions escalated with both Germany and Japan, U.S. officials understood that it was only a matter of time before the United States was formally drawn into the war. With war on the horizon, the Roosevelt administration hastened to resolve the Mexican oil expropriation controversy and other claims that resulted from Mexico's agrarian reforms. Although Mexico had recently taken decisive measures against the Axis and a formal wartime alliance between the two nations was probable, Roosevelt could ill afford to leave the oil issue unresolved.

By November 1941, wartime exigencies had created a new sense of urgency for settling outstanding claims. U.S. leaders ultimately ignored oil company demands and reached a settlement that the oilmen perceived as favorable to Mexico. On November 19, the U.S. and Mexican governments agreed to the Global Settlement, whereby Mexico guaranteed payment of $40 million for agrarian and other general claims. Mexico's leaders also promised $9 million as a down payment on the oil company claims and agreed to allow a panel of experts to determine any additional compensation owed to them. In exchange, the U.S. government agreed to loan Mexico $40 million for fiscal stabilization and guaranteed future silver purchases. It promised an additional $30 million through an Export-Import Bank loan to improve the highway transportation system. Finally, the agreement paved the way for a reciprocal trade treaty between the two nations.[15]

The settlement represented a victory for Mexican nationalism. Under Cárdenas, Mexico had stood up to powerful economic interests in the United States and recuperated its economic sovereignty, while Ávila Camacho's government capitalized on the wartime climate to improve its bargaining power with the United States. But the settlement also advanced the United States' image. By ignoring oil company demands, the United States acted as a truly "good neighbor," intent on treating Mexico fairly. Furthermore, the Global Settlement did far more for winning Mexican support in the war effort than any direct propaganda campaign had so far achieved.[16]

PEARL HARBOR

On December 7, 1941, shock waves spread throughout the Western Hemisphere as Latin Americans reacted to the news that Japan had attacked Pearl Harbor. The reaction of the Ávila Camacho administration was swift and decisive. Most members of the cabinet were relaxing at their weekend retreats that Sunday afternoon. Telephones began to ring as news of the Japanese attack spread across Mexico. Government officials scrambled to confirm the news with the U.S. embassy and met to coordinate their official reaction. Secretary of Public Education Jaime Torres Bodet rushed to the Ministry of Education to address the nation on *La Hora Nacional* radio program. Foreign Minister Padilla returned immediately from his weekend retreat in Cuernavaca to help the president compose a press release stating the government's position. In it, Ávila Camacho referred to the 1940 Havana Conference when he declared that any aggression against a neighbor in the Western Hemisphere was considered aggression against Mexico's sovereignty,[17] and therefore the Pearl Harbor attack required Mexico to sever all relations with the Axis powers. For the moment, however, Ávila Camacho and his cabinet determined that Mexico would remain officially outside of the conflict unless the country was attacked directly.

Concerned about the potential for Japanese attack on the northern Pacific coast, Ávila Camacho created a security zone to protect the sparsely populated regions in Baja California. Some 9,000 Japanese nationals living in Mexico were forced to relocate to Mexico City or Guadalajara.[18] Ávila Camacho assigned former president Lázaro Cárdenas to command the newly created Pacific Defense Zone.[19] Cárdenas's appointment provided important popular enthusiasm to Ávila Camacho's decision to support the United States after the Pearl Harbor attack. Eventually, Cárdenas became secretary of national defense in the Ávila Camacho administration. The image of the popular, revolutionary ex-president commanding such an important defensive position appealed to many Mexicans and brought legitimacy to the argument that Mexico could face a potential Axis threat.

The attack on Pearl Harbor had a significant impact on popular opinion, as it persuaded many ambivalent Mexicans to show indignation toward Japan and the other Axis powers. Mexicans sympathized with the United States as a victim of unprovoked foreign aggression. The attack coincided with insistent efforts by U.S. propagandists to promote anti-Axis sentiments. As a result of Allied censorship and control of newsprint supplies, combined with a growing concern and fear of the Axis, the press reacted with overt sympathy and support for the United States. In addition, local political leaders reinforced the shift toward the Allies by organizing public gatherings. They gave speeches to denounce Japanese aggression and to ensure that all citizens were aware of the Pearl Harbor attack.[20]

As Mexico and the United States finalized the Douglas-Weichers Agreement and set the stage for full economic partnership, Ávila Camacho's administration gradually began a rudimentary program of selling the partnership to the public and swaying popular opinion in favor of the Allies. In order for Ávila Camacho's economic agreements with the United States to succeed, he needed full support from the people. The initial government propaganda focused almost exclusively upon urging the Mexicans to work harder in wartime industries. The underlying theme in this propaganda strategy was that production equals patriotism, and that Mexicans who loved their country and wanted to defend their honor should be productive.[21]

In its earliest stages, the official wartime propaganda campaign was run through the General Information Division with no attempt to consult propaganda or war experts. Eventually, the Ávila Camacho administration established a formal propaganda office and incorporated industrial development into its wartime message. As Ávila Camacho slowly developed a public information strategy at home, he also took steps to bolster diplomatic relations abroad.

THE DECLARATION OF WAR

After Pearl Harbor, most Mexicans did not want to see their country drawn into the conflict, despite the strategic commercial agreement with the United

States. Mexicans tended to view the war as a European conflict that did not concern them. Their reluctance to enter the war changed abruptly in the summer of 1942, however, when government officials responded quickly to German aggression against Mexico. On May 13, an oil tanker, the *Potrero del Llano*, was sunk by a German submarine operating in the Gulf of Mexico. Several crew members died in the attack, and the nation demanded a response.

Ávila Camacho's government initially responded with diplomatic notes of protest demanding an apology and compensation for physical and human losses, to no avail. Then, on May 21, the *Faja de Oro* was torpedoed, killing seven sailors. The press and the government might have overlooked the first submarine attack if the German government had responded to diplomatic protests in a suitable manner, but the second attack sent a clear sign that Mexico was considered an enemy of the Nazi regime and had important consequences for the way Mexicans saw their role in the war.

In a nationwide radio broadcast on May 25, President Ávila Camacho addressed a special session of the National Congress in which he asked for a declaration of war against the Axis. In his passionate address, Ávila Camacho wanted a war declaration that would not require Mexico to commit its military to Europe. In this way, the president remained sensitive to the concerns of many Mexicans who wanted their country to avoid foreign combat.

The tone of his speech was one of reluctance as he commented that Mexico had been given no alternative to these drastic measures. He explained that Nazi aggressors had attacked Mexican territory and sovereignty without provocation. He called on Mexicans to answer the call of national duty to defend democracy against the Axis forces.[22] In this initial wartime address, the president introduced the interpretation that Mexico's involvement in the conflict represented a fight for democracy.

At the same time, Ávila Camacho presented the Congress with a proposal to declare a state of national wartime emergency. The proposal included the suspension of constitutional guarantees such as freedom of speech and freedom of the press. The state of emergency would give the government considerable leverage in fighting the propaganda war against Axis influence in Mexico. He delivered another emotional speech to justify these actions in the name of national unity and regional defense. He characterized the war as a time of total mobilization that required the support of all classes of society. Significantly, he conceded that the enemy was more powerful than Mexico because of its strong national unity.

Mexicans reacted swiftly and patriotically to the German attacks. Initially, most of the public supported Ávila Camacho's decision to declare a state of war. Public opinion polls conducted by *Tiempo* magazine in May 1942 reflected the dramatic shift in public sentiment. In its May 20 poll, *Tiempo* reported that nearly 60 percent of respondents answered no when asked if Mexico should enter the war. Members of leftist organizations and government-employed workers made up the majority of those who favored war; the "man in the street" and other social and political groups clearly opposed Mexico's entrance into the hostilities. Only nine days later, over 80 percent of Mexicans polled in a new survey believed the government's actions were proper.[23]

As soon as the German submarine attacks began, President Ávila Camacho directed his attention toward popular opinion. Presidential reports between May 16 and June 13 included thorough summaries of mainstream press reports and editorial pieces.[24] Articles in the press reflected the popular sentiment expressed by Mexicans in *Tiempo*'s opinion poll. National newspapers supported the declaration of war, and most offered no protest to the suspension of constitutional guarantees. Only *Excelsior* opposed the emergency measures. Its editorials argued that freedom of the press should be restricted only if there were clear evidence that the nation had been betrayed. The paper agreed that other freedoms should be suspended if absolutely necessary to prevent crimes against the country, but argued that those conditions did not currently exist in Mexico. Instead, the country was united around a solid block of patriotism with support for the government.[25] The newspaper opposed the measures because it did not perceive a need for them in a patriotic and united Mexico.

Ávila Camacho weighed his options cautiously, understanding that many Mexicans might oppose a declaration of war. As submarine warfare escalated in the Gulf of Mexico and war appeared more imminent, the government began to seriously consider its own ability to sway public opinion. On the same day that Ávila Camacho asked Congress for a war declaration, he created a special office in charge of national wartime information.

The responsibilities of domestic wartime propaganda fell to the General Information Division of the Ministry of the Interior, headed by José Altamirano, who argued that Mexico should follow the examples of other countries and establish a central office to organize and coordinate an internal propaganda campaign. That was accomplished with the establishment of the Oficina Federal de Propaganda (OFP). Altamirano charged the OFP with two primary objectives: In the context of Mexico's impending declaration of war, the agency aimed to sway Mexicans' opinions against the Axis powers and concomitantly to transform the anti-Axis sentiments into full support for the Ávila Camacho administration.[26]

One of the most important messages developed by the propaganda office encouraged a strong work ethic in all Mexicans to maximize production. This part of Altamirano's plan dovetailed with the incipient propaganda program that the government already had in place. To bolster its commercial agreements with the United States and to make those agreements benefit the national economy, Ávila Camacho's administration needed the general public's support by working harder and producing more. Because Mexico's primary role in the war was to produce strategic goods, this theme quickly came to dominate government propaganda. Particularly throughout the summer of 1942, when patriotic enthusiasm encompassed much of the country, the government tried to capitalize on that zeal by urging high rates of production. It equated production to patriotism in its messages in an effort to convert nationalist energy into increased productive capacity.

The theme of industrialization and production emerged in government posters produced throughout 1942. Corresponding to new economic and trade agreements with the United States, government posters encouraged all Mexicans to work hard to produce goods for the war effort. Ávila Camacho's administration carefully began to craft messages that tied worker productivity to good citizenship. The message emphasized that the country needed industrial and agricultural production, not only for the good of Allied powers, but also for the good of Mexico.[27]

The Radio Division of the OFP developed programs and coordinated efforts between state and the national governments to ensure that radio transmissions reached all major population centers. Its radio spots continued to push the government's message of production. They targeted both the agricultural and industrial sectors and urged them to be more productive for the good of the country. The messages emphasized that only by being productive could Mexicans ensure that the nation would emerge victorious from World War II.

Radio appeals emphasized production in the context of industrialization more than any other theme. They pushed industrialization in several ways. First, government messages argued that industrialization would assure victory in World War II and bring freedom to the world. Second, radio broadcasts emphasized that the nation must industrialize to ensure economic freedom. They argued that new industries would bring complete independence to the country.[28] Particularly on the heels of the economic experience of the 1930s, the theme of economic independence appealed to many Mexicans. This theme illustrates the nationalist nature of government propaganda. It also demonstrates that from its initial involvement in the war, the government saw World War II as an opportunity to unite the country around the idea of industrialization and economic nationalism.[29] The administration further took advantage of the wartime crisis in the world to argue that Mexico's defense of democracy and personal freedoms would equate to financial security for private investors.

Ávila Camacho's emphasis on industrialization posed a challenge to his message of national unity. The agrarian sector had benefited from reforms under Cárdenas, but by 1938 the government had begun to divert resources and attention away from the agricultural sector in favor of an industrialization strategy. After 1940, the Ávila Camacho administration accelerated this

trend. In an attempt to push a message of national unity without surrender-
ing its industrialization priorities, the government developed radio spots that
incorporated both the industrial and agricultural sectors. Propaganda messages insisted that Mexicans could affirm their nationality by increasing production in both sectors and emphasized that Mexico's success in the war
depended equally on industry and agriculture without placing one above the
other. The messages called upon both sectors to rise to the challenges presented in the wartime crisis and to fulfill their patriotic duty. One message
went a step further and presented agriculture and industry as two intricately
intertwined sectors, with the nation dependent on both for prosperity.[30]

By tying the agriculture and industrial sectors together, the government
accomplished several goals. It pushed its message of production in wartime
emergency. This concept emphasized the shift Ávila Camacho's administration was trying to make toward industrialization. More importantly, the
radio features advertised the goal of national unity in the context of wartime
propaganda. The government encouraged agrarians and industrialists to view
each other as allies and patriots. Instead of two separate sectors competing
for government resources, the Ávila Camacho administration wanted agrarians and industrialists to see the advantages of establishing a beneficial relationship. By uniting to confront the wartime crisis, the two sectors would
hopefully forget their past differences and move the nation closer to presenting a unified opposition to its international enemies.

As the war progressed, Ávila Camacho began to face public pressure
regarding inflation, food shortages, and other wartime scarcities. At the same
time, he anticipated new concerns in what Mexico's role would be after the
war. Government officials wanted to ensure the country's economic stability
after the war, and they wanted a voice in the negotiations for an international
peace plan. To resolve domestic anxieties and the country's international
ambitions, Ávila Camacho established a Mexican air squadron to participate
in direct combat.

Squadron 201 trained for a year in the United States and arrived in Manila
Bay on April 30, 1945. After a short precombat instruction period, Mexico's
heroes began participating in combat missions. Members of the "Aztec
Eagles" flew in fifty-nine missions and logged more than 1,200 hours of
flight time. They contributed to major bombing missions in Luzon and For-
mosa and also provided ground support to U.S. airmen. Although the unit
participated in active combat for less than six months, twenty airmen of
Squadron 201 received U.S. medals recognizing their contribution to the war
effort. Seven pilots died during the squadron's combat missions in the Phil-
ippines, and the squadron received the Philippine Presidential Unit Citation
and the Mexican Medal of Valor.[31]

The Aztec Eagles helped the government achieve its domestic objectives of
increasing popular support for the war effort. It allowed the Ávila Camacho

administration to display its improved and modern military proudly. The nation responded to the war heroes with fierce patriotism. Sending a Mexican contingent abroad to fight gave the country a greater, more personal stake in the war. It made problems such as inflation and food shortages seem small compared to the sacrifices being made by the armed forces.

Participation in combat also advanced the government's international goals. The squadron's participation in the war under the Mexican flag gave the government a legitimate argument for a voice at the peace table. Ávila Camacho had pushed his industrialization strategy through a combination of domestic propaganda and reciprocal trade agreements with the United States, but he intended the nation's industrial expansion to be more than just short-term wartime collaboration. Instead he envisioned Mexico's economic future to be based on modern industry.

Throughout World War II, Ávila Camacho had appealed to the Mexican public and largely won their support for the war effort. Building on the success of Squadron 201 in particular, the government sensed that its call to national unity had yielded the intended results. The support Mexicans displayed in rallying behind the Aztec Eagles demonstrated that many in the country looked with pride upon the characteristics that made them Mexican.

As an Allied victory loomed in 1945, the Ávila Camacho administration understood that it needed to use the support and unity established during the war to further its postwar objectives. Specifically, officials hoped to use the incipient industrial base established during wartime to continue to advance the country's industrial potential and modernize the economy. To cement his legacy, Ávila Camacho intended to incorporate the country's growing industrial class into the national unity effort.

Those who had invested time, money, and other resources into expanding the production of war products became increasingly concerned that the government would turn its back on them when the war ended. In 1945, Mexico's industries were relatively new and weak compared to industries in the United States, and the industrialists feared Ávila Camacho would bow to U.S. pressure to engage in open, unprotected trade.

As the war drew to a close, diplomatic exchanges between the United States and Mexico began to focus on trade and trade barriers between the two countries.[32] U.S. leaders viewed Latin America as the best potential market for exports after U.S. industries resumed peacetime production after the war. Mexico in particular had a sizable population that represented a largely untapped market for many U.S. exports. Furthermore, the country had amassed substantial dollar reserves as a result of wartime production and exports to the United States.[33]

Mexico's new group of industrialists had pushed for increased protection against U.S. imports throughout the war, while U.S. propaganda had emphasized a commercial relationship. Although Mexico suffered from consumer goods shortages during the war and the United States was not exporting such products, Mexican industrialists feared that the end of the war would bring a deluge of U.S. imports that would compete with the newer and weaker Mexican industries.[34] They hoped that the distraction of war in Europe and the Pacific would facilitate passage of the new tariff legislation that would be in effect as the war drew to a close, and they pushed for a postwar protective economic policy aimed at securing their new business endeavors from foreign competition.

The demands of the Mexican industrialists paralleled the postwar plans of the Ávila Camacho administration, which placed continued industrialization as a top postwar priority. As early as 1942, the Ministry of National Economy, in cooperation with the School of National Economy at the Universidad Autónoma de México, organized a series of conferences on the war economy. Conference participants debated Mexico's economic role during the war and began to look to potential problems the country could face with a return to peace.[35]

At the same time, Ávila Camacho appointed a commission to study potential peacetime concerns and to formulate a plan to protect the country's interests. By mid-1944, the Comisión Nacional de Planación para la Paz (CNPP) had taken on an increasingly important role in wartime propaganda.[36] Much of its propaganda was directed narrowly to the country's industrial class, while Squadron 201 continued to dominate propaganda directed at the masses.

In the last half of 1944 and throughout 1945, the Ávila Camacho administration began a subtle yet important transition in its wartime messages and policies. Government propaganda eventually became an attempt to win support for the government's peacetime industrialization and economic modernization policy. CNPP rhetoric emphasized that the country needed to prepare itself for a changed world after the war ended.[37] Commission members sent this message to a small circle of industrialists and assured them that the government was taking measures to address the nation's economic challenges after the war. The government's plan included developing new industries during the war and protecting those industries in peace.[38]

The government's industrialization propaganda took on a much more subtle nature as the end of the war approached. Instead of sponsoring festivals, posters, bullfights, and other forms of mass appeal, Ávila Camacho's industrialization propaganda was much quieter and more narrowly directed. In 1945, industrial expansion was a volatile topic and had the potential for rupturing the delicate sense of national unity the government had tried to achieve during the war. Devoting national resources to developing industry necessarily meant that other interests were likely to suffer, but the government could implement its industrialization strategy without widely publicizing its intentions to the country. Unlike declaring war, freezing wages, and implementing the draft, Ávila Camacho understood that he did not necessarily need full national support for industrialization. Industrialization propaganda aimed not to win widespread national support, but rather to appease a small but influential group of industrialists as well as middle- and upperclass consumers who wanted to see their interests protected.

The administration already had support from Mexican industrialists, who stood to gain the most, but also gained the support of the country's middle and upper classes. People who had benefited from the wartime economy had accumulated excess savings due to the large amounts of dollars pouring into Mexico. While the country had faced shortages in the availability of consumer goods—particularly luxury goods such as small and large appliances and automobiles—U.S. wartime propaganda had targeted middle- and upper-class Mexicans, featuring luxury consumer products as part of the American way of life. By 1945, a new consumer culture had emerged among many Mexicans as they began to demand the products that had been featured in the U.S. propaganda.[39] Ávila Camacho used that new consumer demand to gain popular support for his industrialization plans. He promised consumers that national industrial development would give them greater access to the products they wanted to buy. He promoted his strategy to middle- and upper-class consumers as the best way to fulfill their demands for consumer goods, while supporting the nation's economic growth.

A second factor requiring low-key propaganda techniques was the diplomatic pressure the administration received from the United States. The State Department's strong opposition to early attempts by the Mexican government to raise protectionist trade barriers confirmed Ávila Camacho's suspicions that U.S. officials envisioned Mexico as major market for its peacetime industrial production. While Ambassador George Messersmith sympathized and even supported Mexico's position that it needed a certain degree of protection to encourage continued growth of its new industries, officials in Washington were much less sympathetic and pointed to the 1942 Reciprocal Trade Treaty to prevent Mexico from raising tariffs.[40]

Ávila Camacho understood that the United States would play a leading role in determining the nature of a peace agency and therefore the nature of Mexico's place in the postwar world. He could ill afford to alienate U.S. diplomats during such a volatile time in the international system. In an effort not to offend U.S. diplomatic sensibilities and not to alienate large sectors of the Mexican public, Ávila Camacho's approach to promoting industrialization was limited to speeches and publications aimed at a narrow audience as well as policy implementation.

The differences in the U.S. and Mexican visions of the peace culminated at the Inter-American Conference on Problems of War and Peace held at the Chapultepec Castle in Mexico City in March 1945. The conference resulted in the Inter-American Treaty of Reciprocal Assistance and Solidarity, also known as the Act of Chapultepec, which set forth principles of sovereignty and nonintervention that became an important influence on the United Nations Charter.[41] Even though the conference's final act represented the new era of good relations between the United States and Latin America, negotiations during the conference demonstrated their diverging commercial interests. U.S. representatives made declarations and proposed resolutions that would prohibit trade barriers within the hemisphere. They discouraged the development of any new industries that would require protectionist restrictions. Delegates to the conference managed to resolve their differences in commercial policy by using vague language in the final charter.[42] Nevertheless, U.S. and Mexican participation in the conference demonstrated that the two nations had differing visions of the commercial relationship that would develop after the war.

CONCLUSION

Between 1938 and 1945, Mexico evolved from a country deeply divided over its revolutionary past to a society united around its participation in World War II. Mexicans initially reacted to the conflict with ambivalence, as the government moved closer to an alliance with the United States in 1941. Nevertheless, as Axis aggression escalated and eventually culminated in attacks on Mexican oil tankers, the public united behind the president. Manuel Ávila Camacho carefully combined the government's wartime rhetoric with official commercial agreements with the United States and used World War II to justify his domestic industrialization agenda. Government propaganda urged Mexicans to fulfill their patriotic and revolutionary duties by supporting industrialization and working hard to increase production. The participation of Squadron 201 in Pacific combat missions further united the nation around the war. By 1945, Ávila Camacho sensed that a demand for consumer goods had emerged among the country's middle and upper classes. He capitalized on that demand by imposing protectionist measures to reduce competition from U.S. industries. As a result, the government enjoyed a large base of domestic support for its industrialization program.

NOTES

1. José C. Valadés, *Historia general de la Revolución Mexicana: La unidad nacional* (Mexico City: Ediciones Gernika, 1985).

2. T. G. Powell, *Mexico and the Spanish Civil War* (Albuquerque: University of New Mexico Press, 1981), 127.

3. John W. Sherman, *The Mexican Right: The End of Revolutionary Reform,*

1920–1940 (Westport, CN: Praeger, 1997). Sherman's analysis goes beyond the traditional members of the conservative camp, suggesting how divided the country was until World War II.

4. Monica Ann Rankin, "¡México, la Patria! Modernity, National Unity, and Propaganda during World War II" (Ph.D. diss., University of Arizona, 2004), 37–54.

5. Donald Fisher Harrison, "United States–Mexican Military Collaboration during World War II" (Ph.D. diss., Georgetown University, 1977), 54–55; Stephen R. Niblo, "British Propaganda in Mexico during the Second World War: The Development of Cultural Imperialism," *Latin American Perspectives* 10, no. 4 (1983); Stephen R. Niblo, *Mexico in the 1940s: Modernity, Politics, and Corruption* (Wilmington, DE: SR Books, 1999); José Luis Ortiz Garza, *México en guerra* (Mexico City: Grupo Editorial Planeta, 1989).

6. See Avinola Pastora Rodriguez, "La prensa nacional frente a la intervención de México en la segunda guerra mundial," *Historia Mexicana* 29, no. 2 (1979); and Lorenzo Meyer, *México y los Estados Unidos en el Conflicto Petrolero, 1917–1942* (Mexico City: Colegio de México, 1968). For a journalist's account of Mexico during this time, see Betty Kirk, *Covering the Mexican Front: The Battle of Europe versus America* (Norman: University of Oklahoma Press, 1942).

7. Burt M. Connell, *Mexico at the Bar of Public Opinion* (New York: Mail and Express Publishing, 1939).

8. See *El Universal*, April 17, 1940; Rodriguez, "La prensa nacional," 271–72.

9. "El Nazismo en México por la División de Investigaciones Políticas y Sociales," May 23, 1940, GS, Box 83, Folder 10 (2-1/002.4/3 79), Archivo General de la Nación, Mexico City (hereafter referred to as AGN); Kirk, *Covering the Mexican Front*, 275–88.

10. Ezequiel Padilla to Congress, March 8, 1941, quoted in Daniel James, *Mexico and the Americans* (New York: Praeger, 1963), 352.

11. *Excelsior*, April 2, 1941; Rodriguez, "La prensa nacional," 282–84.

12. Stephen R. Niblo, *War, Diplomacy, and Development: The United States and Mexico, 1938–1954* (Wilmington, DE: SR Books, 1995), 75; María Emilia Paz Salinas, *Strategy, Security, and Spies: Mexico and the U.S. as Allies in World War II* (University Park: Pennsylvania State University Press, 1997), 61–66.

13. Jaime Torres Bodet, *Memorias: Equinoccio* (Mexico City: Editorial Porrua, 1974), 268; Rodriguez, "La prensa nacional," 288–89.

14. Paz Salinas, *Strategy, Security and Spies*, 129–31; Rodriguez, "La prensa nacional," 289–91.

15. Text of the agreement can be found in U.S. Department of State Bulletin, November 22, 1941, 399–403. For a discussion of negotiations leading up to the agreement, see Thomas Wood Clash, "United States–Mexican Relations, 1940–1946: A Study of U.S. Interests and Policies" (Ph.D. diss., State University of New York, 1972), 47–54.

16. Jesse H. Stiller, *George S. Messersmith: Diplomat of Democracy* (Chapel Hill: University of North Carolina Press, 1987), 172.

17. Torres Bodet, *Memorias*, 277–79. "Havana Meeting of Ministers of Foreign Affairs of the American Republics, July 21–30, 1940," in *A Decade of American Foreign Policy* (Washington, DC: Department of State, 1950), 411–12.

18. Stephen R. Niblo, "Allied Policy toward Axis Interests in Mexico during World War II," *Mexican Studies/Estudios Mexicanos* 17, no. 2 (Summer 2001), 351–73.

19. Niblo, *War, Diplomacy, and Development*, 75–77.

20. Harrison, "United States–Mexican Military Collaboration," 124; *El Universal*, December 7 and 9, 1941. Headlines reporting the attack on Pearl Harbor came exclusively from the United Press International wire service.

21. Ortiz Garza, *México en guerra*, 179–80.

22. Manuel Ávila Camacho, *Ideario de la nación Mexicana* (Mexico City: September 1942).

23. Howard F. Cline, *The United States and Mexico* (Cambridge, MA: Harvard University Press, 1963), 268–69.

24. "Resumen Diario de la Prensa, May 16, 1942, to June 13, 1942," RP/MAC 550/44-16-33, AGN.

25. *Excelsior* (May 29, June 1, and June 2, 1942); *La Prensa* (May 27 and May 29, 1942); *Novedades* (June 1 and June 3, 1942); *El Universal* (May 29 and June 1, 1942).

26. José Altamirano to Ministry of the Interior, memorandum, May 25, 1942, RP/MAC 545.2/99, AGN. The Oficina Federal de Propaganda appears to have changed names to the Comisión Coordinada de Propaganda Nacional later in 1942.

27. Rankin, "¡México, la patria!" 164–75.

28. Radio broadcasts, summer 1942, DGI/G2 301.2/283, AGN.

29. Martha Rivero, "La política económica durante la guerra," in *Entre la guerra y la estabilidad política: El México de los 40*, ed. Rafael Loyola (Mexico City: Editorial Grijalbo, 1986), 24–27.

30. "Radio Spots, Summer 1942."

31. See William F. Tudor, "Flight of the Eagles: The Mexican Expeditionary Air Force; Escuadrón 201 in World War II" (Ph.D. diss., Texas Christian University, 1997), chaps. 9 and 11.

32. A. García Robles, *México en la postguerra: El marco mundial y el continental* (Mexico City: Ediciones Minerva, 1944), 10–11; Sanford Mosk, *Industrial Revolution in Mexico* (Berkeley: University of California Press, 1954).

33. Valadés, *Historia general*, 84–85.

34. Mosk, *Industrial Revolution*, 33.

35. Alfonso Pulido Islas, "Reporte: Ciclo de Conferencias de Economía de Guerra en México," October 19, 1942, DGI/G2, 301.2/306, AGN.

36. Decree creating the Comisión Nacional de Planación para la Paz, July 1942, RP/MAC, 433/310, AGN.

37. Octavio Véjar Vázquez, "El mundo de la postguerra," speech to Club Rotario y Cámara de Comercio de la Ciudad de Guadalajara, September 26, 1944, RP/MAC, 433/310, AGN.

38. "Primer Congreso Nacional de Economía de Guerra del Proletariado Mexicano: Problemas Económicos de la Post-Guerra," December 1942, RP/MAC 433/310, AGN.

39. Niblo, *War, Diplomacy, and Development*, 13–15; Julio E. Moreno, *Yankee Don't Go Home! Mexican Nationalism, American Business Culture, and the Shaping of Modern Mexico, 1920–1950* (Chapel Hill: University of North Carolina Press, 2003).

40. Clash, "United States–Mexican Relations," 227.

41. "Inter-American Reciprocal Assistance and Solidarity," in *Treaties and Other International Agreements of the United States of America, 1776–1949*, comp. Charles I. Bevans, Vol. 3, *Multilateral, 1931–1945* (Washington, DC: Department of State, 1969).

42. David Green, *The Containment of Latin America: A History of the Myths and Realities of the Good Neighbor Policy* (Chicago: Quadrangle Books, 1971), 175, 203–5.

3

Central America: On the Periphery

Thomas M. Leonard

In early 1939 Central America—Costa Rica, El Salvador, Guatemala, Honduras, and Nicaragua—was not of concern to U.S. military planners. A contemporary assessment concluded that the possibilities of any political, economic, cultural, or military penetration into the region by a power other than the United States were negligible. Despite trade links to Germany and the presence of Nazi and Fascist groups in each of the five republics, the imposition of totalitarian ideologies upon either the people or the governments of Central America appeared remote. Absent any external or internal threats, and because the threat of forced union by one nation over the others was not considered possible, in early 1939 Central America appeared to be in a period of political tranquility. In this ambiance, the U.S. War Department encouraged the completion of the Pan-American Highway and increased economic and cultural activities to further cement the existing favorable U.S.–Central American relationship.[1]

As the world moved toward global war in 1941 and during the war itself, Central America's military, economic, social, and political landscapes changed dramatically owing largely to U.S. policies. This chapter examines the impact of U.S. policies upon the region with specific regard to security, subversion, economics, and propaganda.

MILITARY PLANNING

Global events in 1939 and 1940—the German invasion of Poland, the fall of France, the Japanese march down the Malay Peninsula—brought a new significance to Central America and prompted the U.S. Army to conclude that "a sea landing in Central America and a threat toward the south for an attack upon the Panama Canal was a consideration not to be entirely passed over." At the same time, the United States found the Central American militaries incapable of offering any resistance to such an attack. With their small and poorly trained and equipped armies, the Central Americans were judged to be incapable of meeting the potential challenge.[2]

To fill the void, the United States initiated bilateral military conversations with their Central American counterparts. The primary purpose of these discussions was "to make available to the United States . . . the use of [their] available sea, air and land bases" when necessary for hemispheric defense and to permit the United States to employ its armed forces to assist any republic confronting an external attack or internal sabotage. If no Central American nation requested U.S. assistance to resist such an attack, Washington reserved the right to act following consultation with the other Latin American republics. President Franklin D. Roosevelt put it succinctly when he added that "it is understood that the decision rests with the United States." In other words, the United States became the final arbiter of any threat to Central American security.

Maj. Lemuel Mathewson served as the War Department's liaison officer in the bilateral staff conversations conducted in the capitals of Costa Rica, El Salvador, Guatemala, Honduras, and Nicaragua between August 19 and September 19, 1940. As a result of these conversations, each of the republics agreed to request U.S. armed assistance in case of a military or "fifth column" attack and to permit entry of U.S. troops into the country, even if passing through it to another republic that was under attack. Within each country, the United States obtained the right to use its railways, seaports, airports, and other facilities for military and related purposes. The republics also granted the United States the right to conduct medical, engineering, signal, and aerial photography surveys within their boundaries, to maintain surveillance over aliens and their sympathizers, and to exchange intelligence information with each other. In return, when requested, the United States promised to employ its forces to repel external attacks and suppress internal uprisings, to provide assistance in acquiring U.S.-made armaments, and to train Central American military personnel and to provide military advisers for that purpose.[3]

Following the bilateral discussions, the United States moved quickly to enhance the quality and efficiency of the Central American military forces. In 1941, military assistance agreements were concluded with all but Honduras, where President Tiburcio Carías waited until the war neared its end in 1945 before consenting to military cooperation. The purpose of each U.S. mission was to improve the local military's capability to meet its obligations as spelled out in the bilateral staff conversations. To accomplish this objective, the chief of each U.S. military mission served as head of the local military academy, save Costa Rica where he cooperated with the minister of state police and public safety.[4]

From the start, the task of each U.S. military mission appeared insurmountable. In El Salvador, Guatemala, Honduras, and Nicaragua, the U.S. military missions found the local military academies woefully inadequate and the troops poorly trained and in need of basic support—uniforms, food, medical assistance, and the like. Furthermore, each Central American political leader had his own agenda for the U.S. mission or feared its close contact with the local troops. For example, Nicaraguan strongman Anastasio Somoza cooperated fully with the U.S. defense program, but continually insisted that his Guardia Nacional not be disbanded and that it be trained in jungle warfare to meet future internal security needs—a request consistently denied by U.S. authorities. Somoza also refused to have officers trained as civil engineers to assist with infrastructure projects. Jorge Ubico and Tiburcio Carías, respectively the presidents of Guatemala and Honduras, preferred to keep their officers distant from their U.S. counterparts for fear that contact would result in disloyalty to their leadership. Assuming that his country's geographical location insulated it from the global military conflict, El Salvadoran president Maximiliano Hernández Martínez had little interest in military cooperation with the United States. Although the Costa Rican government cooperated with the defense of its national airport and coastal regions, it always remained cool to the presence of U.S. military forces. In fact, in 1943 the Costa Rican government demanded that U.S. military personnel become as inconspicuous as possible.[5]

The completion of Lend-Lease agreements between the United States and the Central American nations in early 1942 did not effectively modernize the local armies but instead met the demands of U.S. defense strategy for the region that focused upon the German U-boat threat to the Panama Canal, Venezuelan oil, and the Caribbean Sea lanes. The matériel supplied to the Central American republics reflected that strategy. Small water- and aircraft and associated spare parts, along with appropriate ordnance and ammunition, constituted the bulk of supplies provided to the Central American nations. Only a small token of light arms, tanks, and planes were made available to the five republics, and then mostly through the U.S. military missions. As mandated by the Joint Advisory Board, the majority of these supplies were scheduled to arrive in the region after 1942, at a time when the German U-boat threat to the Caribbean had virtually ended. In all, the Central American nations received only $4.1 million in Lend-Lease aid (slightly under 10 percent of all Latin American Lend-Lease assistance) from the program's inception in March 1941 through September 1945, an amount significantly less than the Central American leadership anticipated in 1941.[6]

The need to combat the German submarine presence in the Caribbean Sea and to enable reconnaissance aircraft to reach the northern sectors of the Caribbean prompted the United States to devise a program for upgrading existing Central American airports and for the construction of new facilities. In cooperation with Pan American World Airways, the War Department initiated the Airport Development Program (ADP), which provided for the modernization of the airports in the capital cities of San José, San Salvador, Tegucigalpa, and Managua and to construct or improve air facilities at Puerto Barrios and San José in Guatemala, Puerto Cortés and Puerto Castillo in Honduras, and Fonseca and Corinto in Nicaragua. In addition, smaller airports throughout each country were improved and a number of radar facilities constructed across the isthmus. These properties were to revert to the host governments within a year following the war's end. Importantly, U.S. Army Air Force pilots had responsibility for the reconnaissance flights. Central American pilots were assigned to peripheral duties.[7]

By the end of 1942, the German U-boat threat in the Caribbean region had all but disappeared, and by early 1943, the fear of Nazi sabotage to U.S. interests equally was a thing of the past. Thereafter, until the war neared its end, Central America became less important to U.S. wartime defense strategies. While the military missions continued to function, the availability of military supplies drastically decreased and in some instances became totally unavailable, owing to the demands of the European and Asian theaters.

THE NAZI THREAT

"I want to make it perfectly clear that I make no distinction between German nationals and Germans by birth," Adolf Hitler declared shortly after Germany's defeat in World War I. He promised to implant the German entrepreneurial spirit, to provide the capital to develop their economies and "give them . . . our philosophy." Although Germans had been coming to Central America since the mid-nineteenth century, for those nationals and their descendents living throughout the region in the 1930s, Hitler's claim that they were citizens of the Third Reich and that they would be expected to play a role in his quest for empire proved prophetic.[8] Needless to say, as the war clouds spread over Europe beginning in the late 1930s, U.S. policy makers looked upon them with increasing skepticism.[9]

An intricate set of offices in Berlin connected the German populace in Central America with the German government. The most important office was the Foreign Organization of the German National Socialist Party (the "Auslands" organization), which became part of the German Foreign Ministry in 1937. Auslands was charged with the responsibility to see that German nationals and their descendants living abroad loyally supported Hitler's polices. Through embassy personnel in each country, resident Germans were to distribute propaganda, hold demonstrations that followed the Nazi Party line, and donate money to Nazi causes. Within each country, an elaborate structure was put in place to insure that no German went unnoticed. Threats and intimidation forced those who opposed or wished to remain neutral in the controversies of the 1930s to support the Third Reich. Usually, the threat of retaliation against a relative residing in Germany was enough to bring the foreign resident to do what was asked of him.

Otto Reinbeck, the German ambassador to Guatemala, directed Nazi activities throughout Central America. In each of the five countries, a German consular officer, usually an employee of the Hapag-Lloyd Steamship Company, served as the direct link to Guatemala City. Locally, prominent German merchants, farmers, and representatives of German firms usually assisted with the distribution of propaganda and the collection of monies from Germans residing in the country. The local German Club, with its membership restricted to German nationals and their descendents, served as the distribution center for all printed Nazi propaganda and literature, and it housed a library that contained pro-German materials at the expense of other reading matter. Classrooms at the local German schools emphasized the righteousness of the Third Reich's cause and assisted with the distribution of pro-Nazi propaganda to the students throughout the entire country. In addition, the local German leadership was expected to capitalize upon popular local socioeconomic issues in order to gain the confidence of the general population. Outside the Auslands organization, the German government sought to establish military missions in each of the five countries in hopes of influencing the local officer corps, not only in the German military's tactics but also its philosophy. By 1938, the Germans had in place across the isthmus a sophisticated system of propaganda, espionage, and potentially sabotage.

That same year, the U.S. military attaché assigned to all five republics, Col. Joseph B. Pate, commenced reporting on Nazi activities throughout the region, and the Treasury Department assessed the extent of German economic influence. Their reports were alarming. Nelson A. Rockefeller, who in 1940 became head of the Office for Coordination of Commercial and Cultural Relations between the American Republics—renamed the Office of the Coordinator of Inter-American Affairs (OIAA) in 1941 and the Office of Inter-American Affairs in 1945—recalled that Nazi propaganda had effectively undermined "the morale of the people" so as to "render them helpless" should the Western Hemisphere be invaded. Harley Notter, a key economic adviser in the State Department, believed that the Nazi propaganda convinced Central America's knowledgeable classes that "Germany will win the war and that the prudent thing to do is to be in a position at the time of victory to adjust easily and without risk of retaliation."[10]

In response, the United States undertook a series of actions. Rockefeller's

OIAA conducted a pro-Allied propaganda campaign that is discussed in the final section of this chapter. The U.S. government also determined to bankrupt German business interests and, in the event of war, to have the most dangerous enemy aliens deported and the civil liberties of those Germans who remained on the isthmus severely restricted. A case can be made that the United States overreacted to the Nazi threat, particularly given the fact that the total number of Germans in all Central America was less than 2 percent of the region's total population.[11]

From September to December 1940, a U.S. delegation visited all Latin American countries to identify the extent of German economic influence. The result of their work came on July 17, 1941, when President Roosevelt announced the "Proclaimed List of Blocked Neutrals," or the "Blacklist," as it was commonly known. By May 1942, the United States identified 424 German businesses in Guatemala, 198 in Costa Rica, 122 in El Salvador, 76 in Nicaragua, and 39 in Honduras. Henceforth, these firms no longer could trade with or use funds deposited in the United States. Following the July 1942 Inter-American Conference of Systems of Economic and Financial Controls, the German properties were placed under the control of a government-appointed property administrator.

While hardships were expected in Central America as a result of this policy, the need to deny Germany funds for its war effort was the overriding consideration. The German properties met varied fates over the course of the war. Eventually, the Costa Rican government returned almost all of the properties it administered, and the few it nationalized resulted in court settlements after the war. Its most notable nationalization became the Experimental Agricultural Station at Turrialba. Honduran strongman Carías distributed the majority of the confiscated German properties to his friends, and not until 1955 did the West German government reach a compensation agreement with Honduras on behalf of five families who lost properties during the war. Elsewhere, the dictators—Somoza in Nicaragua, Hernández Martínez in El Salvador, and Ubico in Guatemala—resisted the nationalization of agricultural properties, fearing that it would send a signal to native landowners and result in a challenge to their rule.[12]

Following the Havana Foreign Ministers Conference in July 1940, the United States and the Central American governments cooperated in drawing up lists of the most dangerous enemy aliens in each republic. In case of war, German diplomats would be declared persona non grata and immediately returned to Germany, which was done in January 1942. A second category included the "most dangerous" Germans who openly supported the Third Reich or were suspected of committing acts of sabotage. In all, from the latter two categories, 695 men, women, and children of German descent were brought to the United States from Central America for repatriation to Germany or to be exchanged for U.S. citizens caught behind enemy lines.

Another 230 were sent directly to Germany, until July 1943 when Germany refused the repatriation of its nationals or descendents; as a result, several hundred Germans remained in the Texas internment camps at Crystal City, Kenedy, and Seagoville.

For the Germans who remained in Central America, life's privileges became more restrictive as a result of decisions made at the July 1940 Havana Conference. More serious impositions were agreed upon by the Committee on Political Defense that was established at the February 1942 Rio Conference. Across Central America, German residents were denied the use of shortwave radios and had their mail screened to prevent the introduction of German propaganda. German clubs were closed, and in fact the one in Costa Rica was used as a German detention center. Freedom of assembly was denied and movement within and outside the country greatly limited. Still, by late 1943, after the U-boat threat had been removed from the Caribbean and the tide of war was turning against the Third Reich, the State Department's Bureau of Intelligence Research fretted that the "[Nazi] party structure has not been wholly dismembered" and that the remaining Germans intended "to ride out the storm as best they can, feeling that in the post-war period they will be able to effect a recovery . . . on the skeletons of their commercial existence."[13]

State Department officials did not share the research bureau's fear of a postwar German resurgence in Central America. In fact, as victory became more of reality with each passing month in late 1944 and into 1945, in the State Department there emerged a desire to forgive and forget the un-American activities of enemy nationals. By this time, U.S. policy makers recognized the important roles played by the German merchants and agriculturalists in the Central American economies. As a result of this recognition and in hopes of improving relations with its hemispheric neighbors, at the 1945 Mexico City Conference, the United States readily accepted the Latin American proposal, endorsed by the Central American governments, to prevent the return of only the most subversive Axis elements. For those Central Americans who were shipped to Europe, their only way home was through Spain at their own expense. For those remaining in the United States, the government in Washington paid their travel costs. But they returned home to a Central America greatly different from the one that they had left.

ECONOMIC IMPACT OF WAR

Until the 1930s, the United States did not consider Germany a legitimate economic competitor in Central America, despite the awareness by Washington policy makers that a large number of Germans had migrated to the area since the late nineteenth century. That perception changed with the onset of the Great Depression in 1929 and Germany's subsequent introduction of the *aski* mark system. Rather than working together to address the global depression, the industrialized countries sought to first improve their own economies. Hitler's *aski* mark system must be viewed in that light. Rather than pay for the coffee, cotton, and other primary products purchased from Central America, Germany established a credit system in *aski*, from which the Central Americans could pay for the manufactured products they purchased from Germany. In effect, the Central American demand for finished products kept the money in the German economy to assist with its expansion. But the German government was not beyond intimidation to have its way. For example, in 1937, when Nicaragua indicated that it might restrict the *aski* mark trade, the German government announced that it intended to discontinue subsidies of 30 to 45 percent paid on certain German exports to Nicaragua. As a result of the *aski* mark system in the 1930s, Germany trebled its market share of imports in Guatemala, El Salvador, Honduras, and Nicaragua and doubled it in Costa Rica, mostly at the expense of the United States and, secondarily, Great Britain.

In an effort to improve its depressed economy, the United States pursued trade reciprocity agreements with each of the Central American republics, but the agreements had little benefit to either signatory. The reciprocity agreements provided for a reduction in U.S. tariffs on Central America's primary products, but they already entered the United States on a most-favored-nation status. And while the Central Americans reduced their tariffs on U.S. manufactures and industrial goods, there was little money available on the isthmus for such purchases.[14]

Although Washington had no official statistics to show the value of factories, farms, banks, commercial houses, retail stores, and so forth owned by Germans in Central America, the number of firms on the blacklist as of June 1944 revealed that there 246 in Costa Rica, 120 in El Salvador, 394 in Guatemala, 39 in Honduras, and 112 in Nicaragua. Still, the United States estimated that Germans controlled 60 percent of the Guatemalan coffee industry and about 40 percent of Costa Rica's. In addition, German banks and cartels such as I. G. Farben, Bayer, Bausch and Lomb, and Krupp had operations in the region.[15]

With the outbreak of World War II in September 1939, Central American trade with Europe in general, and Germany in particular, nose-dived, and by early 1942 it was nonexistent. The loss of markets for their primary products meant that the Central American governments lost revenues from export duties and were unable to purchase manufactured products from Europe. Trade with the United States also drastically decreased. At first, merchant ships were diverted from Central America to serve in the convoys supplying Great Britain, and from 1941 until mid-1942, shipping throughout the circum-Caribbean region was sporadic at best, owing to the effectiveness of German U-boats operating in the Caribbean Sea. For an eighteen-month period in 1942 and 1943, shipping came to a standstill on Central America's Caribbean ports. El Salvador suffered the same fate, as few cargo ships made their way either from the Panama Canal or California along Central America's Pacific Coast. The Salvadoran government offset a small portion of these lost markets by reaching trade agreements with Peru and Chile on the southwest coast of South America.

The loss of markets and the importation of goods and strategic materials abroad had a devastating impact upon Central America. Scarcity and inflation became the norm. Across the region, petroleum products, particularly gasoline and automobile tires, were in short supply. During the war, the cost of living soared more than 700 percent in Nicaragua, 200 percent in Honduras, 100 percent in El Salvador, and approximately 75 percent in Costa Rica and Guatemala. While the rural villages and towns were largely self-sufficient, urban centers experienced food shortages. The blocking of funds of the German-owned businesses exacerbated the situation. Career diplomat John M. Cabot understood that the U.S. economic warfare program had been a complete victory in Central America and in fact suggested that the regional economies "probably were permanently crippled." He feared that a U.S. economic protectorate might follow at the end of the war.[16]

The loss of the European coffee market contributed to a resolution at the July 1940 Havana Foreign Ministers Conference calling for the creation of instruments of cooperation for the orderly marketing of commodities of primary importance to the countries of the Western Hemisphere. In response, the United States initiated a conference in September 1940 that subsequently resulted in an international coffee agreement on November 28, 1941, that guaranteed the producing nations a market for a stipulated quantity of coffee at prices that would compensate at least in part for the loss of the continental markets. In application, the agreement provided Central America with a market for virtually its entire exportable coffee surplus, and as a result, the volume of exports in the war years was very similar to the average of the previous five years.

The same could not be said for banana exports from Central America. Following the United States' entry into the war in December 1941, the U.S. government requisitioned banana ships to ferry war supplies to Europe. In addition, because of wartime demands elsewhere, the fruit companies in Central America received inadequate supplies of insecticides, fuel, and other essentials. The loss of export markets impacted all of Central America, reaching its lowest point in 1943. Guatemala, Honduras, and Nicaragua suffered the greatest losses. The shipping shortage and the threat of German U-boats in the Atlantic Ocean abated in 1944, contributing to an increase in banana exports. By the end of the war, only Honduras had reached its prewar level of exports; Guatemala was at approximately 85 percent, Costa Rica 62 percent, and Nicaragua just 8 percent. Even with the market rebound, however, the market loss had contributed to lost government tax revenues and contributed to high unemployment across the isthmus.[17]

The need for strategic materials sent the United States searching in Central America for wild rubber, abaca, cinchona, and mahogany. Wild rubber trees were scattered across the isthmus in dense jungle regions that were difficult to access, but still Honduras and Nicaragua benefited from the U.S. demand. The United Fruit Company received a wartime U.S. government contract to grow abaca—used in the making of marine cordage—in Guatemala, Honduras, and Costa Rica; it produced about 9,000 tons of the fiber annually and was able to meet about 20 percent of the U.S. prewar needs. Cinchona, the source of the drug quinine, was cultivated in Guatemala and Nicaragua. The need for lumber, particularly mahogany for use in the maritime industry, was exploited in Guatemala and Nicaragua. Only El Salvador failed to benefit from the U.S. demand for strategic goods.[18]

Transportation between the Central American countries was abysmal on the eve of World War II. While the idea of Pan-American Highway dated to the 1923 Pan-American Conference in Santiago, Chile, nothing significant had materialized by the outbreak of World War II—at which point the United States recognized the crucial need for connecting itself with Panama for security reasons. In 1941 the U.S. Congress appropriated $20 million for the construction of the Central American portion of the road and, in 1943, another $12 million to complete it. U.S. contractors, using their own equipment and an estimated 6,000 Central American laborers, were to complete the project by May 1943, but the deadline was not met. Several reasons contributed to the project's failure. The region's lengthy rainy season hampered construction, but the shortage of construction materials, lack of gasoline and spare parts, shipping disruptions, and the like added to the problem. The removal of the Axis threat from the isthmus and the turning of the war's tide by 1943 lessened the security need.[19] The reasons that prompted the haste in 1941 for the highway's construction disappeared by 1943, causing the Army Corps of Engineers to cancel construction with only 24 percent of the roadway completed in Central America.

The cancellation of the Pan-American Highway project paralleled the U.S. cancellation of strategic materials contracts with the Central American governments. At the end of the war in 1945, the loss of U.S. investments in strategic materials, termination of the Pan-American Highway project, the unknown future regarding European markets for coffee and bananas, high government debt due to the loss of tariff income, and the loss of German entrepreneurs raised questions about the future direction of Central America's economy. For sure, Central America's trade patterns shifted toward the United States. With the war's end, the Central Americans had a favorable trade balance with the United States, owing to the wartime unavailability of goods the Central Americans relied upon from its northern neighbor.[20]

THE FIGHT FOR DEMOCRACY

On April 18, 1944, Col. Fred T. Cruse, the U.S. military attaché assigned to the embassy in Guatemala, reported on his recent discussions with the "leading men" of Central America, most of whom he had known for fifteen years. According to them, the war was over, given the stoppage of work on the Pan-American Highway, disappearance of U.S. troops from the region, and emphasis on postwar planning by the local governments. "This means that politics and other personal concerns are once again regarded as the only things that matter," Cruse declared. Furthermore, Cruse noted that these "resentments and personal ambitions," held in check during the war, "are now growing and coming more and more out into the open." Cruse concluded that the attitude in all the countries, save Costa Rica, was that the dictators "[had] been in long enough" and that they "should give someone else a chance."[21]

At the time, Cruse did not know the accuracy of his observation. Within days of writing his letter, Salvadoran dictator Maximiliano Hernández Martínez came under attack, and by midyear he and Guatemalan dictator Jorge Ubico had been overthrown. Subsequently, Anastasio Somoza, Nicaragua's longtime strongman, declared that he would not be a presidential candidate in 1947. In May 1944 left-leaning Teodoro Picado became president of Costa Rica. Only the Honduran dictator Tiburcio Carías appeared to have weathered the storm.

Cruse's observation reflected the conventional wisdom regarding Central American history, one characterized by elitist rule with the support of the military. Struggle for political power was described as the "outs" wanting "in"—and the former's willingness to use force to attain their goal. The dean of Central American historians, Ralph Lee Woodward Jr., added that the changes of 1944 were brought about by the "generation of rising expectations," those middle-sector groups that blossomed in the 1920s as a result of Central America's agro-export industries. These lawyers, accountants, medical professionals, small merchants, journalists, teachers, and students understood that the political system denied them entry. In 1944, their time had arrived to enter the political arena. According to this theory, the elites could well afford to permit the middle sector's entry into the system because it constituted only a small portion of the electorate and apparently had little or no interest in the welfare of the poor urban worker or rural peasant. Voting requirements in each country support this view.

While citizens of the Central American countries received the right to vote at age 18 in some countries, and 21 in others, landholding patterns and voting restrictions across the isthmus limited their effective participation in elections. Except in Costa Rica, the elites controlled approximately 70 percent of the productive lands in these agriculturally based societies. In effect, the mass majority of rural workers did not own land, often a requirement for obtaining the right to vote. Home ownership also bypassed most urban unskilled workers. Literacy requirements as a voting prerequisite also existed in Costa Rica, Guatemala, and Honduras. Fifty-eight percent of Costa Rica's population was literate, enabling it to far outdistance its neighbors—30 percent in El Salvador, 20 percent in Nicaragua, and 15 percent in Guatemala and Honduras. Thus the articulate voting base in each country, save Costa Rica, was restricted to the elite and the emerging middle sector.[22] Within this context, the middle sector initiated the political changes in 1944.

Missing from the discussion is the impact that U.S.-generated pro-Allied propaganda and news stories, emanating from the United States, may have had upon Central America's political upheaval in 1944. Executive Order 8840 of July 30, 1941, established the OIAA under the direction of Nelson Rockefeller to increase hemispheric solidarity and the spirit of Inter-American cooperation. After the Pearl Harbor attack on December 7, 1941, the OIAA developed and maintained a strong information program throughout the war, utilizing radio, motion-picture, and press media. Walt Disney was enlisted to produce films especially for Latin America. Coordination committees, composed of U.S. citizens residing in each country and linked to the U.S. embassy, were established in each capital to distribute posters and reading materials, hold discussions, show films, and sponsor cultural events from sporting events to art exhibits, all supporting the Allied cause.[23]

In all but Costa Rica, newspapers labored under government censorship, but they all reported on the Allied advances in the North Africa, Europe, and the Pacific through dispatches from the Associated Press and United Press International. Photographs usually depicted successful Allied assaults, naval shelling and bombing missions, and the surrender of Axis troops along with their destroyed vehicles and equipment. While all of this might be expected, the papers also carried President Roosevelt's annual messages to Congress and any of his special announcements, press conferences, and "fireside chats," along with pronouncements by Under Secretary of State Sumner Welles and Secretary of State Cordell Hull. The anniversary of U.S. independence always received special recognition. Special magazines such as *En Guardia*, *La Guerra y Las Americas*, and *La Guerra Industrial* were heavy on photographs of the battlefield victories and factories producing war matériel. A number of themes characterized these stories: that the United States was leading the fight for democracy against totalitarianism; that Central America contributed materially to the war effort; and that the "four freedoms" found in the 1941 Atlantic Charter were to be for all the people of the world. Carías, Hernández Martínez, Somoza, and Ubico repeated these themes in editorials and in their annual congressional messages.[24]

Daily radio news programs, originating in the United States, repeated the same themes in each of the republics. Other programs came to include "Song of the Americas," a collection of Walt Whitman's poems and stories about freedom and democracy, and "Music and Words of Freedom," music and commentary on democracy. As the war progressed, increased emphasis was given to addressing the anticipated postwar socioeconomic needs of these countries, such as "Mirando al Horizonte," an intellectual program on the peace and prosperity to come after the war. OIAA printed pamphlets that explained the conversion of factories from civilian to wartime production, a theme also prevalent in the advertising by U.S. companies in Central American newspapers. Other pamphlets offered printed versions of the Roosevelt, Welles, and Hull speeches.[25]

Clearly, the U.S.-sponsored propaganda in Central America emphasized democracy, civil and human rights, and economic and social mobility. In fact, official U.S. policy in 1944 made it known to the regional dictators that it favored doing business with representative and democratically elected governments.[26]

OIAA films shown in Nicaragua mirrored what was seen in the other republics, including *Victory in the Air*, about Curtis Wright Cyclone planes; *Heavy Bombers*, about B-17 Flying Fortresses; and *Men of West Point*, which depicted training at West Point.[27]

Despite the effort, not all policy makers agreed that the U.S. propaganda and information campaigns were having any significant impact upon the masses of Central Americans, given their illiteracy and concern with everyday needs. For example, State Department analyst J. F. Melby noted that the four dictators tightly controlled their nations, including the disorganized opposition groups. Only the withdrawal of U.S. support would threaten the dictators' position. In Costa Rica, Melby concluded, the war was having little impact upon the country's internal affairs, and peaceful, comparatively honest elections were expected to be the continued norm. Oklahoma journalist Reginald Dawson shared Melby's viewpoint. Dawson authored a pamphlet that circulated in the United States and made its way to Central America. In his "Letter of a North American Newspaperman to the President of the United States," Dawson criticized the prodemocracy efforts made by the United States in Central America, where no one knew "about any of the freedoms that you have proclaimed all over the globe."[28]

Melby and Dawson misjudged Central America's political realities, however. In El Salvador, in the months leading up to Hernández Martínez's "reelection" on March 1, 1944, opposition flysheets and pamphlets specifically noted the absence of a free press, a right to free assembly, and honest elections. Notably, on the same day that *La Prensa Grafica* reported about the

Atlantic Charter, August 7, 1943, its publisher José Quetglas penned an editorial asserting that democracy provided the right to not only protest against a government but also to freely exercise the right to vote and to have civil rights.[29]

In Guatemala, Ubico exercised greater control over opposition groups. In April and May 1944, university students informed embassy officials that every time they gathered to protest, the National Police were at their doorstep. Yet, it was the students' demands for a greater voice in the affairs of the College of Pharmacy that mushroomed into a general strike that included "[medical] internees, doctors, teachers and other professional groups in protest against the curtailment of civil liberties." Partisan elements seized the moment, forcing Ubico to choose between bloodshed and resignation. On July 1, 1944, he chose the latter. Although Guatemala City's *El Imparcial* did little more than credit students and women for initiating the return to constitutional government, the Salvadoran papers paralleled the two movements as triumphs of the ideals of humankind.[30]

While *El Imparcial* ignored the ideals of World War II in writing about events in Guatemala, it emphasized those ideals when reporting about the various protests in Honduras on July 4, 1944. Significantly the Honduran papers did not mention the demonstrations in Tegucigalpa, San Pedro Sula, and Nueva Ocotepeque, which were ostensibly on behalf of the U.S. Independence Day, but were filled with banners demanding constitutional government and civil liberties in Honduras. In each, women wore United Nations headscarves. The July 4 demonstrations were the culmination of a clandestine movement that began in May 1944 following the ouster of Hernández Martínez in El Salvador, when secretly printed flysheets circulated in the larger cities demanding the implementation of the Four Freedoms in Honduras. As he had in the past, President Carías used the military to brutally suppress the July 4 demonstrators. Ironically, Carías used Franklin Roosevelt's reelection in 1944 and the wartime restriction of civil liberties in the United States to justify his own *continuismo* and iron fist in Honduras.[31]

Somoza understood the elite landowners' opposition to him, but misjudged the extent of it from the middle and lower socioeconomic sectors. Just as Somoza openly praised Roosevelt to serve his own purposes, the elites used Roosevelt's idealistic war objectives to serve their own goal—Somoza's ouster from office. Nicaraguan exiles residing in Mexico City, like their counterparts from El Salvador, Guatemala, and Honduras, often chastised the United States for combating dictatorships in Europe and Asia but not Central America. Oftentimes their mimeographed flysheets could be found in Nicaragua's major cities, but seldom was there a mass circulation of them. Occasionally, when Nicaragua's embryonic and Communist-led labor movement marched in demand of better wages and working conditions, they carried banners declaring that "Roosevelt Has Said That the Tyrants of the

Earth Will Be Wiped Out." When Hernández Martínez was ousted on May 17, 1944, and Ubico a month later, students and women marched before the U.S. Embassy in Managua demanding U.S. support to achieve the same goal in Nicaragua. The United States did not act—but Somoza did. He withdrew his support from the movement to pass a constitutional amendment that would have extended his presidency in 1947. For the moment, a political calm returned, but not the Nicaraguans' dislike of the dictator. Still, Somoza continued to speak in favor of FDR, applauding his reelection in November 1944 and expressing appreciation for current U.S. policy that encouraged democracy in all Latin America.[32]

Traditionally democratic Costa Rica held its regularly scheduled presidential election on February 2, 1944, which was won by National Republican Party candidate Teodoro Picado over Democratic Party nominee Leon Cortés. *Personalismo*, social reform, and the war-instigated hardships such as food shortages and inflation were the major issues—not World War II, on which the country was decidedly pro-Allied. The ideals of World War II were not an issue; instead, the role of government in addressing the Ticos' socioeconomic issues was. Picado's victory continued Costa Rica's movement down the socialist road.[33]

The middle and upper sectors played a significant role in instigating Central America's political upheaval in 1944. As the readers of newspapers and other publications, the listeners of radio stations, and the moviegoers, these sectors were the region's most articulate. They best understood the closed political systems in which they lived and were frustrated by their historic inability to change it. While many reasons indigenous to the region called for change, World War II's idealistic goals offered new reason and hope for changing the political arena in 1944.

CONCLUSION

As throughout much of its history, Central America did not occupy the center stage of U.S. policy during World War II. Yet, with the exception of military planning, the region was greatly impacted by U.S. actions. At the war's start, the Central American military was unprepared to meet the challenges of regional defense, and the subsequent U.S. effort to modernize and incorporate the armies into regional defense plans was resisted by the isthmian governments. In contrast, the Central American governments readily cooperated with the United States in the deportation of German nationals and their descendents and in limiting the civil liberties and controlling the properties of those who remained in the region following the outbreak of war.

The anti-Axis policies, however, removed one of the most vibrant groups that contributed to the economic life of each republic. This loss, coupled with the loss of markets for their primary products, wreaked economic havoc across Central America and during the war contributed to the nascent labor movements that grew in strength afterward.

While the economic dislocations caused by the war contributed to the regional elites' pressure for political change, they found an ally in the broad-based middle sector that was greatly influenced by the idealistic goals espoused by the Allies throughout the war. These ideals found expression in Central America's political arena in 1944.

NOTES

1. "A Study of Central America, Panama and Colombia," January 26, 1939, File 2-1939-9, U.S. Army War College Archive, Carlisle Barracks, Pennsylvania.

2. Caribbean Defense Command, *The Caribbean Defense Theater in the Defense of the Americas*, File 8-2.8, Office for the Center of Military History Archive, Washington, DC, 23, 58–59.

3. Stetson Conn and Byron Fairchild, *The United States Army in World War II: The Western Hemisphere; The Framework of Hemispheric Defense* (Washington, DC: GPO, 1960), 172–86.

4. The texts of these agreements can be found in Charles I. Bevans, comp., *Treaties and Other International Agreements of the United States of America, 1776–1949* (Washington, DC: Department of State, 1971), 6:1063–67 (Costa Rica), 7:545–50 (El Salvador), 8:535–38 (Guatemala), 8:961–65 (Honduras), 10:415–29 (Nicaragua).

5. Thomas M. Leonard, "Central America and U.S. Strategic Planning, 1939–1941," *MesoAmerica*, forthcoming.

6. For the texts of the Lend-Lease Agreements, see Bevans, *Treaties and Other International Agreements*, 6:1070–73 (Costa Rica), 7:554–57 (El Salvador), 8:539–44 (Guatemala), 8:936–39 (Honduras), 10:420–23 (Nicaragua). For Lend-Lease assistance to Central America, see U.S. Department of State, *Twenty-Third Report to Congress on Lend-Lease Operations* (Washington, DC: GPO, 1946). For a discussion of the Lend-Lease program, see Warren F. Kimball, *The Most Unsordid Act: Lend-Lease, 1939–1941* (Baltimore: Johns Hopkins University Press, 1969).

7. Conn and Fairchild, *Framework of Hemispheric Defense*, 172–206, 238–64; U.S. Bureau of Yards and Docks, *Building the Navy's Bases in World War II: History of the Bureau of Yards and Docks and the Civil Engineer Corps, 1940–1946* (Washington, DC: GPO, 1947), 2:35–71.

8. "Axis Penetration of South America," Papers of Nelson A. Rockefeller, Personal Files, Rockefeller Archive Center, North Tarrytown, New York (hereafter referred to as the Rockefeller Archive), Washington Series, CIAA, Box 6, Folder 49, 4.

9. Literature describing the German threat before the outbreak of war includes Alton Frye, *Nazi Germany and the American Hemisphere, 1933–1941* (New Haven, CT: Yale University Press, 1967); Leslie B. Rout Jr. and John F. Bratzel, *Shadow War: German Espionage and United States Counterespionage during World War II* (Frederick, MD: University Publications of America, 1986); Carlton Beals, "Totalitarian

Inroads in Latin America," *Foreign Affairs Quarterly* 17 (October 1938): 78–89; Richard R. Behrent, "Foreign Influence in Latin America," *Annals of the American Academy of Political and Social Science* 204 (July 1939): 1–8; and Lawrence Martin and Sylvia Martin, "Nazi Intrigues in Central America," *American Mercury* 53 (July 1941): 66–73.

10. Letter to Congressman John Stefan, May 8, 1947, Rockefeller Archive, Group III, Box 2, Folder 9; memorandum of December 12, 1940, National Archives and Records Administration of the United States (hereafter referred to as NARA), RG (Record Group) 59, Lot Files, Office of Inter-American Affairs, 1918–1947, General Memoranda, Box 4.

11. A most critical account of U.S. policies can be found in Max Paul Friedman, *Nazis and Good Neighbors: The United States Campaign against the Germans of Latin America in World War II* (New York: Cambridge University Press, 2003).

12. In Guatemala, the ruling junta that replaced Jorge Ubico in June 1944 nationalized the German properties, which were among the first lands redistributed to the peasants in the subsequent Jacobo Arbenz administration. See Jim Handy, *Revolution in the Countryside: Rural Conflict and Agrarian Reform in Guatemala, 1944–1954* (Chapel Hill: University of North Carolina Press, 1994).

13. "Condition of German Groups in the Other American Republics," NARA, RG 59, Office of Intelligence Research, Division of Research for the American Republics, Vol. 5, July–December 1943. For the Havana Conference, see U.S. Department of State, *Foreign Relations of the United States: Diplomatic Papers, 1940*, Vol. 5, *The American Republics* (Washington, DC: GPO, 1940), 180–256. For the Rio Conference, see U.S. Department of State, *Foreign Relations of the United States: Diplomatic Papers, 1942*, Vol. 5, *The American Republics* (Washington, DC: GPO, 1942), 6–45.

14. For a discussion of U.S.-German economic competition in Central America, see Thomas D. Schoonover, *Germany in Central America: Competitive Imperialism, 1821–1939* (Tuscaloosa: University of Alabama Press, 1998). For a discussion of German trade with Central America in the 1930s, see Victor Bulmer-Thomas, *The Political Economy of Central America since 1920* (Cambridge: Cambridge University Press, 1987). For a discussion of the U.S. Trade Reciprocity Program, see Dick Steward, *Trade and Hemisphere: The Good Neighbor Policy and Reciprocal Trade Agreements* (Colombia: University of Missouri Press, 1975).

15. "Economic Penetration of Latin America," Rockefeller Archive, OIAA, Box 11, Folder 85.

16. John M. Cabot, memoranda of July 8 and 21, 1943, NARA, RG 59, ARA, Lot Files, Box 8.

17. Bulmer-Thomas, *Political Economy*, 91–92, 350n15.

18. "Statistics-Imports from Other American Republics," July 4, 1944, Rockefeller Papers, CIAA, Box 12, Folder 99; "A Brief Account of the Activities of the Procurement Agencies of the U.S. Government," August 14, 1944, Rockefeller Papers, OIAA, Box 12, Folder 100.

19. F. W. James, "A Quarter Century of Road Building in the Americas," *Bulletin of the Pan American Union* 79 (November 1945), 609–18; Organization of American States, *The Pan American Highway System* (Washington, DC: Organization of American States, 1969).

20. "Confidential Data on Other American Republics," undated, NARA, RG 59, Office of Intelligence Research.

21. Cruse letter to Col. W. W. Cox, April 18, 1944, NARA, RG 165, MID, Regional Central America.

22. For a fuller discussion, see Ralph Lee Woodward Jr., *Central America: A Nation Divided*, 3rd ed. (New York: Oxford University Press, 1999). Statistics from memorandum of November 14, 1942, NARA, RG 59, Lot Files, ARA, Box 7; and "Literacy Project," undated memorandum, Rockefeller Papers, CIAA, Box 5, Folder 40.

23. The official history of the OIAA is Office of Inter-American Affairs, *History of the Office of the Coordinator of Inter-American Affairs* (Washington, DC: GPO, 1947).

24. This information is drawn from NARA, RG 229, Records of the Department of Press and Publication, and the author's six-month research trip in Central America, where newspapers were examined at national archives and national libraries.

25. "CIAA Transcription Programs in Production," "Short-wave Broadcasts to Other American Republics," and "Proposed Special Advertising for Spanish Language," all undated, Rockefeller Papers, CIAA, Box 9, Folder 73.

26. For a discussion of the political events in Central America during 1944, see Thomas M. Leonard, *The United States and Central America, 1944–1949: Perceptions of Political Dynamics* (Tuscaloosa: University of Alabama Press, 1984).

27. NARA, RG 229, OIAA, Department of Information, Regional Division, Coordinating Committee, Nicaragua, Folder "Press, Pictures and Posters."

28. NARA, RG 59, Lot Files, ARA, Box 8, February 20, 1943.

29. *La Prensa Grafica*, August 15, 1943.

30. "Triunfo del civismo y ed la cultura fué la manifestación ayer," *El Imparcial*, July 3, 1944; "Los sucessos de Guatemala" and "La verdad sobre lo de Guatemala," Biblioteca Manual Gallardo, Santa Tecla, El Salvador, Apuntos 1–44.

31. "La causa del Pueblo Hondureño," *El Imparcial*, July 8, 1944; "Matanzas en la República de Honduras," *La Prensa Grafica* (San Salvador), July 5, 1944.

32. Memoranda of May 17 and 24, June 27 and 28, and July 9, 1944, NARA, RG 84, Post Records; memorandum of November 8, 1944, RG 59 817.911/8–44.

33. "Costa Rican Presidential Election," February 7, 1944, Rockefeller Archive, CIAA, Box 9, Folder 74.

4

Panama: Nationalism and the Challenge to Canal Security

Orlando J. Pérez

Panama occupied the most important strategic location in Latin America during World War II, and protecting the canal that dissected the country was of vital importance to the U.S. war effort. Concomitantly, Panamanian political dynamics greatly concerned U.S. officials. In the years immediately preceding U.S. entrance into the war, Panama had undergone significant political changes that threatened U.S. interests. The rise of middle-class sectors linked to xenophobic nationalist political ideas—and thought to be susceptible to Axis influence—alarmed the United States. The United States therefore aided in the overthrow of the Panamanian government two months prior to the Japanese attack on Pearl Harbor. After December 1941, the new Panamanian government complied with U.S. interests on the isthmus and, although tensions between the two countries continued to focus upon Panama's insistence on receiving greater compensation for its assistance, Panamanian cooperation became the key to securing the Western Hemisphere from the Axis powers.

This chapter first examines the rise of nationalism as a major force in Panamanian politics in the decades before World War II, followed by a discussion of the administration of Arnulfo Arias (1940–41) and U.S.–Panama relations on the eve of the war. Third will be an analysis of U.S.–Panama wartime relations, paying particular attention to the defense of the Panama Canal. The conclusion explores Panama's response to the war and its implications for the country's domestic economic and political situation.

ECONOMIC CRISIS AND THE RISE
OF NATIONALISM AS A POTENT
POLITICAL FORCE

By the early 1930s, the impact of the world depression served to exacerbate tensions between Panama and the United States. Panamanians found themselves competing for unskilled jobs on the "silver roll"[1] with West Indian blacks whose forefathers had been imported by the U.S. Panamanian Canal Company to supply manual labor for canal construction. Panamanians now condemned the foreigner—whether U.S. technician or West Indian laborer—as an invader who seized the benefits of the waterway while Panamanians suffered economic deprivation.

The ill effects of the Depression were especially acute in Panama City and Colón, where Panama's emerging middle class lived, depending upon the prosperity of the canal for their livelihood. Just like the working-class Panamanians who competed with blacks in the Canal Zone, the middle classes of Panama City and Colón resented U.S. policy and sought greater commercial benefits from the canal. Similarly, both groups tended to be xenophobic, expressing hostility toward the encroachment of Anglo-Saxon norms in isthmian life.

Middle-class nationalist aspirations found expression in the *Acción Comunal* (precursor of the *Panameñista* movement) coup of 1931. Founded in 1923, this group represented an important opposition to the Liberal presidency of Florencio Harmodio Arosemena (1928–31), whom it accused of having organized electoral fraud to capture the presidency and engaging in widespread corruption. The basic ideological tenants of Acción Comunal were nationalist and fervently anti-U.S.; the slogan adopted by the organization was *"Patriotismo, Acción, Equidad y Disciplina"* (Patriotism, Action, Equality, and Discipline).[2]

Another important element of the organization's ideology was a strong anti-immigration stance. Isidro Beluche Mora explains that Acción Comunal's nationalism was based on the belief that Panama's unique geographic position exposed it to "a mass of immigrants willing to enrich themselves to the detriment of national citizens and erase the characteristic elements of Panamanian national identity."[3] Arnulfo Arias would echo these sentiments in his inaugural address in 1941, and they would form the basis of many of the most xenophobic policies of his administration. Arias's overtly racist policies were in line with Nazi ideas and compounded U.S. suspicion of his administration.

By 1931, accusations of financial corruption and political scandals involving President Arosemena had reached a high pitch. On January 2, Acción Comunal launched a coup that successfully unseated the Panamanian president. After the coup, a transitional government was established to rule until the elections of 1932. Harmodio Arias, brother of Arnulfo Arias, won those elections.[4] The Acción Comunal coup was the first violent overthrow of a sitting president in Panamanian history, but it would not be the last.

One of the significant consequences of the coup was the proliferation of paramilitary groups at the service of political candidates and parties. Taking advantage of changes in U.S. policy that renounced direct military intervention, government and opposition parties formed paramilitary organizations to intimidate and harass opponents and keep supporters in line. Once the election was over, the winning candidates would "incorporate" these paramilitary forces into the National Police, thus increasing their control and the politicization of the police force.[5] This process eventually led to the National Police becoming the arbiter of national politics. As historian Michael Conniff notes, "Whoever controls the *Policía Nacional* writes Panama's political history."[6]

As the subversive activities of Latin American Nazi and Fascist sympathizers gained momentum in the 1930s, the United States became concerned about the need for hemispheric solidarity. By the late 1930s, Secretary of State Cordell Hull observed, "Axis penetration had made rapid, alarming headway under various guises."[7] Particularly alarming for the secretary was the growth of business ties between Latin Americans and Germans, who, according to Hull, developed "their businesses and [were] digging in socially, commercially, and politically."[8]

In his March 1933 inaugural address, President Franklin D. Roosevelt enunciated the Good Neighbor Policy. That same year, at the Seventh Inter-American Conference in Montevideo, the United States expressed a qualified acceptance of the principle of nonintervention; in 1936 the United States approved this principle without reservation.[9] Therefore, by the late 1930s the rise of nationalism as a potent political force in Panama, changes in U.S. policy toward Latin America, and U.S. concerns about Fascist influence in the region worked to significantly change the terms of U.S.–Panamanian relations.

In October 1933, President Harmodio Arias paid a visit to the United States. The visit paved the way for negotiations to change the 1903 Hay–Bunau Varilla Treaty.[10] As a result of the conversations between Roosevelt and Arias, the United States pledged that it would give sympathetic consideration to future arbitration requests involving economic issues so long as they did not affect the vital operations of the canal. On March 2, 1936, Secretary of State Hull and Assistant Secretary of State Sumner Welles joined the Panamanian negotiators in signing a new treaty—the Hull-Alfaro Treaty.

The new treaty provided a new context for relations between the two countries. It ended the protectorate by abrogating the 1903 treaty guarantee of the republic's independence that had given the United States the right to intervene in Panama whenever it deemed necessary. The annuity was increased to $430,000 to be paid retroactively to 1934.[11] Several provisions dealt with long-standing Panamanian grievances over their commercial access to and activity in the Canal Zone, particularly the inability of the Panamanian commercial elite to penetrate the zone market and the "unfair" competition from subsidized zone prices. As a result, the 1936 treaty forbade private commercial enterprises unconnected with canal operations within the zone. The treaty also forbade the duty-free entry into the zone of Panamanian goods and other foreign-made goods that passed through Panama. To regulate the entry of goods from the zone into Panama the republic established customhouses at the zone's entrances.[12]

With the abrogation of the U.S. right to unilaterally intervene in Panama, one of the most contentious issues in the negotiating process dealt with the defense of the canal. The U.S. concern centered on the possibility that an "unfriendly" Panamanian government might grant concessions to a foreign power. Thus, Washington wanted to maintain its ability to secure the canal and adjacent lands with military intervention, if needed.

For Panama, restoration of "sovereignty" over its entire territory was the most important factor. Article X of the treaty recognized the concept of joint responsibility for canal defense, but underscored the right of both nations to act unilaterally in the event that their "common interests" were threatened. The treaty, however, stipulated that actions taken by one party to protect its interests that might affect the territory of the other party must be a "subject of consultation between the two Governments."[13]

While Panama ratified the treaty almost immediately, the U.S. Senate took another three years—and then only when an imminent threat of a real "international conflagration" prompted it to do so and only after assurances that the United States could act "without consulting" Panama if an emergency developed.[14] The importance of Article X and the ability of the United States to act unilaterally became evident once World War II started. Under the provisions of the treaty, the U.S. moved to aggressively defend the canal from foreign threats, including the leasing of hundreds of military defense sites throughout the isthmus.

PANAMANIAN POLITICS ON THE EVE OF WAR

Immediately after Great Britain and France declared war on Germany on September 3, 1939, following the German invasion of Poland, invitations were dispatched to the Latin American nations for a conference to be held in Panama. The Panama Conference opened on September 23, with Under Secretary of State Sumner Welles heading the U.S. delegation. The Panamanian government, now headed by Juan Demóstenes Arosemena, brother of

Florencio, enthusiastically supported U.S. positions in international affairs.
President Arosemena (1936–39) sought to use Panama's cooperation as
leverage to wrest significant concessions from the United States. In particular, he wanted to increase the local merchants' access to the post exchanges
that supplied goods to the U.S. armed forces stationed in the Canal Zone. As
stated earlier, the threat of an international conflagration had already
prompted the U.S. Senate to ratify the 1936 Hull-Alfaro Treaty, which called
for greater commercial links between Panamanian businessmen and the
Canal Zone. Arosemena demanded that those provisions be enforced as soon
as possible.[15]

Before the conference adjourned on October 3, the delegates adopted resolutions embodying the principles of neutrality and provisions for inter-
American political and economic cooperation. Resolution XIV, usually
known as the Declaration of Panama, provided for the establishment of a
Neutrality Zone, from which all belligerent warships were to be excluded,
extending about three hundred miles seaward from the coast, starting at the
Canadian-American boundary in the Atlantic and continuing around North
and South America to the Canadian-American boundary in the Pacific. Each
nation was authorized to patrol waters adjacent to its own coast to secure
compliance with this resolution.[16]

When President Arosemena died unexpectedly in December 1939, U.S.
officials feared a rise to power of Arnulfo Arias, and in an effort to thwart
any effort by Arias, the U.S. Army Air Force returned the first presidential
designate, Ambassador to the United States Augusto Samuel Boyd, to Panama to be sworn in as president.[17] U.S. officials hoped that Boyd's ascension
would serve as a "stumbling block to Arias in the 1940 elections."[18]

During his brief presidency (1939–40), Boyd continued to support U.S.
efforts to strengthen its military position on the isthmus and made efforts
to distance Panama from the Axis powers. For example, Panama recalled its
ambassadors from Italy; sought to continue diplomatic contacts with the
deposed governments of Poland, Holland, and other German-occupied territories; and reduced its representation in Berlin significantly.

In 1940, rather than challenging Arias, Boyd—to the great disappointment
of the United States—did everything within his power to assist the Arias
candidacy. In retrospect, one U.S. State Department official noted, "Boyd
virtually assured the election of Arnulfo Arias in the recent presidential election by permitting the National Police and other governmental agencies to
overawe and intimidate the electorate in favor of Arias."[19]

ARNULFO ARIAS AND THE RISE OF THE
PANAMEÑISTA PARTY

Arnulfo Arias and his older brother Harmodio came from a rural, lower-
middle-class family in the interior. Both studied abroad, Arnulfo pursuing

medicine at the University of Chicago and at Harvard University. While the United States had maintained very good relations with Harmodio—evidence exists that the United States acquiesced to the 1931 Acción Comunal coup partly because it considered Harmodio a man of "honesty, integrity, and ability"—the same cannot be said for Arnulfo. At one point, a U.S. intelligence official said Arnulfo had a "totalitarian complex" and was part of the "irresponsible" elements of Acción Comunal.[20] Arnulfo emerged as the most forceful leader of the organization and led its paramilitary forces.

Arnulfo Arias spent most of the period of his brother's 1932–36 presidency as Panamanian ambassador to Italy, where he came to admire the discipline and nationalism of both Mussolini and Hitler. Upon his return from Europe, Arias's xenophobic and nationalist rhetoric intensified and became virulently anti-American. This sudden change of attitude puzzled many U.S. officials. Previously, while Arias espoused nationalistic rhetoric, he had still maintained friendly relations with the United States. U.S. officials surmised that Arias's attitude change resulted from having "reached some understanding with the Berlin and Rome Chancellories."[21]

Arias made the first of his five runs for president in the 1940 elections. He founded the National Revolutionary Party, which became the political arm of the Panameñista movement and the political successor to Acción Comunal. The elections proved to be among the most violent in Panama's history. Both Arias and his opponent, noted diplomat and former interim president Ricardo J. Alfaro, funded paramilitary forces. Arias, however, had the advantage. With the overt support of President Boyd came the support of the National Police. In the end, Alfaro boycotted the elections and Arias won by default.

By the time Arnulfo Arias assumed the presidency in 1940, he faced considerable opposition from Washington, where he was viewed as a "pro-Axis" sympathizer. The U.S. ambassador to Panama, Edwin Wilson, reflected this opinion when he cabled the State Department: "What has developed in Panama is about as near an approach to Hitlerism as the characteristics of Latin Americans and the peculiar circumstances affecting Panama could be expected to permit."[22]

In his inaugural address on October 1, 1940, Arias did nothing to allay Washington's concern. In this speech, Arias reiterated his party's creed of "Panama for the Panamanians" and said this did not preclude the "assimilation or incorporation of desirable foreigners." Arias went on to argue against the "demagogic" idea that "all men are born equal and free." He based his argument on the "biological and evolutionary basis of our existence." Arias dedicated a large portion of his inaugural address to discussing the problem of immigration, which he tied to the imperative of "improving the biological conditions" of Panamanians. For Arias, the problem of immigration was directly tied to U.S. policy during the construction of the Panama Canal when the United States imported large contingents of people of "color, alien to [Panama's] culture," mostly from the West Indies and Asia.[23]

Perhaps the most significant action taken by the short-lived Arias administration was the promulgation of a new constitution. On November 22, 1940, a month and a half after Arias had taken power, the National Assembly, controlled by Arias's forces, issued a law establishing the new constitution. Instead of waiting for the next Assembly, four years hence, on November 26 Arias issued Decree no. 141, which assumed for the executive the "supreme representation of the State" in order to call for a plebiscite to approve the new code. In the December 15 referendum, an overwhelming majority of voters approved the constitution.[24] The document became effective on January 2, 1941.

While the Constitution of 1941 contained many progressive features, such as suffrage for women, a social security system, and other social welfare reforms, the document also consolidated power in the hands of the president. Among other things, it increased the presidential term from four to six years, expanded the power of the executive to issue decrees, and provided for the National Assembly to delegate extensive powers to the president in "emergencies." Perhaps the most controversial portions of the new constitution were the anti-immigrant provisions. Article 23 denied entrance to Panama to immigrants "of the black race whose native language is not Spanish, of the yellow race, and the races originating in India, Asia Minor, and North Africa."[25]

Among the most insidious provisions of the new code was the denial of citizenship to children born in Panama of individuals within the categories of "prohibited" immigration. When many in the West Indian community and others protested the provision, Arias reportedly said that he did not consider these people "a bad Colony, on the contrary they were hardworking people, who did not trouble the police courts too frequently." He later added, "At any rate, I will not do as the Nazis do: I will not shoot them." The foreign minister declared, "The Panamanians are anxious to guard against the danger that Panama, situated at the crossroads of the world, should degenerate from a Spanish-speaking, white nation into a cosmopolitan congeries, a babel of tongues, an utterly bastardized race."[26]

In addition to the constitutional provisions, the president went further by prohibiting the allocation of business licenses to all prohibited races,[27] a law aimed particularly at Chinese-Panamanian merchants. Additionally, a new press law restricted foreigners from commenting on Panamanian affairs, thus providing criminal penalties for Panamanians of West Indian origin who protested their mistreatment.

Arias's policies and pronouncements alarmed the United States, and also generated substantial opposition in Panama. Sectors of the commercial elite feared the new constitution would damage their business interests. Particu-

larly important was opposition from his brother, former President Harmodio Arias, who used his newspaper, the *Panama American*, to launch
attacks on the president.[28] There is evidence that Harmodio and others had
approached the U.S. embassy seeking support for a coup to topple the president as early as January 1941.[29]

Given the United States' stated objective of nonintervention laid out in the
Good Neighbor Policy, the U.S. was reluctant to be seen to overtly sanction
or support a coup. However, given the fears of Axis influence and Arias's
refusal to agree to the leasing of sites for U.S. military bases, the United
States did not hesitate to support the coup that occurred on October 7, 1941.

President Arias provided his opponents with the "rope to hang him with"
when, on October 7, he surreptitiously left Panama to visit his mistress in
Cuba. The Panamanian constitution required the president to inform the
Supreme Court prior to leaving the country. Thus, when U.S. intelligence
officers informed his opponents that the president had left the country,[30] the
opposition, which by now included powerful elements of the National
Police,[31] moved quickly to declare that the president had "abandoned" his
office and to name Ricardo Adolfo de la Guardia, the minister of government and justice, to the presidency.

The overthrow of President Arias marked the second time in ten years
that a Panamanian president had been removed by a coup and marked
another sign of the growing influence of the National Police. The coup also
reminded nationalists in Panama of the power the United States would use
to influence Panamanian politics. Having established the importance of the
Panama Canal for U.S. strategic interests, and given the rising international
tensions, the United States was not about to stand by and allow a Panamanian president to thwart its plans for defending the waterway.

PANAMA DURING THE WAR

The United States quickly moved to recognize de la Guardia's government.
John Major quotes a U.S. intelligence officer as saying that "the accession to
authority . . . of a man of known pro-U.S. sentiments . . . would be acceptable
if not welcomed." Some U.S. officials were so concerned about anti-American
activity in Panama that they suggested "a thorough fumigation" whereby
children would be "indoctrinated" in U.S. values "so that never again will
we ever face the danger of having to tolerate an anti-America Administration
in Panama."[32]

President de la Guardia's attitude was decidedly pro-American. Shortly
after assuming the presidency, de la Guardia reversed Arias's refusal to arm
Panamanian-flagged vessels. On December 10, 1941, three days after the
Pearl Harbor attack by Japanese forces, Panama declared war on Japan and

Germany[33] and initiated the process of incarcerating German and Japanese nationals. In addition, the government prohibited the immigration of persons from Axis-occupied territories.[34] This provision and the arrests were part of a U.S. initiative to rid the isthmus of Axis influence. As the U.S. embassy stated, "The request to have these enemy aliens in the Republic of Panama detained and interned was made by the United States Government, because of reasons connected with the defense of the Panama Canal." In fact, Max Paul Friedman argues that as early as October 1941, shortly after the overthrow of Arnulfo Arias, the government of Panama "agreed to a U.S. proposal to establish camps for interning the Panamanian Japanese in the event of war." The Panamanian government expressed certain reservations with regard to German and Italian nationals, many of whom had married members of Panama's oligarchy and were considered prominent citizens. In the end, the United States obtained Panama's acquiescence to the internment of Axis Europeans, with "a very few exceptions in the case of German and Italians married to Panamanians concerning whom the Government could give assurances that they would constitute no danger." Apparently one of these Germans was married to the foreign minister's aunt.[35]

Disputes between Panama and the United States would ensue regarding deportation of well-connected Germans. In the end, as reported by Friedman, many of the Germans deported and interned were not members of the Nazi Party nor did they have any provable connections with the German government or its intelligence agencies. In fact, a report by the U.S. Justice Department alluded to the fact that U.S. officials in Panama and the Panamanian government were rounding up Axis nationals "without inquiry as to the loyalty or danger of the particular alien." Friedman concludes that this approach undermined the premise of the deportation policy—to defend the Panama Canal—since it led to "the internment of more Jewish refugees than Nazi Party members, while the majority of the Nazis were left behind in Panama."[36]

A question arose as to where the "enemy aliens" would be interned. Guatemala's government asked that they be sent to the United States, and by December 16, State Department officials were seriously considering that request. On January 13, 1942, Panama agreed to transport interned Axis nationals to the United States with the caveat that they remain under Panamanian "jurisdiction."

The plans for the internment of Japanese and other Axis nationals were laid out during the Emergency Advisory Committee for Political Defense in Rio de Janeiro in January 1942. This meeting consisted of the United States and the foreign ministers of countries in South and Central America. The U.S. officials expressed their desire to intern those who they considered "dangerous Axis nationals." The United States assured the countries that it would pay for the shipping and interning facilities of the internees. In the end, a total of 247 Germans were deported from Panama to the United States between 1941 and 1945.

Expropriation of property was also common. Many Germans were interned and deported precisely because they ran successful businesses. Most Latin American countries complied enthusiastically since they could use the expropriation for their own political and economic purposes. For the United States, expropriation was a matter of immediate and future national security, in the sense that no one could be certain how Germany would emerge from the war and whether or not it would use those assets to engage in military activities in the future. But expropriation also allowed for the expansion of U.S. economic interests in the region, particularly in areas such as air travel, wholesale commerce, mining, and industrial development. While the State Department was wary of overt support for U.S. private firms to acquire former German assets, it did little to stand in the way. In the case of Panama, U.S. officials could report that by 1945 "there is not a single known Axis enterprise in operation."[37]

In addition to the measures against Axis nationals, the de la Guardia government undertook several measures to assist in the "defense of the Panamanian population." For example, it established a Civil Defense Commission to coordinate the efforts at protecting the homeland, including the recruitment of thousands of citizens to serve as volunteers across the nation to detect suspicious activities and aid the National Police in their defense functions. Additionally, the government established a Superior Board of Disciplinary Organization "destined to awaken the consciousness of duty in our youth and prepare them for service to the fatherland, under any emergency." The board, under the jurisdiction of the Ministry of Education, sought to promote patriotism, nationalistic feelings, and especially anti-Axis sentiments among the young. The administration also created a National Board of War Censorship to monitor and control radio broadcasts.[38]

In other actions directly related to the war, Panama sought to establish a more reliable air passenger and mail service by contracting with the Salvadoran-based Transportes Aéreos Centroamericanos (TACA) to operate regular commercial flights throughout the isthmus.[39] This contract would later place Panama and the Canal Zone government in conflict, as the latter supported a deal with Pan American World Airways to operate a civilian airfield in the Canal Zone. Because it viewed such an action as detrimental to its national economic interests, the Panamanian government argued that the 1936 treaty prohibited a commercial firm from operating in the Canal Zone; U.S. government officials countered that the new airfield was necessary for the war efforts. Beyond the airport's location, U.S. military authorities sought to control Panama's airspace in time of war and peace. As early as October 1939, the United States regulated use of the Canal Zone's airspace, barring Panamanian planes and those of the European combatants from flying over the zone. In the end, a new joint Aviation Board was created to regulate flights across the isthmus, but Panamanian board members were expected to follow the lead of their U.S. counterparts.

The war had a major impact on Panama's economy. Commercial transit through the canal dropped by more than a third between 1940 and 1945, resulting in a two-thirds decrease in toll revenues. In contrast, Panama's domestic production rose, with many exports destined for the European and Pacific war theaters. Production of milk, sugar, and slaughtered cattle nearly doubled between 1939 and 1946. The government accelerated the take-off by quadrupling expenditures, but the real catalyst was the influx of dollars. Between 1930 and 1943, U.S. capital investments dropped sharply in every Latin American country except oil-rich Venezuela and Panama. The latter enjoyed the higher percentage increase of the two, as investment multiplied threefold to $514 million, mostly in banking and utilities. The number of enterprises controlled by U.S. companies increased from 22 in 1929 to 79 in 1943. Additionally, an estimated 12.5 percent of the Panamanian workforce was employed in the Canal Zone. In 1939, there were 3,511 "gold roll" (U.S. rate) workers in the zone and 11,246 "silver roll" (local rate) workers. By 1942, those numbers had climbed to 8,550 and 28,686, respectively.[40] The influx of workers to the Canal Zone and to Panama City and Colón was so large that the Panamanian government complained of the scarcity of teachers and other skilled employees. The government nonetheless took steps to take advantage of the situation by strengthening English-language education in the schools and emphasizing vocational training in commercial and business administration so as to encourage the development of small businesses and provide skilled employees for the increased number of commercial enterprises.[41]

Panamanians were employed in the construction of a third set of locks for the canal,[42] numerous highways, and hundreds of defense sites across the country. The highway construction included a stretch of road from Panama City to the Rio Hato air base in the west and a road between Panama City and Colón, known as the Transisthmian Highway. Along with the increased number of Panamanians, the United States imported thousands of workers from Central America and the West Indies. The additional workers and military personnel prompted the U.S. government to purchase huge amounts of food and other goods, thus helping to spur activity in Panama's agricultural sector.

During World War II, the Panama Canal's security remained the United States' most important concern in the Western Hemisphere. Panamanians saw this imperative as an opportunity to wrest significant economic concessions from the United States.

SECURING THE PANAMA CANAL

Because the mobility of the U.S. Navy fleets between the Atlantic and Pacific Oceans was a cornerstone of continental defense plans, the Army considered its mission of guarding the Panama Canal as secondary only to continental defense. In the mid-1930s the canal seemed completely invulnerable to attack. The extent of U.S. military power in the Canal Zone, plus geographic features such as the deep jungles beyond the zone, led many in the U.S. government to believe that land or sea attacks on the canal were unlikely to threaten the security of the waterway.

The emergence of air power by the late 1930s, however, alarmed U.S. military planners and caused a reconsideration of canal defense strategy. Following their reassessment of the situation in 1939, Army and Navy planners decided that the continental United States and the Canal Zone could be subjected to invasion or large-scale surface attack only if such an attack were backed by air power. While the Atlantic and Pacific Oceans provided a sense of security from the Axis powers, an attack could still be launched from land bases within the Western Hemisphere. This possibility took on new meaning because of the German influence in neighboring countries, which could lead to the establishment of Axis air bases for the launching of air strikes against the Panama Canal.[43] Therefore, a primary objective of U.S. hemispheric defense policy was to prevent the building of any hostile air bases in the Western Hemisphere from which the continental area or the Panama Canal might be bombed or from which a surface attack or invasion might be supported. To ward off a potential attack, the U.S. military planners wanted to obtain territorial sites throughout Panama that could be used to station U.S. troops and equipment. These bases would not only be used in the event of an attack, but could be used to preemptively destroy planes before they reached the canal area.

Had the original 1903 canal treaty been in effect at the beginning of the war, the United States would have had no problems obtaining the land and building the bases. The 1903 Hay–Bunau Varilla Treaty stated that the United States had in perpetuity the "use, occupation and control of other lands and waters outside of the zone . . . which may be necessary and convenient for the . . . protection of the said canal."[44] However, the 1936 Hull-Alfaro Treaty required the United States to obtain the acquiescence of Panama before any additional lands for canal defense would be ceded to U.S. control.

In September 1939, a week after hostilities began in Europe, the United States presented Panama with a list of ten sites, most about one acre in size, that the War Department considered essential for building military bases. The War Department initially asked for a 999-year lease. Understandably, the Panamanians fretted over the impact long-term leases would have on their sovereignty over national territory. Additionally, they feared that significant concessions would nullify the gains obtained in the 1936 treaty. Concerns over Panamanian sensitivities led the U.S. State Department to lower the time frame for the leases to ninety-nine years and to guarantee that Panama still held sovereignty over the territories and jurisdiction over Panamanian citizens working at the sites. Additionally, Panama would receive an annual payment and have the right to inspect each base. Along with those concessions, the United States submitted an additional list of sites for warning stations, landing fields, and searchlight positions. In the end, it requested more than 100 sites across Panama to be used for the canal's defense.

Negotiations dragged on for two years. On February 13, 1941, the anti-U.S. government of Arnulfo Arias advised the United States that such a request could only be attended under the provisions of Article X of the 1936 treaty, which required the United States to officially declare that an imminent threat existed against the canal. On the same day, U.S. Secretary of State Cordell Hull issued the required statement, declaring:

> The Government of the United States has . . . reached the conclusion that, in accordance with the terms of Article X of the Treaty of 1936 . . . an international conflagration has broken out bringing with it the existence of a threat to the security of the Panama Canal which requires the taking of measures for the defense of the canal on the part of the Government of the United States.[45]

On February 18, Panama responded with a memorandum that included twelve specific demands in exchange for the base leases:

1. Transfer, without cost, of the sanitation systems in the cities of Panama and Colón
2. Transfer of all lands belonging to the Panama Railroad in Panama City and Colón, valued in approximately $12 million
3. Both governments to intensify their efforts at preventing contraband from the Canal Zone into Panamanian territory
4. Construction of a bridge across the canal
5. U.S. assumption of a third of all costs to improve and maintain all roads and highways used by its military in Panama
6. The cessation of importing Caribbean blacks to work in the Canal Zone
7. U.S. military police and zone police restricted to the use of only billy clubs outside of the zone
8. Excess electricity from canal operations to be distributed to Panama City and Colón, as requested by the Panamanian government
9. The United States to assume the total cost of the road to Rio Hato,[46]

and therefore to pay the $2 million borrowed by Panama for this purpose from the U.S.-operated Export-Import Bank

10. The United States to transfer the railroad station in Panama City to the government of Panama
11. The United States to pay Panama an indemnity if the flow of U.S. troops during wartime interrupted regular canal traffic
12. The United States to provide workers for building an oil pipeline between Panama City and the Balboa port.[47]

The estimated cost of meeting these demands was estimated to be $25–30 million. This was one of several obstacles that contributed to the prolongation of negotiations. There also was disagreement on the length of the leases for the new military sites. The U.S. military sought them for at least a ten-year period and the State Department wanted them until the danger to the canal passed, whenever that might be, while Arias insisted that they be terminated immediately upon the war's end.

Another contentious issue between Panama and the United States was the latter's request to arm ships registered in Panama. President Arias refused, which disrupted U.S. plans to use U.S.-owned ships flying a Panamanian flag of convenience to supply the British. Ships going into and coming out of the canal into the Caribbean Sea were being tailed, and sometimes attacked, by German U-boats. Arias's refusal to arm Panamanian-flagged ships and his hard-line negotiation for the base leases led many in the U.S. government to conclude that Arias had to go. In the words of one: "The present conditions are considered dangerous to the security of the canal and it is believed that they should be corrected as soon as possible. A local revolution to throw out the crooked pro-Axis officialdom would be preferable to intervention by U.S. forces."[48] Occupation of the sites began in March 1941, well before any agreement had been reached between the two nations.

As described earlier, the U.S. wish was granted through a bloodless coup on October 7, 1941. With the new president, Ricardo Adolfo de la Guardia, negotiations for the bases moved quickly and positively for the United States. On May 12, 1942, the United States and Panama signed an agreement for the lease of 134 sites to be used for the protection of the canal. The accord called for the occupation of the sites to end one year after the end of World War II. The United States agreed to pay $50 per hectare annually for the bases, except Rio Hato, for which it would pay $10,000 per year. Finally, Panama received promises for the completion of various public works projects, including the Rio Hato road, the bridge over the canal, and a third set of locks for the canal itself.

Ironically, despite de la Guardia's acquiescence to the United States, Washington's generosity had its limits. Throughout the war, the United States turned away repeated Panamanian entreaties to receive Lend-Lease assistance. A State Department official is quoted as saying it was "desirable to keep something dangling before the noses of our Panamanian friends. There is no profit to us in giving the present administration all of the gravy."[49] However, in order to reward de la Guardia's commitment in supporting U.S. interests in Panama, and in an effort to bolster the president's position domestically, Washington did provide the new government with hundreds of automatic weapons and pistols, boats, and other war materials, in addition to a permanent U.S. military mission to assist in training the Panamanian National Police.

RISING DOMESTIC OPPOSITION
DURING THE WAR

The modernization of the National Police and the support of the United States secured de la Guardia's position but did not eliminate rising domestic opposition, led primarily by Arnulfo Arias's supporters.[50] The president had managed to extend his term in office when, in January 1942, the National Assembly failed to appoint the three designates (*designados*) in the line of succession. The president's supporters feared that the selection would allow Arias's forces to appoint one of their own and thus provide an opportunity for the former president to maneuver against de la Guardia and return to office or run the country via a surrogate. Nonetheless, political instability and potent opposition plagued de la Guardia throughout his term. Gambling interests tied to the former Panameñista administration designed a plan to overthrow the government as early as November 1941. The most serious threat came in September 1943, when dissident police officers and civilians plotted an armed revolt. The coup was put down by loyal police forces that used the equipment provided by the United States, with the acquiescence of its embassy in Panama City.[51]

Students became another source of opposition to the administration. Soon after its founding in 1935, the University of Panama became a hotbed of nationalist feelings and dissent against the government. In October 1943, the newly established Federation of Panamanian Students coordinated the opposition to the de la Guardia administration. In December 1944, the Federation and other student organizations formed the Patriotic Youth Front. Its leadership came from the middle-class and professional sectors, public employees, university students and graduates, and liberal professors. Subsequently, teachers unions and the emerging trade unions joined the student organizations. These forces represented the growing middle- and working-class sectors eager to wrest control of the government from the commercial elites that had dominated Panamanian politics since 1903. Many of these groups were inspired by the Panameñista movement and upheld its nationalistic—

although not necessarily its xenophobic and anti-immigrant—ideology. The mounting opposition only served to bolster the power of the National Police as de la Guardia sought to remain in power as long as possible with the assistance of the armed institution. The United States provided tacit support to the administration, particularly during the war, because it saw in de la Guardia a trusted ally and because it wanted to avoid a political crisis in the middle of the international conflagration.

By late 1944, however, it was clear that de la Guardia could no longer remain in office. At first, his administration tried to stay in power by suspending the constitution and calling elections for a National Constituent Assembly in May 1945, which he and his supporters intended to control. When finally held on May 6, 1945, however, the opposition won an overwhelming victory.[52] The Constituent Assembly was installed on June 15, 1945, with the subsequent election of Enrique J. Jiménez as chief executive.

Jiménez had served as Panamanian ambassador to the United States, where he was considered a U.S. ally. In Panama, however, Jiménez's electoral victory frustrated the aspirations of the middle- and working-class sectors to increase their power within Panamanian politics. This fact, and the economic recession that ensued after the war, provided for very difficult times for the new president. Crime rates increased in the terminal cities of Panama and Colón; students, teachers, and workers all intensified their protests; and Panameñista forces organized paramilitary organizations to promote violence against the government. Arnulfo Arias's return to Panama in October 1945 intensified the crisis as he moved to mobilize his supporters. In December, Arias and many of his supporters were arrested after the National Police disrupted an attempted coup. Arias was jailed for a few months before President Jiménez pardoned him in a futile attempt to placate the opposition.

At the war's end, one of the critical questions in U.S.–Panamanian relations was the future of the military bases outside the Canal Zone used by the United States during the world crisis. The 1942 base leasing agreement called for the United States to abandon the sites a year after the signing of the peace settlements. Technically, this meant that by September 1, 1946, one year after the Japanese surrender, the bases had to be abandoned. The United States, however, sought to extend the leases for ten additional years. At the end of August 1946, the State Department informed Panama of the U.S. desire to negotiate an extension of the bases lease. Foreign Minister Ricardo J. Alfaro immediately expressed Panama's opposition and stated that any consideration of U.S. bases in Panama should be made after the United States complied with the provisions of the 1942 accord and removed its bases.

Negotiations ensued for over a year. During that time span, the Soviet Union entrenched itself in Eastern Europe and, to the United States, appeared as a threat to Western Europe. The nations of the Western Hemisphere also became increasingly concerned with the possibility of another war and agreed to the Inter-American Treaty of Reciprocal Assistance, better known as the Rio Treaty. The treaty expanded and reiterated the earlier commitment of all nations in the region to come to the assistance of another nation if they were attacked by an extraregional power or if their independence was threatened.

Against this backdrop, Panama and the United States reached an agreement, which was signed on December 10, 1947, by U.S. Ambassador General Frank T. Hines and acting foreign minister Francisco Filós. The Hines-Filós Treaty called for the United States to maintain control over 13 sites comprising 10,500 hectares, was down from the initial request of 75 sites covering 32,000 hectares. Importantly, the treaty also provided for a joint Panamanian-U.S. commission to determine the uses of the sites, other than military, which remained exclusively in U.S. hands. The duration of the leases was set at five years for most of the sites, except Rio Hato, the largest, which was to be occupied for ten years.[53]

Two days later, the government sent the treaty to the National Assembly for ratification. Ten days of massive protests followed. Students, teachers, workers, and other groups who stood against the treaty led them. The protests were organized by a variety of groups, including the Federation of Panamanian Students, the National Association of Professors, the Federation of Panamanian Workers, and the Patriotic Youth Front. Arnulfo Arias and the Socialist Party joined forces to oppose the treaty as well. In a reflection of public opinion, on December 22 the National Assembly unanimously rejected the Hines-Filós Treaty.

This incident marked the coming of age of a nationalistic movement led by students and other professional sectors that continued to challenge U.S. presence in Panama for the remainder of the twentieth century. This movement would make its presence known again in the mid-1960s, when riots in the Canal Zone precipitated the worst crisis in U.S.–Panama relations up to that time. Additionally, many of the leading members of the student organizations became prominent members of the populist military regime led by Gen. Omar Torrijos, which negotiated the 1977 canal treaties that led to the return of the Panama Canal to Panamanian control on December 31, 1999.

Another important process that emerged from the events of the 1930s and 1940s was the rise of the National Police as a significant political force. The police, later to be called the National Guard, became the real arbiter of political power in Panama—a process that marked Panamanian politics until the U.S. invasion of December 20, 1989.

CONCLUSION

Panamanian politics were transformed in significant ways in the 1930s and 1940s. This period saw the emergence of a middle and professional class that challenged the commercial elite that had dominated politics on the isthmus since its separation from Colombia in 1903. The leading political force during this period was Arnulfo Arias and his Panameñista movement. Arias challenged the dominant bourgeoisie with a highly nationalistic appeal that frequently mobilized popular support. In 1940, Arias founded the National Revolutionary Party as the political party expression of the Panameñista movement. His program called for a new governing alliance, composed of the most dynamic sector of the bourgeoisie (i.e., industrialists), small agricultural producers, and rural peasants. The slogan adopted by this movement was "Panama for the Panamanians."

The period also saw the rise of the police as a key arbiter of politics, as the commercial elite sought to control the emergence of middle-class and nationalist threats. By the end of the 1940s the police force was acting to promote its own interests, particularly the political ambitions of its commander, José Remón Canteras. Another important force that emerged in this period was the student and labor movements that helped shape national politics by insisting on a new more symmetrical relationship between the United States and Panama.

The importance the United States placed on canal defenses was vindicated by the performance of the waterway. More than 23,000 transits were recorded between July 1941 and June 1945, an average of sixteen per day. The ability to move troops and supplies easily and quickly between the Atlantic and Pacific theaters was invaluable to the U.S. war efforts. Ironically, the course of the war and the way it ended placed the strategic importance of the Panama Canal in jeopardy. The development of a two-ocean navy and larger warships too big to pass through the canal reduced the waterway's military advantage. The start of the atomic age would make conventional canal defense virtually useless. The United States, however, continued to insist on dominance in the Canal Zone until the 1970s.

In the end, World War II reinforced both the close strategic ties between the two nations and the dominance of the United States. The negotiations for military sites and the eventual rejection of their extension illustrated both the ability of the United States to obtain key concessions from the Panamanian government and the limits of U.S. power in the face of a determined and mobilized population. These lessons would replay themselves in the postwar decades as Panama and the United States sought to balance the interest of the latter with the sovereign rights of the former.

NOTES

1. Payment for Panama Canal workers was divided between those paid in gold—the "gold roll"—and those paid in silver who were on the "silver roll." The former

was exclusively the domain of U.S. citizens, while the latter was for non-U.S. citizens. All Panamanians—white or not—were paid in silver.

2. Isidro A. Beluche Mora, *Acción Comunal: Surgimiento y estructuración del nacionalismo panameño* (Panamá: Editorial Condor, 1981), 33–44. For a discussion of the major programmatic tenets of Acción Comunal, see Jorge Conte Porras, *Arnulfo Arias Madrid* (Panama: Litho Impresora Panamá, 1980), 69.

3. Beluche Mora, *Acción Comunal*, 44.

4. For a detailed description of the coup, see Porras, *Arnulfo Arias Madrid*, and Thomas L. Pearcy, *We Answer Only to God: Politics and the Military in Panama, 1903–1947* (Albuquerque: University of New Mexico Press, 1998).

5. Pearcy, *We Answer Only to God*, 67, 83–84.

6. Michael L. Conniff, *Panama and the United States: The Forced Alliance* (Athens: University of Georgia Press, 1992), 91.

7. As quoted in Walter LaFeber, *The Panama Canal: The Crisis in Historical Perspective*, expanded ed. (Oxford: Oxford University Press, 1979), 86.

8. Lars Schoultz, *Beneath the United States: A History of U.S. Policy toward Latin America* (Cambridge, MA: Harvard University Press, 1998), 308.

9. Schoultz, *Beneath the United States*, 304–5.

10. This treaty set the basis for the "construction of a canal for ships across the Isthmus of Panama to communicate the Atlantic and Pacific Ocean." The treaty, in Article 2, gave the United States in perpetuity "the use, occupation, and control of a zone of land and land under water for the construction, maintenance, operation, sanitation, and protection of said Canal." Article 3 granted the U.S. "all rights, power, and authority within the zone . . . which the United States would possess and exercise as if it were the sovereign of the territory . . . to the entire exclusion of the exercise by the Republic of Panama of any such sovereign rights, power, or authority." In return, Panama received a one-time payment of $10 million and an annuity of $250,000 beginning nine years after the exchange of the instruments of ratification. Furthermore, the new treaty in its first article stated, "The United States guarantees and will maintain the independence of the Republic of Panama." In Article 7, the United States was granted the "right and authority . . . for the maintenance of public order in the cities of Panama and Colón and the territories and harbors adjacent thereto in case the Republic of Panama should not be, *in the judgment of the United States*, able to maintain such order" (emphasis added). See Ernesto Castillero Pimentel, *Panamá y los Estados Unidos, 1903–1953: Significado y alcance de la neutralización de Panamá* (Panama, 1988), xlix–l, liii, xlix–li.

11. The devaluation of the dollar in 1934 reduced its gold content to 59.6 percent of its former value, which meant that the value of the $250,000 annuity stipulated by the 1903 treaty was nearly cut in half. The Panamanian government refused to accept the annuity for a number of years in protest. See Pearcy, *We Answer Only to God*, 76.

12. These provisions would be the key Panamanian grievances during World War II against what they perceived were abuses by Canal Zone and U.S. military authorities in denying Panamanian commercial interests access to the zone, while allowing U.S. commercial enterprises unfettered access to the same.

13. Castillero Pimentel, *Panamá y los Estados Unidos*, xc.

14. LaFeber, *The Panama Canal*, 88.

15. Patricia Pizzurno Gelós and Celestino Andrés Araúz, *Estudios sobre el Panamá republicano, 1903–1989* (Panama: Manfer, 1996), 260–61.

16. The resolutions adopted at the conference can be found in S. Shepard Jones and Denys P. Myers, eds., *On American Foreign Relations, July 1939–June 1940* (Boston: World Peace Foundation, 1940), Vol. 2. See also William L. Langer and S. Everett Gleason, *The Challenge to Isolation, 1937–1940* (New York: Harper & Bros., 1952), 206–18; and Joseph Alsop and Robert Kintner, *American White Paper* (New York: Simon and Schuster, 1940), 68–73.

17. At the time, the Panamanian constitution called for the National Assembly to name three designates (*designados*) in order to take over the executive in the event the sitting president became incapacitated, was removed, or died.

18. Pizzurno Gelós and Andrés Araúz, *Estudios sobre el Panamá republicano*, 268.

19. Pearcy, *We Answer Only to God*, 86.

20. John Major, *Prize Possession: The United States and the Panama Canal, 1903–1979* (Cambridge: Cambridge University Press, 1993).

21. LaFeber, *The Panama Canal*, 93.

22. Major, *Prize Possession*, 265.

23. Ricaurte Soler, *El pensamiento político en Panamá en los siglos XIX y XX: Estudio introductoria y antología* (Panama: Universidad de Panama, 1988), 368, 370, 372.

24. It is estimated that more than 90 percent of the electorate voted in the affirmative. Jorge Conte Porras, *Procesos electorales y partidos politicos* (San José, Costa Rica: Litografía e Imprenta LIL, 2004), 192.

25. Pizzurno Gelós and Andrés Araúz, *Estudios sobre el Panamá republicano*, 278.

26. Michael L. Conniff, *Black Labor on a White Canal: Panama, 1904–1981* (Pittsburgh, PA: University of Pittsburgh Press, 1985), 99.

27. Pearcy, *We Answer Only to God*, 89.

28. Apparently, in early 1941 Harmodio Arias was asked to fire the paper's editor and appoint one loyal to President Arias.

29. Major, *Prize Possession*, 266.

30. At the time, Panama's international airport was located within the Canal Zone, so when the president boarded a plane bound for Havana, a U.S. intelligence officer recognized him and alerted his superiors.

31. President Arias had alienated the National Police by creating a National Secret Police that would answer only to him and the minister of government and justice and by appointing a Guatemalan officer, Lt. Col. Fernando Gómez Ayan, as chief of staff.

32. Major, *Prize Possession*, 267.

33. The Panamanian government justified the declaration of war on the provisions of the 1936 Hull-Alfaro Treaty and those of the Declaration of the Third Meeting of Ministers of Foreign Affairs of the American Republics, which in part stated, "The American Republics reaffirm their declaration to consider any act of aggression on the part of a non-American State against one of them as an act of aggression against all of them, constituting as it does an immediate threat to the liberty and independence of America." See "Confronting the Fascist Threat: The Delegates to the Third

Meeting of Ministers of Foreign Affairs of the American Republics," in Robert H. Holden and Eric Zolov, *Latin America and the United States: A Documentary History* (New York: Oxford University Press, 2000), 162–65.

34. Pizzurno Gelós and Andrés Araúz, *Estudios sobre el Panamá republicano*, 291.

35. For a complete analysis of the treatment of German citizens and others in Latin America during World War II, see Max Paul Friedman, *Nazi and Good Neighbors: The United States Campaign against the Germans of Latin America in World War II* (Cambridge: Cambridge University Press, 2003). The quotes presented in this paragraph can be found on page 108.

36. Friedman, *Nazi and Good Neighbors*, 111.

37. Friedman, *Nazi and Good Neighbors*, 187.

38. Pizzurno Gelós and Andrés Araúz, *Estudios sobre el Panamá republicano*, 289–90.

39. Pizzurno Gelós and Andrés Araúz, *Estudios sobre el Panamá republicano*, 290.

40. Major, *Prize Possession*, 380.

41. Pizzurno Gelós and Andrés Araúz, *Estudios sobre el Panamá republicano*, 293.

42. See Major, *Prize Possession*, 209–10, 284–85, 306–7, and 312–14. The effort to expand the capacity of the waterway was abandoned soon after the war for budget and strategic reasons.

43. At the start of the war, German airline companies had major investments in Colombia, Brazil, and other countries in South America.

44. LaFeber, *The Panama Canal*, 255–56.

45. Castillero Pimentel, *Panamá y los Estados Unidos*, 299.

46. Rio Hato, lying sixty miles southwest of the port of Balboa in Panama City, was the largest of the military installations at 19,000 acres. The area had been leased from a private owner since the 1920s for the use of Canal Zone flyers.

47. Castillero Pimentel, *Panamá y los Estados Unidos*, 300–302.

48. Official from the Office of Naval Intelligence, quoted in Pearcy, *We Answer Only to God*, 93.

49. Quoted in Major, *Prize Possession*, 267–68.

50. Arias himself spent the war in exile in Argentina.

51. Pizzurno Gelós and Andrés Araúz, *Estudios sobre el Panamá republicano*, 312–13.

52. Conte Porras, *Procesos electorales*, 205–6.

53. Pizzurno Gelós and Andrés Araúz, *Estudios sobre el Panamá republicano*, 334–35.

5

The Dominican Republic: The Axis, the Allies, and the Trujillo Dictatorship

Eric Paul Roorda

The history of the Dominican Republic's participation in World War II has much to do with the personality and policy of the country's dictator, Rafael Trujillo (*R.* 1930–61), who was president, general, and admiral. Trujillo was also an enigma. A protégé of the U.S. Marine Corps, Trujillo received his military training during the U.S. occupation of 1916–24 and cultivated friendships and alliances with U.S. military men. But he also admired Adolf Hitler, whose wardrobe and militarized rallies he emulated. Like Hitler, Trujillo ordered acts of racial genocide; in the Dominican case, the violence was committed against Haitians. Despite Trujillo's fascist proclivities, the United States needed his cooperation in the war effort. With the imperative of defending shipping and the approaches to the Panama Canal in mind, U.S. military representatives formed an alliance with Trujillo and sent an unprecedented amount of military aid to the Dominican Republic. Trujillo used the war to tighten his control of the country, accelerating the military buildup of Dominican society that began with his rise to power. The Dominican Republic declared war against the Axis countries on cue, the first country in Latin America to do so. But Trujillo's Dominican Republic was one of the less savory members of the coalition formed to defeat fascism around the world, and its participation, like that of Stalin's Soviet Union, undercut the black-and-white, good-vs.-evil construction of the war that its proponents, then and now, have offered.[1]

Dominican militarism spread across the country during the first seven years of Trujillo's rule. As chief of the U.S. Marine Corps–trained Dominican armed forces, he seized power easily in February 1930 and quickly killed his rivals or forced them into exile. The Dominican presidential elections of 1930 and 1934 were a sham, but further solidified Trujillo's power by lending a façade of legitimacy to his tenure in office. The *generalísimo* cultivated his relationships with U.S. military men he had served under during the Marine occupation, and they in turn praised the shipshape order their protégé imposed on the Dominican Republic. But Trujillo could not warm up to the resident U.S. diplomats, who opposed the violence and increasing repression of the dictatorship and prevented arms sales to the Dominican Republic. Undeterred by the State Department's disapproval of matériel shipments, Trujillo augmented his military capacity bit by bit throughout the 1930s, adding small arms for a growing infantry, naval patrol boats, and a fledgling air force, often doing so with behind-the-scenes assistance from his Marine Corps friends, who made contacts with arms dealers on his behalf.[2]

The pervasive military milieu of 1930s Dominican life resembled that of some other contemporary societies around the world such as Germany, Italy, and Japan. Another dimension of the increasingly powerful Trujillo regime that was similar to the rule imposed by Hitler, Mussolini, and the Japanese Imperial forces was racism. Much like the Aryan, Roman, or Yamato race supremacy espoused by other militarist nations at the time, the superiority of Hispanic blood became the creed of *trujillista* racial ideology. In each case where racist dictatorships took over, the victimization of racial Others began, with, for example, Jews, Ethiopians, and Chinese becoming the targets of violence by German, Italian, and Japanese forces. Under the Trujillo regime, people of Haitian descent were the scapegoats of a racist interpretation of Dominican history, much as the widely believed anti-Semitic myths blamed Jewish people for Germany's troubles. In October 1937, Trujillo ordered the death of all Haitians resident in the Dominican Republic, initiating a weeklong slaughter carried out by machete-swinging soldiers and civilian accomplices, known as the Haitian Massacre. That systematic genocide of many thousands of Haitians preceded by two months the Japanese "Rape of Nanjing" in China, which took place soon after the invasion of Shanghai that marked the onset of the regional war in Asia. Inasmuch as "whitening" the Dominican population was a motive for the killings, the Haitian Massacre can be considered one of the first mass racial atrocities of World War II.[3]

To repair the damage done to his international reputation after the Haitian Massacre became public, Trujillo donated a beautiful tract of coastal land at Sosúa to create a colony for 100,000 Jewish refugees from Europe. This act of apparent generosity brought a great deal of positive publicity, coming as the Evian Conference was seeking new homes for the displaced. There were few invitations from Depression-wracked countries around the world, so Trujillo's message of welcome to so many Jewish victims was notable and hopeful. But Trujillo reneged on his offer, ultimately accepting only a few hundred families from Germany and Austria. Sosua never became a new Canaan in the Americas for the survivors of anti-Semitism. In the meantime, the dictator cordially greeted visiting ships of the Third Reich.[4]

THE COURTSHIP OF GENERAL TRUJILLO

Dominican foreign policy was receptive to overtures for cooperation from both the Allied and Axis powers. With war looming in Europe, the United States overlooked Trujillo's misdeeds in order to court him as an ally in the impending conflict. The dictator's associates in the Marine Corps lobbied successfully to overcome State Department opposition to naval "goodwill" visits, sending a parade of increasingly larger vessels to call at Ciudad Trujillo, as Santo Domingo had been renamed, in the late 1930s. The naval visits acted out the budding military alliance between the United States and the Dominican Republic on a variety of stages. Officers were hosted at official receptions, ship's baseball teams played Dominican teams at the stadium, enlisted men and noncoms feasted on local food and beer as guests of their Dominican counterparts, and Dominican dignitaries were invited to tour the visiting ships. On one of these occasions, when the mighty battleship *Texas* came to the Dominican capital, Trujillo renamed a coastal road "Avenida United States Marine Corps," occasioning a binational parade of Dominican and United States marines in their nearly identical uniforms, marching along the waterfront, while forty-two U.S. Navy airplanes roared overhead. In July 1939, Trujillo made his first visit to the United States, coming as the guest of Marine Corps mentors and friends.[5]

The Axis offered competition for Trujillo's attention during the late 1930s. Benito Mussolini of Italy had been the first foreign leader to honor Trujillo with a military decoration, but he also threatened Trujillo with war in 1935 in an incident over the tobacco interests of an Italian national named Amadeo Barletta. Letting the incident pass, Mussolini dispatched a diplomatic minister to represent him in Ciudad Trujillo. Commendatore Mario Porta arrived later in the same month as the Haitian Massacre, October 1937, and with his English wife began to entertain lavishly. He was joined by an Axis counterpart, a minister from the Third Reich, in August 1939. Trujillo had been soliciting an official representative from Hitler's government since 1935, when he had named his son-in-law to be minister to Germany and sent his own daughter to Berlin to represent him. In 1938, Trujillo appointed two brothers with fascist views, Arturo and Roberto Despradel, to be foreign minister and minister to the Third Reich, respectively, the latter presenting his credentials to Hitler personally at his Berchtesgaden retreat in the Bavarian Alps. Now, with the accreditation of Dr. Hans Roehrecke, the German dictator reciprocated the overture. Hitler's move was intended "to exploit the generally pro-Nazi and anti-American sympathies of the Trujillo regime," judged the British minister in the Dominican Republic at the time.[6]

In the meantime, dueling visits to Samaná Bay by U.S. and German naval ships in 1938 underscored the strategic potential of that deepwater anchorage in the northeast corner of the Dominican Republic. It was apparent to naval observers and diplomats alike that German naval intelligence coveted access to Samaná Bay in the event of a war in the Atlantic, because it would be perfect as a submarine refuge. When the German battleship *Schlesien* and an escort tanker entered the bay in 1938, President Franklin D. Roosevelt himself asked the U.S. Navy to dispatch a destroyer immediately from Guantánamo Bay in Cuba to keep the Germans company. While calling at Samaná, which the Americans rarely visited but which was an annual destination for a Third Reich ship, the *Schlesien* sent a contingent overland to the capital for a round of diplomatic pleasantries. Later in 1938, the U.S. Navy sent a cruiser to survey the bay en route to a visit to Ciudad Trujillo, then followed up in early 1939 by conducting part of its Fleet Problem XX maneuvers around Samaná, with Trujillo's permission. The aircraft carrier *Langley* and twelve other warships used the bay during the exercise, which was designed to test Caribbean defenses.

After the invasion of Poland in September 1939, rumors circulated that Dominican Coast Guard vessels were engaged in refueling German submarines in Samaná Bay. A French destroyer sank one of the few cutters in the Dominican armed forces after a collision near there in October 1939. The French claimed the Dominicans were transferring oil to U-boats and temporarily detained a Dominican merchant ship at Martinique while they investigated the incident.

The Axis courtship of Trujillo continued with seeming success as the "phony war" in Europe endured through the winter of 1939–40. Trujillo conferred the nation's highest award, named the Order of Duarte for the Dominican Republic's founding patriot, to an Italian prince in February 1940. Even the U.S. envoy seemed seduced by the diplomatic blandishments of Mario Porta and Hans Roehrecke, whom he hosted as the guests of honor at a dinner that month. The day after Italy's declaration of war on France in June, which Roosevelt denounced in Mussolini's "stab in the back" speech, U.S. chargé d'affaires Eugene Hinkle dined at the Italian Legation in Ciudad Trujillo. For a while, the political ambience in the capital was very strange, reported the amazed British minister, because it seemed as if the Americans were siding with the Axis. But with the departure of Hinkle, that bizarre moment in diplomatic history was over.

Relations between Trujillo and Hitler caromed back and forth wildly during this time. In May 1940, Trujillo banned the film *Confessions of a Nazi Spy* at the request of the German legation. But a month later, when the German minister published congratulations on Nazi victories in Europe he had received from Dominicans, Trujillo censured him and threatened jail time for any Dominican who said positive things about the Axis. Ironically, Trujillo also used the German minister's diplomatic gaffe as a pretext for cutting off all immigration to the country, ostensibly to prevent more Nazi agents from gaining entrance—though his mandate also ended the trickle of Jewish refugees to the crude haven of Sosua. The German–Dominican relationship also soured partly over the issue of cinematic portrayals of dictatorship. Charlie Chaplin's scathing lampoon of Hitler in the 1940 film *The Great Dictator* was banned in the Dominican Republic until the summer of 1941, but then Trujillo allowed it to be shown. His action was partly in reprisal for the exhibit in Nazi-controlled Europe of a *March of Time* newsreel portraying him as a brutal buffoon. The Dominican government shut down a front operation for German espionage, the Dominican-German Scientific Institute, and began keeping tabs on Nazi sympathizers, who would be deported to the United States after the Dominican Republic entered the world war.

Trujillo gradually ended his dalliance with the Axis powers, opting instead for the emoluments of cooperation with the United States, which under the leadership of Roosevelt was busily preparing for war on the Allied side. The advantages of this choice came in the form of military hardware and government loans. A military alliance between the Dominican Republic and the United States took shape after the spring 1940 Blitzkrieg and the fall of France. Military staff talks began in June 1940, and the following month, Trujillo's envoy to the Havana Pan-American Conference, Foreign Minister Arturo Despradel, pledged "the land, the seas, the skies, and the men" of the Dominican Republic to defend the hemisphere. The State Department upgraded its representation to the level of ambassador, and the U.S. Navy and Army established attaché offices in the new embassy in Ciudad Trujillo. After years of denying requests for arms shipments, a small flotilla of patrol boats arrived from the U.S. Coast Guard. Additionally, loans from the Export-Import Bank flowed to the Dominican Republic for military equipment purchases, civic improvements, and hotel development.[7]

DECLARATIONS OF WAR

The real jackpot of wartime matériel for the Trujillo regime came in the form of the Lend-Lease Act, passed in March 1941, which authorized Roosevelt to send military equipment to defend the countries he decided were vital to U.S. defense. The Dominican Republic, located on the important Panama Canal approach through the Mona Passage, was on FDR's list of important countries, receiving approval as the first Latin American recipient in May. Much of the forthcoming aid served to develop Dominican air and sea power in order to combat submarines. Antisubmarine patrols were a natural priority for the Dominican Republic during the war, requiring airplanes for spotting U-boats and naval cutters for fighting them.

The Dominican share of Lend-Lease was a minuscule part of the Act's initial funding of $7 billion—less than $1.6 million—but it was gigantic by the republic's historic standards. Matériel from the United States brought unprecedented strength to the naval and air forces of the country: twelve more coastal patrol boats and nineteen airplanes, accompanied by fifteen pilots and mechanics to instruct Dominican personnel. In addition, U.S. funds constructed a network of modern air bases around the country, some of which doubled as commercial airports. Trujillo himself had a fascination for air power, and the war gave him a chance to begin building what would become the most potent air force in all of Latin America during the postwar years. Although it would have trouble near the end of the Lend-Lease program in obtaining spare parts, the Dominican Air Force cultivated other sources to supply airplanes after the war, becoming independent of the United States. The initial Lend-Lease bounty also included four Scout vehicles with mounted machine guns, but the regime's request for three thousand Enfield rifles for the Dominican army, a force that had been growing steadily since Trujillo took power, was not granted. Trujillo tried to get the rifles he needed to expand his army from other sources, such as Mexico and Brazil, but he ended up constructing his own munitions factory after the war.[8]

The bilateral military staff talks, Havana Conference pledges, and flow of Lend-Lease assistance solidified the Dominican–American alliance by late 1941. Within forty-eight hours of the attack on Pearl Harbor on December 7, the Dominican Republic became the first Latin American country to declare war on Japan. Declarations of war against Germany and Italy followed four days later. Trujillo prided himself on this distinction, and his supporters in the United States frequently stressed Dominican wartime cooperation in his defense. The "Dominican Lobby" of pro-Trujillo voices comprised influential Americans in many walks of life: generals and admirals, senators and representatives, journalists and paid publicists, lawyers and businessmen. After a decade of chilly ambivalence from the official diplomatic establishment in Washington and its envoys, the declarations of war brought a period of warm relations between the governments of the Dominican Republic and the United States, during which Trujillo's group of Yankee friends worked to strengthen ties with the Dominican Republic and increase military aid.

At the outset of the Dominican participation in the war, the country could muster only 3,220 soldiers and 900 police, armed with about 2,400 old Spanish 7mm rifles and 1,860 vintage-1898 Krag Jorgensens left behind by the

U.S. Marines in 1924. Of all these weapons, perhaps 750 were in reliable working condition. To support this meager armory of small arms, the infantry possessed fewer than eighty Browning and Thompson machine guns, while the artillery consisted of about forty cannons and mortars. The air force operated a single Curtiss Wright and six assorted small planes, including four Piper Cubs. There were a grand total of four antiaircraft guns to repel an air assault. The Dominican Navy had only seven coastal patrol boats to its name, which did not count the most impressive and ornate vessel in the country: the president's private yacht. When the war broke out while Trujillo was in the United States, he was forced to abandon his yacht and fly back to the island, compliments of the U.S. military. The three-masted *Angelita* returned safely to Ciudad Trujillo, but other Dominican ships were not so fortunate when the war came to the Caribbean between 1940 and 1942.

THE WAR AT SEA

The first hostile action of the war to take place in Dominican waters occurred on the night of May 5, 1940, six months after war was declared in Europe. One of several German freighters stranded in Curaçao tried to elude British and French naval patrols by steaming into the neutral waters of the Dominican Republic on its way north through the Mona Passage and on to Germany. The *Hannover*, with a cargo of minerals and wood, encountered the British cruiser *Dunedin* and French cruiser *Jean d'Arc* within Dominican territorial waters, but the warships ordered the merchantman's surrender nonetheless. The German captain ordered his crew to scuttle and burn their vessel before embarking in lifeboats, but a British boarding party closed the scuttling valves that had been opened and extinguished the fires. Two of the three German lifeboats were captured as well, but the third made it to Punta Cana on the eastern tip of the Dominican Republic after two hours at sea, with thirty-seven sailors on board. The merchant mariners clambered ashore to be greeted by the local peasants, who had stayed awake all night watching the action between the freighter and the two cruisers offshore.[9]

The British towed the captured German ship to Jamaica, where it was converted to a small aircraft carrier and renamed HMS *Audacity*.[10] In the meantime, the German merchant crewmen who had made it to Dominican soil walked overland for two days until a sympathetic rancher sent them on to the capital by truck. They were interned on an old estate called Cambelén outside San Cristóbal, Trujillo's hometown not far west of the capital. It was a large house and farm that had been the home of a former president and archbishop, in a pleasant location near the mouth of the Nigua River just off the highway, convenient for people to come see the new residents. Press coverage of the Germans' presence caused a sensation in the country, and visitors were many. The Germans were allowed to move about freely on an "honor system" when not at work in the fields of their temporary home, and it was said that several of them fathered children with local women. Despite the hospitality shown them, the elitist Germans disdained the Dominicans, calling the republic "a little country of monkeys."

One of the thirty-seven sailors died of malaria, and sixteen of the most skilled merchant mariners were allowed to depart for Haiti in October 1940 under the care of the German minister in Port-au-Prince, who sent them along to Colombia.[11] That left twenty involuntary German visitors in the Dominican Republic, receiving suspicious visits from members of the German colony. The Cambelén estate became a meeting place for the Dominican branch of the Nazi Party.

In August 1941, the *Hannover*'s radio operator was caught setting up a clandestine transmitter with a Nazi sympathizer prominent among the German expatriates. Afterward, the sailors were restricted in their independent movements, but they were still allowed to travel to the capital in the company of a soldier. In October, one of the mariners escaped from Cambelén, then turned up at the German Legation in Ciudad Trujillo, working as a "cook." He was arrested and returned as soon as he left the legation grounds. By then, Trujillo's relations with the resident German minister and the government he represented had deteriorated, and the remaining sailors were seen as a threat to the dictator personally, living as they did adjacent to the highway he traveled to his farm outside San Cristóbal. So the *Hannover* crew was placed under closer guard in a camp in the northern coastal mountain range, near El Cumbre. When the Dominican Republic declared war against the Third Reich in December, they were joined at the camp by a group of reputed Nazi sympathizers from the German community in the Dominican Republic. In May 1942, two years after the capture of the *Hannover*, the remaining merchant mariners were deported by ship into U.S. custody, along with twenty-seven of their compatriots and an assortment of other foreign nationals who were suspected of being enemy agents by the U.S. naval attaché: two Italians, a White Russian, a shady Swiss "count," and a Japanese citizen.

German submarines first entered the Caribbean Sea in mid-February 1942. The first survivors from torpedoed vessels came ashore at Puerto Plata on the north coast of the Dominican Republic that month, including thirty-one rescued by the Dominican Coast Guard from the British freighter *McGregor*. By the end of March, six submarines had destroyed forty ships in the Caribbean area alone. U-boat warfare sank sixty more ships in April, then sent 105 to the bottom during the month of May 1942. Two of the ships on that grim roster were the pride of the Dominican merchant marine fleet, the steamers *San Rafael* and *Presidente Trujillo*.

The *San Rafael* was hit on the second day of May as it neared Kingston, Jamaica, on a voyage from Tampa, Florida, with a cargo of construction supplies for an Allied air base. Two of the crew died—the first Dominican casualties of World War II—but the others survived a seven-day passage in two lifeboats to the Caymans and Isle of Pines. The freighter was one of nine ships destroyed by U-125 before it, too, was sunk by Royal Navy vessels off the coast of Newfoundland exactly one year after the sinking of *San Rafael*.

The *Presidente Trujillo* was torpedoed only eighteen days after the *San Rafael*, ten miles outbound from Fort-de-France, Martinique, after delivering beef. Although rowboats came out from the shore within an hour of the attack to pull fifteen survivors from the water, another twenty-four Dominican sailors went down with the ship, which had been en route to San Juan, Puerto Rico. The *Trujillo* was one of the twenty-three victims of U-156, including the *McGregor* the previous February off the Dominican north coast town of Gáspar Hernández. The most infamous of U-156's kills was the elegant *Laconia* of the Cunard Line, torpedoed with the loss of more than one thousand, mainly civilian, lives. The horrendous scale and circumstances of the *Laconia* sinking were such that the Allies suppressed the full news of the event until after the war had ended, for fear of demoralizing the citizenry. U-156 succumbed to an attack by a Catalina PBY airplane east of Barbados ten months after the sinking of the *Trujillo*.

The loss of the *San Rafael* and *Presidente Trujillo* had a demoralizing effect on the Dominican population. On the one hand, it stoked popular animosity toward the Axis nations, so recently the competitor for Dominican allegiance. But it also produced a public backlash against U.S. leadership, which had mustered the Dominican nation to war but was incapable of protecting its few seagoing assets. After the loss of the country's only two modern merchant ships in May, two large schooners capable of hauling bulk cargoes were apprehended by U-boats in the early summer. The Nazis took the Dominicans' food supplies before blowing up their schooners. The *Nueva Altagracia* was destroyed by U-126 near the coast of Curaçao, after a farewell in Spanish from a German on board the submarine who previously had lived in Samaná. U-166 blew the *Carmen* apart fifteen miles from Cabarete on the north coast of the Dominican Republic, killing one member of the crew.

Other schooners had happier fates, such as Captain Alegría's *Pearl of the Ozama*. The wooden vessel was stopped in July 1942 by a U-boat commanded by a former captain of the Horn Line, which had provided passenger steamship service between Germany and the Dominican Republic before the war. The German recognized Captain Alegría from his days in Dominican ports, so he did not destroy the schooner, though he warned that he would if he saw it again. The Dominican captain declined his Nazi acquaintance's offer of payment for the food taken off his vessel and returned quickly to port, where he spent the next three months making "repairs" until the U-boat danger had waned in the Caribbean. The famous Captain Alegría was not the only lucky one; other Dominican coastal craft lost their food, but not their vessels or their lives, to German submarines that surfaced in order to forcefully reprovision from them. In addition to factual incidents of provisions being heisted from fishermen and schooner crews, wild rumors of pro-Nazi Dominicans supplying German U-boats with food, water, and fuel abounded during the war. None of these tales, many of which involved Samaná Bay, have proven to be true.

The Horn Line discontinued its trans-Atlantic service to the Dominican Republic when the war broke out. The country also lost passenger steamship service to other destinations during the war. The Porto Rico Line had offered the most connections between the island and both San Juan and New York, with a consistent schedule of port calls by a trio of modern liners capable of carrying almost four hundred passengers each: the *Borinquen*, *Coamo*, and *Iroquois*. But after Pearl Harbor, the U.S. government requisitioned all three for convoy use, and only the *Borinquen* survived the Battle of the Atlantic.

As a result of these shipping losses, shortages in the Dominican Republic quickly worsened from their already meager Depression levels. The scarcest commodity was oil. Nazi submarines targeted sea traffic near the refining facilities of Curaçao in their devastating assault on Allied tonnage, choking off the petroleum supply to places such as the Dominican Republic within the first several months of the war.

Along with the worsening privations of the economy, the sight of humble smallcraft burning in coastal waters and filthy, scorched survivors struggling ashore brought the world war home to the people of the Dominican Republic. Fortunately for the Dominicans, however, the Allies countered the submarine offensive as the summer of 1942 wore on, and no other Dominican ships were lost to Nazi U-boats, which sank a total of only fifteen merchant vessels in August. There was still significant danger—two Dominican schooners actually took fire from Allied aircraft by mistake during that summer—but the worst of the war was over quickly for the Dominican Republic.

The government built six new wooden schooners in Dominican shipyards to reinforce the heavy early losses to its already weak merchant marine and to maintain the island's tenuous links with the outside world. Beginning in 1943, the United States purchased all edible exports the Dominican Republic produced, such as corn and sugar, through Lend-Lease and the Foreign Economic Administration and shipped them to other places in the Caribbean where food supplies were low. Market prices of Dominican agricultural products spiraled upward during the war, bringing financial relief to a Dominican government that had been strapped for funding for fifteen years.

Nonetheless, the wartime shortages of durable goods, gasoline, and other commodities made life difficult for the average Dominican citizen.

THE WAR ON THE GROUND

There was no combat on Dominican soil in the military sense, but the war was fought there by other means. One offensive the republic could mount against the Axis went forward on economic ground. As soon as Great Britain declared war against Germany, its foreign office began to compile blacklists of businesses around the world that had connections to the Third Reich. When the United States joined the war, it compiled its own blacklists against enterprises with Axis ties. These lists were used to boycott the aggressors' global interests. In the case of the Dominican Republic, the U.S. blacklist duplicated the British roster of ten German-connected and three Italian-connected firms. Having itself declared war on Germany, Italy, and Japan, the Dominican government seized many of the businesses on the list, and others besides. One of the commercial properties commandeered by the government was the tobacco firm of Amadeo Barletta, whose business Trujillo had tried to seize in 1935, leading to the war scare with Mussolini. Now Trujillo had his way, and Barletta relocated to Havana. Those who were involuntarily deported also lost their property to the Dominican government in this economic war. German physician and philanthropist Carl Theodor Georg, who operated a hospital in San Pedro de Macorís at his own expense, was accused of operating a clandestine radio station from the hospital. Dr. Georg was deported to detention in the United States, and his hospital became a Dominican government facility.[12]

Bits of evidence about German espionage point to a fairly active underground around the country in the late 1930s and early 1940s. By the end of that period, the Dominican branch of the National Socialist Workers Party operated in five cities, each of them home to a local German Colony of expatriates or descendents of recent immigrants: Puerto Plata and Montecristi on the north coast, Santiago in the central Cibao Valley, and, on the south coast, San Pedro de Macorís and the capital. The Nazi Party numbered perhaps fifty active members during the period of Dominican neutrality, out of a German-born population of approximately 150 and a German-descended group of another three hundred people in the entire country.

Nearly four hundred Italians, and perhaps as many Italo-Dominicans, lived in the Dominican Republic, as well, but they were more assimilated than the Germans and, lacking cohesion, they offered little support for Mussolini's fascism. The Spanish community was divided between the 1,500 or so of them who lived in the country prior to the Spanish Civil War, a prosperous urban group who supported Francisco Franco, and around four thousand refugees welcomed by the Trujillo regime as part of its efforts to bring in light-skinned immigrants, many of whom were recently in the ranks of the defeated Republicans. The "old" Spanish colony supported an underground Falangist organization that had greater fifth-column potential than the minor Nazi movement, but it never plotted against Trujillo or contributed to the Axis and so was not persecuted by the regime during the war.

Nearly five hundred German and Austrian Jews resided at the Sosua Refugee Colony near Puerto Plata on the north coast, as well. Their Spartan community, perched on cliffs beside a bay, was widely suspected to be a base for Nazi infiltrators. If so, the spies posing as Jewish refugees received a hard assignment, because they had to scrape out a living from the soil under the tropical sun and sleep in barracks reminiscent of sugar workers' shacks.

In August 1940, according to an FBI report, a Gestapo officer from Heinrich Himmler's inner circle named Heinrich Karl Fritz Cordes visited Ciudad Trujillo, where he was guest of honor at a dinner held at the Third Reich's legation and attended by members of the German Colony. His mission was to train the German legation staff to make radio transmissions, in order to remove German cables from the commercial wires; the *Hannover* radioman helped with the training. The need for independent communications had been underlined to the Nazis two years earlier, when the German code was stolen from an agent in Ciudad Trujillo and taken to Cuba by the thief. The thief, himself a German, had been assassinated in Havana just three months before the Gestapo man's visit to Ciudad Trujillo. The circumstances of the killing indicated complicity, if not active agency, in the murder by Germans in the Dominican Republic. Cordes was also reported by the FBI to have worked with the leading Dominican Nazi and one of the stalwarts of the German Colony, Karl Hertel, in planning a sabotage school in the Dominican Republic.

Also in the summer of 1940, the U.S. naval attaché received reports of a plot against Trujillo being floated by the Nazis in the country. The source of the intelligence was Maj. Miguel Angel Paulino, one of the dictator's most notorious secret police officers, who earned a brutal reputation as leader of the paramilitary group known as "The 42" during the coup year of 1930 and since then was known for using his revolver on prisoners. According to the scheme as related by Paulino, who claimed to have penetrated the Nazi organization in the Dominican Republic, a front operation was to be set up in the form of a shipping office managed by Hertel, who was already working as an agent for a Hamburg firm. The office would funnel money, arms, and ammunition from Germany for the purpose of staging a revolution against Trujillo, who was ailing with a severe anthrax infection at the time, and installing Paulino in his place. The Dominican Republic could then be used as a beachhead for Nazi domination of Latin America. The conspiracy simmered until April 1941, when Paulino was fired by Trujillo prior to his embarkation on an international trip. The same month, Hertel was jailed for a day, after which his Dominican associates saw fit to steer clear of him. Employers took notice of the official hostility, too; other prominent Nazi Party members were fired from their jobs at the electric company, a sugar mill, and the newspaper *La Nación* in the next few months.

The five Japanese citizens living in the Dominican Republic in 1939 were subjects of suspicion, as well, prompting all but one of them to depart the country before Pearl Harbor. When the Dominican Republic declared war on Japan, the authorities arrested the last Japanese national in the country, the proprietor of a small shop in Ciudad Trujillo, and sent him to the internment camp in the mountains at El Cumbre. More than forty Germans already occupied the camp's little cabins on the crest of the cordillera, which were not unlike the shacks being inhabited by forcibly interned Japanese-Americans at desolate locations in the United States at the same time. The unfortunate Japanese man and everyone else at the El Cumbre camp—almost fifty Nazi and Fascist sympathizers and the remaining crew members of the *Hannover*—were deported in the custody of the United States in May 1942. After they left, the bulk of Axis espionage activities seem to have ceased. Thereafter, Dominican exiles occasionally accused Trujillo himself of secretly aiding the Axis, but aside from some diplomatic flirtation with Francisco Franco in Spain and Antonio de Oliveira Salazar in Portugal carried out by the Dominican minister to both Iberian countries, there was little substance to these allegations. Just because the dictator looked, sounded, and acted like a Fascist tyrant did not mean he could not be a member of the nations united to defeat Fascism.

WARTIME DIPLOMACY

The Dominican infantry and artillery forces expanded as a result of the war, further militarizing the society and economy of the nation. The more numerous and better equipped ground troops of the Dominican Republic played a major role in maintaining Trujillo's power. These forces assisted in defeating invasion attempts designed to unseat Trujillo in the postwar years, joining the expanded navy and awesome new air force as the unquestioned arbiters of power in the country. The certainty of his tenure in office afforded the dictator by his military, which had been bolstered so impressively during World War II, permitted Trujillo to develop the luxury of megalomania in his declining years. Long before hosting his "international peace fair" or trying to kill the president of Venezuela with a car bomb, however, signs of Trujillo's grandiose delusions of himself as a pivotal global leader were manifest in his wartime foreign policy.

One of the motivating factors for the expansion of the Dominican infantry during the war was the threat of war with Haiti. The simmering dispute with the nation next door also helps to explain the regime's frantic search for rifles, the scarcity of which limited the growth of Dominican ground forces. After a long history of border wars and the more recent Haitian Massacre, the friction with Haiti intensified after Elie Lescot became president there in 1941. Lescot had been on Trujillo's payroll of foreign allies during the 1930s and gained the presidency partly with his financial backing. But the new Haitian leader charted a course independent of the Dominican dictator when he took office, including a buildup of the Haitian Army, which had been powerless to respond at the time of the 1937 Haitian Massacre. During the summer of 1943, Trujillo ordered another one thousand men recruited to the army, despite the lack of rifles for them, because he was worried about the strength of Lescot's forces, numbering five thousand men armed with Springfield rifles recently acquired from the United States.

Trujillo's envy of Lescot's well-equipped army merged with his resentment of the Haitian's warm reception in Washington, D.C., in October 1943, when President Roosevelt hosted him overnight at the White House. By contrast, Trujillo had traveled to the United States six times between 1939 and 1941, but only once had he received an audience with the president, and then only for a brief tea visit. Not only had he never seen the inside of the Lincoln Bedroom, Trujillo encountered mainly frosty cordiality from civilian officials in Washington, some of whom could barely conceal their disdain for the man, knowing what they did about his cruelty and avarice. Roosevelt felt compelled to intervene personally in the tiff between Trujillo and Lescot in February 1944, asking them to abstain from war. But Trujillo could not resist the urge to embarrass his former protégé in March 1945 by publishing Lescot's past correspondence with him, which revealed the Haitian president's treasonous acceptance of Trujillo's bribes. The ensuing scandal contributed to Lescot's fall from power.[13]

The personal travels of Trujillo are one useful map of Dominican relations during the period leading up to Pearl Harbor, when the inexperienced dictator discovered the outside world for himself. During those tense years, the man who had grown up in poverty in San Cristóbal and had never set foot beyond his native country began to navigate international waters, literally and figuratively. His travels abroad reinforced his relationships with Allied comrades-in-arms ties, gave him a taste for expensive, cosmopolitan amenities, and filled him with a sense of self-importance. His first trip away from the shores of the Dominican Republic was his visit to the United States in July 1939, when the military was actively courting his strategic cooperation in a series of staff talks. His itinerary on that occasion reflected his priorities and those of his uniformed hosts, including Arlington National Cemetery, Quantico Marine Base, and the Military Academy at West Point. His next venture beyond the land of Quisqueya was also a military excursion, this time to observe U.S. naval maneuvers near Culebra, an island east of Puerto Rico, in February 1940. The salute he received from the Atlantic Fleet on that memorable day may have guaranteed his future wartime cooperation once and for all.

Trujillo's second trip to the American mainland also helped to solidify the Dominican-American alliance, this time putting the bilateral financial house in order. Despite a painful outbreak of anthrax on his neck, Trujillo came personally to sign a treaty ending the U.S.-supervised customs receivership in the Dominican Republic. President Theodore Roosevelt had insisted on the creation of the receivership in 1904, as part of his effort to control the Dominican foreign debt, and as such it became the first practical exercise of the Roosevelt Corollary to the Monroe Doctrine. In his corollary, the first Roosevelt said the United States would act as a police force in cases of "impotence or chronic wrongdoing" in Latin America. The receivership, as a relic of Gunboat Diplomacy, was the "last sore thumb" of the Good Neighbor Policy, by which the second Roosevelt pledged nonintervention in the region in 1933. The "sore thumb" metaphor was chosen by Secretary of State Cordell Hull, who joined Trujillo to sign the treaty ending the Dominican Receivership in September 1940. The Trujillo-Hull Treaty was the occasion for a national holiday upon Trujillo's triumphant return in October, although the "March of Victory" staged to celebrate the agreement seemed to the U.S. ambassador to have been in bad taste.

Having made a fortune in the tyranny business, Trujillo found many ways to enjoy and display his wealth on three trips to New York in one year, during which he stayed at the Hotel Carlyle or rented a penthouse apartment on Park Avenue. He also sought out expensive medical care for his various physical maladies during stays abroad. The suspicious autocrat established a pattern of behavior upon his return from his trips abroad, one of which unmasked a plot that had been hatched in the dictator's absence, followed by the punishment of the alleged plotters. The first of Trujillo's three sojourns away lasted from December 1940 until March 1941, nearly four months of conspicuous consumption and elbow-rubbing with members of the informal "Dominican Lobby." He returned to the Big Apple again in May 1941 and then escaped the heat of his home country to autumnal New York in November 1941. He was there when he heard the news of the Pearl Harbor attack.[14]

CONCLUSION

The Dominican Republic's status as an ally during World War II undercut the idealistic war aims enunciated by Franklin Roosevelt and Prime Minister Winston Churchill, among others. Under the circumstances, the parroting of democratic rhetoric by the grimly authoritarian Trujillo dictatorship injected unintended irony into the Allies' stock phrases praising freedom and international solidarity. For example, a 1944 official history of the Dominican Republic included a chapter on "The Dominican Republic at War with the Axis," which was illustrated with an artist's rendition of the sinking of one of the modern Dominican steamers. The narration stated, "The alliance between the Dominican Republic and the United States is complete and total, and the great nation to the north has found in the Dominicans, lovers of liberty whose cooperation has become necessary for the speedy attainment of the war's goals."[15]

The extensive development of the Dominican military during World War II, a buildup that continued unabated after the war with the assistance of arms-dealing countries such as Brazil and Sweden, disturbed the Caribbean peace even as the global conflict ended. Military might, much of it surplus merchandise such as P-51 Mustang fighters and B-26 Marauder bombers, maintained Trujillo as the unassailable master of the Dominican Republic and allowed him to indulge his resentment of critics overseas, such as Rómulo Betancourt of Venezuela and Ramón Grau San Martín of Cuba, in plots to menace, undermine, or assassinate them. Trujillo's war-based military complex, most notably its air capability, kept neighboring Haiti in a near-constant state of tension. The threat of being bombed by the Dominican Republic extended to Cuba, Mexico, and Venezuela, among other places, as long as Rafael Trujillo, erstwhile Allied leader, retained his capricious control until 1961.

NOTES

1. For the broader context of wartime Dominican history, see Eric Paul Roorda, *The Dictator Next Door: The Good Neighbor Policy and the Trujillo Regime in the Dominican Republic, 1930–1945* (Durham, NC: Duke University Press, 1998).

2. The indispensable sources for research on the Dominican Republic during World War II are the documentary compendia edited by Bernardo Vega, *Los Estados Unidos y Trujillo, Año 1945* (1982), *Nazismo, fascismo y falangismo en la República Dominicana* (1985), and *Trujillo y las Fuerzas Armadas Norteamericanas* (1992; all Santo Domingo: Fundación Cultural Dominicana). The volumes comprise information from archives in the Dominican Republic, Germany, Great Britain, and the United States.

3. Roorda, *Dictator*, 127–43. For the background to the massacre, see Lauren H. Derby, "Magic, Money and Haitians: *Raza* and Society in the Haitian-Dominican Borderlands, 1900–1937," *Comparative Studies in Society and History* (July 1994), 488–526.

4. Roorda, *Dictator*, 143–48.

5. Roorda, *Dictator*, 170–82.

6. British Minister Alexander Paterson to Anthony Eden, quoted in Roorda, *Dictator*, 205.

7. Roorda, *Dictator*, 203–8. For the larger picture of wartime cooperation, see John Child, "From 'Color' to 'Rainbow': U.S. Strategic Planning for Latin America, 1919–1945," *Journal of Interamerican Studies and World Affairs* (May 1979): 233–59.

8. For more on the Dominican military build-up, see Vega, *Fuerzas Armadas*, and Roorda, "The Cult of the Airplane among U.S. Military Men and Dominicans during the U.S. Occupation and the Trujillo Regime," in Gilbert M. Joseph, Catherine C. LeGrand, and Ricardo D. Salvatore, eds., *Close Encounters of Empire: Writing the Cultural History of U.S.-Latin American Relations* (Durham, NC: Duke University Press, 1998), 269–310.

9. The story of U-boat activity involving the Dominican Republic is told in Vega, *Nazismo*, 227–41. For background to the Dominican Merchant Marine, see René de la Pedraja, *Oil and Coffee: Latin American Merchant Shipping from the Imperial Era to the 1950s* (Westport, CT: Greenwood Press, 1998).

10. Less than two years after its capture, on only its second Allied convoy, the former *Hannover* was sunk by a German submarine.

11. Secret Service report filed by "Bunny," quoted in Vega, *Nazismo*, 167.

12. The details of wartime espionage are contained in Vega, *Nazismo*. For the wider context of German spying and blacklisting, see Alton Frye, *Nazi Germany and the American Hemisphere, 1933–1941* (New Haven, CT: Yale University Press, 1967).

13. Robert D. Crassweller, *Trujillo: The Life and Times of a Caribbean Dictator* (New York: Macmillan, 1966), 160–63.

14. Roorda, *Dictator*, 173–81.

15. José Ramón Estella, *Historia Gráfica de la República Dominicana*, 2nd ed. (Santo Domingo: Editora Taller, 1986), 366–67.

6

Puerto Rico: Quiet Participant

Andrew Lefebvre

Puerto Rico's involvement in World War II had more to do with its strategic location than with any other issue, including the anti-Axis sentiment that permeated the island. Although they were U.S. citizens, the people of Puerto Rico were disenchanted with their island's status as an autonomous territory of the United States. In the forty years following the Spanish-American War in 1898, the U.S. government had not given any consideration to granting Puerto Rico statehood or independence, because of the island's strategic importance. Puerto Rico is the easternmost island of the Greater Antilles island chain, lying between North and South America and between the Mona and Virgin passages into the Caribbean Sea. Its location serves as a guard to the eastern approaches to the Panama Canal and to vital Caribbean and Atlantic shipping routes.

The ambiguous status of Puerto Rico fostered an unstable political climate on the island, which encouraged some members of the Puerto Rican elite to experiment with subversive political groups. U.S. policy regarding statehood or Puerto Rican independence, as well as links with Spain and the island's Spanish heritage, generated resentment toward the United States. Residual feelings for Spain promoted adherence to Falangism, a Spanish form of fascism. This support created an intelligence nightmare during World War II, as U.S. officials worried that these Puerto Rican subversives would transmit valuable military information to the Axis. The U.S. government was also concerned with the remote possibility of Axis military strikes against the island's military installations.

These problems did not prevent Puerto Rico from being of invaluable assistance to the Allied war effort, however. The resentment among some

Puerto Ricans did not prohibit the majority of the island's population from performing its duty and helping the Allied cause. Puerto Ricans helped wherever needed and some even volunteered for service in the U.S. armed forces. The commonwealth played to perfection its part as a strategic outpost. The war's economic impact on Puerto Rico strengthened a political movement that sought to improve the island's economic and social basis prior to making the battle for statehood or independence a priority. Puerto Rico's economic relationship with the United States had been problematic ever since the U.S. acquisition of the island in 1898, and the island's economy had its share of ups and downs during the war, with the people enduring shortages of everyday items ranging from food to nylons to gasoline.

POLITICAL AND ECONOMIC BACKGROUND

The United States received Puerto Rico as an indemnity from the Spanish-American War of 1898. Capt. Alfred Thayer Mahan convinced the U.S. government that the Navy would need a coaling station in the West Indies in order to protect the planned trans-isthmian canal, and naval officers focused upon Puerto Rico for several reasons, the most important being its position as the gateway to the Caribbean; whoever possessed Puerto Rico controlled access to the Caribbean. Furthermore, Puerto Rico was easier to control than Cuba because of its smaller size and lack of an organized native army to offer resistance.[1]

Puerto Rico's geographical location justified the U.S. invasion of the island in 1898 and its strategic importance far outweighed the arguments against imperialism in the House of Representatives and Senate. The humanitarian pretext used for the Spanish-American War immediately switched to expansionism following the U.S. military intervention. The conquest of Puerto Rico was not intended to directly promote capital gain, but instead to broaden the United States' sphere of influence. Secretary of the Navy Theodore Roosevelt, a Mahan disciple, believed that the United States needed a formidable navy in order to compete as a world power and that the addition of the Caribbean into the U.S. sphere of influence would bring with it the necessity for a "proper navy." Roosevelt also understood Puerto Rico's strategic importance to the proposed isthmian canal.

In the four generations following the Spanish-American War, Puerto Ricans have failed to benefit from the U.S. supervision of the island. Under the terms of the 1900 Foraker Act, the U.S. government appointed all administrative officials and reserved the right to overrule all legislation approved by the locally elected legislature. Economically, by the onset of the Great Depression in 1930, the island remained predominantly an agricultural society.

The rising tide of Puerto Rican nationalism became evident by the 1910s and was not stemmed by the U.S. passage of the Jones Act in 1917, which provided U.S. citizenship for the Puerto Ricans. Puerto Rican nationalism came to center stage during the 1930s and soon became enmeshed in U.S. wartime policies.

Supernationalist Pedro Albizú Campos inherited the leadership of Partido Nacionalista in the 1930s. Albizú Campos denounced the electoral process as a farce and sanctioned the use of violence and terrorism as political tools. His threat became a reality following the police killing of three Nationalist demonstrators in October 1936. In response, Albizú Campos vowed that a continental American would die for each of the dead Nationalist party members. The following February, Nationalist gunmen assassinated Col. Francis Riggs, the chief of the Insular Police, making Albizú Campos's threat a partial reality and landing the Nationalist leader in prison.

Luis Muñoz Marín founded a more moderate party in 1938. The Partido Popular Democrático (PPD) realized that either independence or statehood was a lofty goal for Puerto Rico's immediate future. The party preferred to seek Commonwealth status—internal self-government short of statehood—for Puerto Rico. The PPD won the 1940 insular election with 40 percent of the popular vote and also won control of the insular Senate. In order to garner enough support for the 1940 election, Muñoz Marín turned to the poor rural classes for support. He spoke only colloquial Spanish while campaigning, chose the simple slogan "Bread, Land, and Liberty," and promised land redistribution and economic prosperity.[2]

Muñoz Marín's electoral victory came shortly before the appointment of Rexford Tugwell as governor of Puerto Rico on September 19, 1941. As a New Dealer, Tugwell was concerned with helping the poor of Puerto Rico. He also argued that Puerto Rico's economic underdevelopment should not continue; not only did it serve as fuel for anti-American sentiment, but it would hinder the U.S. war effort. Although he and Muñoz Marín did not always agree, they did share a vision of a better Puerto Rico in which the population shared equal access to opportunities. Muñoz Marín believed that statehood or independence did not matter if the island's immediate economic and social problems were not rectified.[3] He also realized that more could be gained from the United States by not casting it in the role of an oppressor.

Tugwell helped to pave the way for Muñoz Marín's reforms by lobbying for greater autonomy for the elected Puerto Rican government and a decisive U.S. answer regarding the island's political status. In 1942, Tugwell suggested to President Franklin D. Roosevelt that Puerto Rico elect its own governor, reasoning that Puerto Rico was important enough to the war effort that it should have greater local autonomy. As it stood at the time, the locally elected Puerto Rican House and Senate severely limited the governor's ability to pass legislation, and the governor could veto local legislation. To overcome the political stalemate and to enable Puerto Rico to more effectively assume its role as the gateway to the Caribbean and more fully cooperate against the Axis, Tugwell argued that Puerto Rico needed extensive modernization and industrialization.[4]

Unlike most Caribbean nations, Puerto Rico did not have a choice about joining the Allied cause, since it was a U.S. possession. The United States courted other countries, such as the Dominican Republic and Mexico, in order to convince them that it was in their best interest to help fight the Axis. The Germans assisted in the decision-making process with their U-boat campaign in the Caribbean that adversely impacted neutral shipping. However, Puerto Rico, as a U.S. territory, was required to assist the United States in its Caribbean defense strategies. Given Puerto Rico's involuntary involvement in the war, the significance of Tugwell's attempts to maintain political and economic stability on the island became self-evident. His efforts contributed to the widespread Puerto Rican support for the Allied war effort.

The island responded well to the challenge of World War II. Relations between Puerto Ricans and continental Americans were cordial at worst and at times exceptional. The Puerto Ricans welcomed U.S. servicemen to the island and opened up their homes and families in an effort to make their stay in Puerto Rico amicable. Puerto Rican women participated in the many events hosted by the armed forces to socialize, play games, and dance with the servicemen, a phenomenon that spawned many romances and marriages.[5]

Part of this successful integration into the Allied war effort was due to Muñoz Marín's reforms. He made good on his election promises of land redistribution and economic prosperity, accomplishing both largely because of the rum trade with the United States. During the war, the United States lost its traditional sources of hard liquor due to the naval blockade. To compensate, it turned to Puerto Rico. This could not have come at a better time for Puerto Rico, then in a state of desperation. The unemployment rolls skyrocketed from 99,100 in July 1941 to an unprecedented 237,000 in September 1942, and food and petroleum stockpiles had reached disastrous levels.[6] In an effort to correct these problems, the U.S. Congress allowed the island government to keep 70 percent of the taxes received from the sale of rum. As a result, the island enjoyed a period of economic prosperity. Puerto Rico's revenues jumped from $1.7 million in 1941 to $13.9 million and $65.8 million in 1942 and 1944, respectively. The increased tax revenues permitted Muñoz Marín to institute his land redistribution program.[7] Economic prosperity and the implementation of some of its electoral promises gave the PPD a landslide victory in the 1944 insular election. The PPD received 383,280 of a possible 591,978 votes, for a 65 percent majority over the newly formed

Progressive Republican Union, a coalition of the Liberal and Republican parties.[8]

SPAIN'S INVOLVEMENT WITH THE AXIS

With the coming of World War II, Spain had a government like that of contemporary Italy—highly centralized and undemocratic, essentially a Fascist dictatorship—with Generalissimo Francisco Franco as Supreme Leader.[9] Franco also headed the Falangist Party, which was founded in 1933. Built with military-style discipline and rank structure, it conformed to the Nazi and Italian fascist models. Its Falange Exterior operated outside of Spain, where it carried out tasks that were military in nature, including assault, vigilance, suppression, espionage, and counterespionage. In these military aspects, the Falange was identical to the German Nazis and Italian fascists.[10] The Falange Exterior operated throughout Latin America, but none of its chapters was more dangerous to U.S. sovereignty than that of Puerto Rico.[11]

Initially, Spain declared its neutrality with the outbreak of World War II in 1939, but changed its status to that of nonbelligerent on June 12, 1940.[12] Despite its professed status, however, Spain's collaboration with the Axis—and particularly with Adolf Hitler's Third Reich—is common knowledge. Clearly Franco was an active partner of the Axis belligerents—Hitler, Mussolini, and the Japanese militarists. While he did not fulfill Hitler's every wish, he served him to an extent incompatible with neutrality, let alone Allied interests. Spain exported to the Axis precious metals, military equipment, and supplies and opened its airfields and ports to the German Luftwaffe and Kriegsmarine.[13]

Most notably, representatives of Franco's government collected information of potential use to the Axis governments and forwarded it to them. This had special implications for Puerto Rico, where a large Spanish population resided. Information passed on to the Germans about U.S. naval operations in the Caribbean could threaten the security of the Panama Canal, Venezuelan oil shipments, and convoy routes, all essential for the U.S. war effort. The political climate of the island mattered. Widespread sympathy for the Falangist cause among Puerto Ricans might jeopardize the secrecy of U.S. naval operations and assist saboteurs.

Without a doubt, Franco had numerous powerful admirers among Puerto Rico's upper classes. Many of these were resident Spaniards who chose to keep Spanish citizenship after the 1917 Jones Act. The majority of the Spanish citizens in Puerto Rico held positions of influence, in business or in politics. Other Puerto Ricans who admired Franco included Puerto Rican Nationalists and their sympathizers, who thought that anyone opposed to the United States conformed to a worthwhile ideology.

The wealthiest of the Spanish residents were by far the most influential. Spaniards had large investments in business in Puerto Rico. Spaniards living in Spain owned $6.2 million in assets, and Spanish residents in Puerto Rico owned another $29.2 million. The FBI's San Juan Field Division compiled a list of the controlling partners of businesses in Puerto Rico, and the membership of the two main Falange-influenced clubs in San Juan, Casino Español and Casa de España, constituted a large part of this list. Almost a third of both boards' members (8 of 27 and 5 of 17, respectively) owned controlling interests in Puerto Rican businesses. José Maria del Valle, a president of Casino Español and acting president of the Casa de España owned just over a million dollars' worth of properties and businesses by himself.[14]

An estimated 75 percent of the approximately 5,300 Puerto Ricans who held Spanish citizenship were pro-Franco—a fact that concerned U.S. officials. Although most of the Puerto Rican Falangists were not militant, they actively distributed pro-Axis propaganda and expressed pro-Axis sympathies. These Spaniards constituted a threat to the United States because they were wealthy, influential landowners with ties to several industries.

Alfonso Miranda Esteve founded the Puerto Rican chapter of the Falange, which most prominent and wealthy Spaniards in Puerto Rico supported. In September 1938, he wrote to Secretary of State Cordell Hull and the chief of the Office of Arms and Munitions Control, Joseph C. Green, informing them that the Puerto Rico Falangists aimed "to create a favorable attitude towards Catholic and Nationalist Spain."[15] The Falange was most popular in the largest cities and towns of Puerto Rico. Its membership spread throughout San Juan, Ponce, Mayagüez, Arecibo, Bayamón, and Caguas. The Falange "helped General Franco financially, celebrated his victories, and worked intensively spreading Falangist propaganda."[16]

Puerto Ricans belonged to numerous social clubs where they mingled with other social elites, business members, and influential men. Casino Español, located in San Juan, was one of the most prestigious of these clubs, with membership from both the Spanish and non-Spanish communities. The latter, however, were not allowed to hold office or participate in the club's business affairs. Although some 700 Loyalist members left the club during the Spanish Civil War, the membership roster at the end of October 1941 included 307 Spanish and 952 non-Spanish members, the majority of whom favored Franco. The club's two honorary members, Franco himself and Mariano De Amuedo, the Spanish consul, also reflected this view.[17]

In 1938, Casino Español hosted the officers of the German warship *Meteor*. An article in *El Imparcial* described the occasion by noting that the Spaniards joined the German officers in a toast to Franco, and a contemporary photograph of the meeting clearly displayed the men toasting with pictures of Franco and Hitler in the background. Notably, the German officers were in full military dress uniform. Casino Español's acting president, C. Conde, denied the report in a letter to Governor Blanton Winship, however. According to Conde, the German scientists came to the club as a response to a visit to the *Meteor* arranged by the German consul for some of the club's members. Conde insisted that no toasts were made "which could be construed to hurt the feelings of outsiders. The members of the Spanish Club are persons of different political and religious ideals." Conde continued, "The officials have invariably observed a neutral attitude in keeping with the regulations of the Club since its establishment very many years ago."[18]

In San Juan, the FBI received many complaints about the Auxilio Mutúo, a prominent Spanish hospital and health clinic, founded in the 1860s. Reportedly, the hospital's policies showed excessive favoritism to Franco and his supporters. The FBI placed the hospital's chief operating officer, Dr. Amalio Holdan, under surveillance because of his friendship with the Spanish consul and his participation at a function at the Mallorquina restaurant on July 17, 1942, to celebrate the anniversary of the Spanish Rebellion. The FBI also kept the majority of the hospital's board of directors under surveillance because they were known Falangists.[19]

The only known anti-Franco club in Puerto Rico was the Asociación Pro Democracia Española. Founded as a Spanish Republican organization on December 2, 1938, the San Juan–based association drew its membership principally from the island's middle-class businessmen and university professors. One of its most prominent objectives was "to offer the services of the organization to the United States of America in its fight against Fascism."[20]

The amount of advertising space purchased in the Falange's periodical *Avance* illustrates the size of and respectability of the Falange in Puerto Rico. Obviously these businesses did not think that advertising in a Falangist magazine would taint their reputations. Advertisements originated from companies across the entire island, in various cities and towns, including San Juan, Ponce, Caguas, Mayagüez, Santurce, Humacao, and Bayamón. Each of these centers had its own chapter of the Falange. There was also an advertisement from Menedez + Compañía Shipping Co. Puerto Rico y República Dominicana. This company advertised for international shippers, including Red "D" Line, International Merchants Marine Company, American Exports Line, Canadian National Steamship Co., and the Compañia Chilena de Navigacíon Interocéana.

Advertisements in *Avance* ranged from shoes and furniture to construction equipment and importers. There was a large complement of Spanish-owned stores and products. The most surprising advertisements were those for well-known international products. These included ads for popular beers and U.S. shoe brands:

Budweiser
la legitima cerveza

J + R Tennent's Scotch Pilsner Beer
brewed in Scotland
Distinga su gusto y personalidad tomando
*Cerveza "Tennent" Inglesia Freiria
Anos & Co. Agentes*
San Juan, Puerto Rico

The Packard Shoe a *"El Popular"*
San Juan, Puerto Rico

*Sientase, Joven
Use zapatos* "Pathfinder"
Almacenes Rodriguez
San Juan, Ponce, Mayaguez, Humacao[21]

Businessmen who supported the Falange and Franco sent money to Spain that helped to finance the Nationalist factions in the Spanish Civil War and Spain's guarded efforts in World War II. A 1942 FBI report described the contents of a Spanish newspaper article in *Fara de Vigo* reporting that the Puerto Rican Falange had contributed more than $500,000 to Franco's efforts between June 18, 1936, and November 1937. In that seventeen-month period, Puerto Ricans donated $100,000 to acquire new airplanes, $2,000 to repair devastated towns, $2,000 for the building of the cruiser *España*, $25,000 in medical supplies, and another $400,000 cash. The report credited the Puerto Rican Chamber of Commerce with sending an additional $10,000.[22] Less scrupulous businessmen such as Puerto Rican Falange leader Seguno Cadierno and, in 1943, an importer of Spanish brandy, Sobrinos de Esquierdo, Inc., transferred money to Spain through U.S. dollar credits by falsifying import/export receipts and orders.[23]

On August 15, 1937, the Spanish Ministry of Exterior Affairs ordered that Falangists receive primary consideration for all foreign commissions and services in an effort to homogenize the diplomatic corps.[24] The Spanish consul in San Juan, Mariano De Amuedo, was one such appointment. In 1945, De Amuedo predicted that after the war Puerto Rico would become a dominion of Spain such as Canada was to the United Kingdom. This raised U.S. suspicions about his possible involvement in Puerto Rican politics. More suspicious was the discovery by the U.S. Office of Strategic Services (OSS) that De Amuedo had purchased, in cash, a $7,500 draft and an another $500 in traveler's checks at the San Juan branch of the Bank of Nova Scotia, which was not De Amuedo's regular bank. When queried by a bank official, De Amuedo explained that he planned to go on vacation to the United States.

However, De Amuedo did not earn enough as consul to spend $8,000 in cash casually. This event implied that he was either sending the money to the Falange or paying agents for their services.[25]

THE ROLE OF THE CATHOLIC CHURCH

Although the Roman Catholic Church did not show open and unmitigated support for the Nazi regime, it did not openly abhor it, leaving the Church open to criticism during World War II. Given the friendship of the Vatican for Falangist and fascist causes in general, and given the fact that Franco and the Falange had powerful friends and admirers among Puerto Rico's Roman Catholic clergy, U.S. authorities viewed many Church officials in Puerto Rico with suspicion.[26]

The roots of this support can be traced to Spain, where the Jesuits remained a tool of the Falange even after it was outlawed by the Second Republic. Additionally, during the Spanish Civil War, the Vatican launched a public crusade against Communism, and Pius XI gave Franco's Nationalist forces his blessing for their battle against Communism.[27] This evidence exposes the Catholic Church in the grasp of fascism, but how did this affect Puerto Rico?

Since the Catholic Church supported the Falange, it became one of the most influential sources of Falangist propaganda abroad. The presence of Spanish priests in Spanish-speaking countries around the world gave the Falange a very large sphere of influence. During the Spanish Civil War, the Catholic priests in Puerto Rico, most of whom were either adherent members or sympathizers of the Falange, celebrated masses in the name of Franco and prayed for a quick rebel victory.[28]

Various sources estimated that 99 percent of the Catholic clergy in Puerto Rico was pro-Franco and pro-fascist. Because the Spanish Church, in concert with Rome, approved all assignments to Puerto Rico, priests who demonstrated these tendencies could not easily be removed from service. The Paulist Order best illustrates the point. The Holy See had granted the Paulist Order certain rights *ad perpetuam*. Priests in Puerto Rico spread the Order's message through sermons and through publications such as the biweekly pamphlet *La Milagrosa*, which was distributed by the Order. While most of the Paulist activity took place in the urban centers of San Juan and Ponce, *La Milagrosa* was distributed across the island. The Office of Naval Intelligence (ONI) discovered evidence of Spanish priests actively cooperating with the Falange's local chapters. ONI suspected that the priests also served as couriers for the Falange, mostly in transferring money back to Spain.[29]

Spanish priests in Puerto Rico also subscribed to the Falangist propaganda and other publications from Spain. In 1943, when the Falange in Puerto Rico was supposedly defunct, there was an upward trend of pro-Axis propaganda entering Puerto Rico. For example, during a three-day period in March 1943, the censorship board confiscated 420 different publications as they entered Puerto Rico, including *La Nueva España, Región, Proa, Signo, El Diario Vasco, Ya, La Tarde, La Vos de Asturias,* and *Diario de Navarra.* The recipients included most Catholic Orders and priests in Puerto Rico: the Paulist and Augustine Orders; the Centro Universitario Católico in Río Piedras; the director of the Colegio Ponceno, a Catholic organization in Ponce; an array of parish priests; the former German consul in Puerto Rico, Henry Frese; and the Falange leader of the time, Seguno Cadierno.[30]

THE ROLE OF MEDIA

The FBI also accused the secular media of playing an influential role in spreading Falangist propaganda across Puerto Rico, but most often on flimsy evidence. Two such cases involved *El Mundo* and *Puerto Rico Ilustrado.*

El Mundo was a respected, conservative Puerto Rican newspaper. The news it reported was exactly that—news. *El Mundo* did not receive reports from the German news agency Trans Ocean, and its interpretation of various wartime events was nothing out of the ordinary. The FBI appeared to rest its case upon the Falange advertising its social events in *El Mundo* prior to World War II![31] Because the Falange was a legal organization at that time, and because anyone could buy space in the classifieds to announce events, the FBI argument lacks credibility.

The FBI also condemned the magazine *Puerto Rico Ilustrado,* which was owned by the same people as *El Mundo,* but *Ilustrado* seemingly suffered guilt by association. As with *El Mundo,* nothing printed in *Ilustrado* gave the appearance that it was a Falangist appendage. It printed articles about current events and news, as any other news magazine would.

Only *Avance* actually served as a Falangist propaganda tool, until it ceased publication in 1940. It included the aforementioned articles about the religious significance of the Falange and its creed, which was a distortion of the Apostle's Creed. *Avance* ran advertisements to raise funds for the Nationalists by selling "photographs of the leader of New Spain his Excellency Señor Francisco Franco Báhamonde." The pictures cost sixty cents each, and the proceeds were sent to Spain.[32] Its articles were blatant propaganda. An article from April 1937 claimed that the Spanish Civil War was actually the "defense of the essence of Western Civilization against the barbaric Soviets" and that "all nations, Authoritarian and Democratic States alike, must be deeply alarmed by the audacity of the maneuvers of the Internationals for a world tolerable of Marxism."[33]

PUERTO RICO AND U.S. DEFENSE STRATEGIES

As a gatekeeper to the Caribbean Sea, Puerto Rico played a significant role in U.S. defense planning. San Juan became the headquarters of the Caribbean Sea Frontier, a region that included the entire Caribbean west to the Panama region. Commanded by Rear Adm. John H. Hoover, Puerto Rico and its outlying naval stations served as the first line of defense in protecting the southern approaches to the Panama Canal and aiding in the protection of the Venezuelan oil and refineries and Caribbean trade in general. The construction of the Roosevelt Roads Naval Station provided a deepwater port in the region, without which the U.S. Navy would have had to anchor in Panama or the Chesapeake Bay, thus reducing its effectiveness in controlling the Caribbean.[34]

Prior to the outbreak of the European war, the U.S. Army Air Force also recognized Puerto Rico's importance as a staging area for planes and supplies going to South America and then on to Europe. A southern route was essential because the North Atlantic was impassable during the winter months. The principal warm weather route was from the United States to Brazil via Puerto Rico, Martinique, Trinidad, and Dutch Guiana; the secondary route sent planes to Brazil via Panama, Colombia, and Venezuela.[35] Puerto Rico's importance in air transportation led to the construction of a major air base at Borinquen Point. Known alternately as Puerto Rico Air Base No. 1 and Borinquen Field, it opened on September 6, 1939, and was capable of handling all types of aircraft ranging from fighter planes to B-17 bombers.[36]

An estimated 65,000 Puerto Ricans served in the U.S. armed forces during the war. A large portion of these troops—23,000 of them—volunteered for service. Although they faced discrimination, most Puerto Ricans eagerly contributed to the war effort. Initially, Puerto Ricans were thought of as intellectually inferior to their continental colleagues. However, the military hierarchy soon realized that Puerto Rican troops were at a disadvantage largely due to language constraints. The majority of instruction and testing was in English, a language foreign to the Spanish-speaking Puerto Ricans. The fact that the ratio of officers to enlisted men was 45 to 1 indicates some form of discrimination against them.

Three Puerto Rican regiments served outside the island. The 65th Infantry Regiment served in countries ranging from Panama to Germany. The 295th Infantry Regiment, formerly the Puerto Rican National Guard, saw service on various islands in the Caribbean Basin, from Jamaica to Curaçao. The third infantry regiment, the 296th, trained for battle against Japan in the Pacific, but the war ended while they awaited deployment in Hawaii.[37]

Puerto Rico's strategic value declined as the war continued. After the German U-boat threat to the Caribbean transit routes ended in late 1942, U.S.

security interests shifted to other war zones. The security around piers in San Juan harbor was demonstrative of this change. Early in the war, the piers were patrolled by the U.S. Coast Guard and some recruits from continental police and fire departments. By the war's end, the piers were patrolled by continental women in security uniforms.[38]

CONCLUSION

Puerto Rico's participation in World War II went beyond its strategic geographic location. Puerto Ricans volunteered and fought in the U.S. armed forces. U.S. officials also gained a greater appreciation of the island's need for economic development, a factor that resulted in closer relationships between Puerto Rican and continental politicians. Like their continental counterparts, Puerto Ricans endured the shortages of basic commodities and goods—a factor that helped to unite the islanders to support the Allied war cause rather than squabble about domestic problems.

The presence of Falange- and Axis-friendly people in Puerto Rico captivated the attention of the U.S. intelligence community. Each of the major U.S. intelligence-gathering organizations—the Federal Bureau of Investigation, the Military Intelligence Division, the Office of Naval Intelligence, and the Office of Strategic Services, aided by the Puerto Rican Insular Police—investigated possible Falangist activities and maintained extensive files on the Falange and its sympathizers in Puerto Rico. Although the government of the United States utilized substantial resources to investigate the Falange, there were no arrests or military reinforcements sent to the island as a result of the threat. This speaks volumes about what the United States really felt regarding the nature of the Falange: it was worth watching but did not constitute a critical priority. Still, the existence of the Falange and its considerable influence in Puerto Rico was sufficient enough to justify the U.S. investigatory actions.

The Roman Catholic Church in Puerto Rico often used its pulpit to spread pro-Falange and Axis propaganda. Many members of the clergy subscribed to fascist and Falangist publications for the purpose of educating their flock. These activities, when combined with pronouncements by the media, diplomats, and businessmen, made the island's residents subject to Falangist influence.

The Falange represented a potential threat to U.S. security in Puerto Rico, the hub of U.S. naval interests in the Caribbean. There was no smoking gun regarding the Germans, Japanese, or Italians—all of whom could legally have their own people there until early January 1942, when the United States commenced its supervision of the deportations of Axis spies from Latin America. In fact, Spanish activity was greatly reduced following a memo dated September 8, 1942, ordering the Falange Exterior to cease and desist.[39] However, the threat to U.S. and Allied interests remained a serious one.

NOTES

1. Kal Wagenheim, *Puerto Rico: A Profile* (London: Pall Mall Press, 1970), 65.

2. For a discussion of Puerto Rico's development in the early twentieth century, see Raymond Carr, *Puerto Rico: A Colonial Experiment* (New York: New York University Press, 1984), 25, 62–65; Federico Ribes Covar, *Historia cronológica de Puerto Rico* (Panama: Editorial "Tres Amèricas," 1973), 448; Ronald Fernandez, *The Disenchanted Island: Puerto Rico and the United States in the Twentieth Century*, 2nd ed. (Westport, CT: Praeger, 1996), 141, 142; Arturo Morales Carrión, *Puerto Rico: A Political and Cultural History* (New York: W. W. Norton, 1983), 244.

3. Lynn-Darrell Bender, ed., *The American Presence in Puerto Rico* (Puerto Rico: Publicaciones Puertorriquenas, 1998), 79–81.

4. Morales Carrión, *Puerto Rico*, 252–55.

5. Edwin R. Dooley Jr., "Wartime San Juan, Puerto Rico: The Forgotten American Homefront, 1941–1945," *Journal of Military History* 63, no. 4 (October 1999): 933–34.

6. Morales Carrión, *Puerto Rico*, 251.

7. Fernandez, *Disenchanted Island*, 145.

8. Morales Carrión, *Puerto Rico*, 255.

9. Samuel Hoare, *Complacent Dictator* (New York: Alfred A. Knopf, 1947), 33.

10. "The Falange Party," June 11, 1941, National Archives and Records Administration of the United States (hereafter cited as NARA), RG 165, "Records of War Department and Special Staffs, Office of the Director of Intelligence G-2, Subordinate Offices—Latin American Branch," Spanish Falange to Falange General, entry 188, NM-84 (hereafter cited as RG 165), Box 1000.

11. Other countries that had extensive evidence of Falange movements included Mexico, Cuba, Peru, Venezuela, and Panama.

12. U.S. Ambassador to Spain Weddell to Secretary of State Hull, June 13, 1940, in U.S. Department of State, *Foreign Relations of the United States: Diplomatic Papers, 1940* (Washington, DC: GPO, 1940), 797.

13. Max Gallo, *Spain under Franco* (New York: E. P. Dutton, 1974), 107.

14. [FBI Special Agent] Lowell Dunham, "Survey of Spanish Activities in the San Juan Field Division," August 28, 1942, pp. 2–3, and October 12, 1942, pp. 1–8, NARA, RG 38, Chief of Naval Operations, "ONI Security Classified Administrative Correspondence, 1942–1946" (hereafter cited as RG 38), Box 231.

15. "Exhibit I," from Falange (Puerto Rico) to U.S. Department of State, December 11, 1939; letter from Alfonso Miranda Esteve to Cordell Hull, September 12, 1938; and letter from Miranda Esteve to Joseph C. Green, September 22, 1938—all in Archivo General de la Administración, Alcalá de Henares, Caja 60, "15 D.N. Servicio Exterior, America-Latina, Correspondencia, Puerto Rico y Uruguay, 1937–1946."

16. Office of Assistant Chief of Staff (G-2) to Lt. Col. E. B. Harry, April 10, 1943, NARA, RG 165, Box 1000, pp. 1–2.

17. Dunham, "Survey of Spanish Activities," August 28, 1942, pp. 2–3.

18. Letter from Conde to Winship, April 4, 1938, Archivo General de Puerto Rico, Oficina del Gobernador, Caja 191, Tarea 96–20, "Consulate of Spain."

19. Dunham, "Survey of Spanish Activities," August 28, 1942, pp. 4–5, and October 12, 1942, p. 11.

20. Dunham, "Survey of Spanish Activities," August 28, 1942, p. 8.

21. *Avance* 1, no. 5 (March 31, 1937): 3–33; *Avance* 1, no. 20 (December 1, 1937): 16.

22. J. Edgar Hoover to Harry L. Hopkins, "The Spanish Falange in Puerto Rico," April 28, 1942, Franklin Delano Roosevelt Archives, FBI files Puerto Rico, Box 143, p. 4.

23. "Spanish Pro-Axis Propaganda," May 5, 1943, NARA, RG 165, Box 1002.

24. "Situación del personal de la carrera diplomatica que presto servicio en FET y de las JONS," August 15, 1937, Archivo del Ministerio de Asuntos Exteriores, Madrid (hereafter cited as AMAE), LegR. 1020, Exp. 65.

25. Memorandum from Sr. Ygual, Spanish consul general in Shanghai, to Foreign Minister Serrano Suñer, December 1, 1940, AMAE, Personal File no. 4; memorandum from De Amuedo to Minister of the Exterior, May 19, 1945, AMAE, LegR. 1656, Exp. 4, "Informacion Política"; Col. P. J. Parra to Headquarters, Antilles Department, Office of the Assistant Chief of Staff (G-2), October 27, 1945, NARA, RG 165, Box 999.

26. Guenter Lewy, *The Catholic Church and Nazi Germany*, 1st Da Capo ed. (Boulder, CO: Da Capo Press, 2000), 207.

27. "The Spanish Falange," ARA, Box 1000, p. 1; Lewy, *The Catholic Church*, 312.

28. Office of Assistant Chief of Staff (G-2) to Lt. Col. E. B. Harry, 2.

29. "Tenth Naval District: Counter Intelligence Section B-7 Monthly Summary," month ending November 30, 1942, NARA, RG 38, Box 241, p. 10.

30. "Spanish Pro-Axis Propaganda," 1.

31. Hoover, "Spanish Falange in Puerto Rico," 5.

32. *Avance* 1, no. 4 (March 15, 1937): 28.

33. "España, contra el Soviet: El significado real de nuestra guerra," *Avance* 1, no. 6 (April 15, 1937): 15.

34. Alejandro Torres Rivera, *Militarismo y decolonización: Puerto Rico ante el siglo 21* (San Juan: Congreso Nacional Hostosiano, 1999), 47; Michael Gannon, *Operation Drumbeat: The Dramatic True Story of Germany's First U-Boat Attacks along the American Coast in World War II* (New York: Harper and Row, 1990), 308; Samuel Eliot Morison, *History of the United States Naval Operations in World War II*, Vol. 1, *The Battle of the Atlantic, September 1939–May 1943* (Boston: Little, Brown, 1961), 144–54.

35. Stetson Conn and Byron Fairchild, *The United States Army in World War II: The Western Hemisphere; The Framework of Hemispheric Defense* (Washington, DC: Office of the Chief of Military History, Department of the Army, 1960), 250.

36. Stetson Conn, Ross Engelman, and Byron Fairchild, *The United States Army in World War II: Guarding the United States and Its Outposts* (Washington, DC: Office of the Chief of Military History, Department of the Army, 1964), 325.

37. Morales Carrion, *Puerto Rico*, 257–58.

38. Dooley, "Wartime San Juan," 927.

39. Memorandum from Foreign Minister Gómez Jordana to all members of the Falange Exterior, September 8, 1942, AMAE, Caja 1370, Exp. 9, "Política Exterior—Problema de Actuación de Falange en el Extranjero."

Panamanian troops on parade in the capital city in 1941.

A nine-year-old Panamanian girl offers a drink of water to U.S. soldiers on maneuvers in Panama in 1943.

U.S. naval personnel turn over the command of a coastal patrol vessel to Central American naval forces in 1943.

Nicaraguan senior officers inspect new antiaircraft weaponry at a U.S. military installation in 1943.

Soldiers of the Brazilian Expeditionary Force prepare to embark for combat in Italy during World War II.

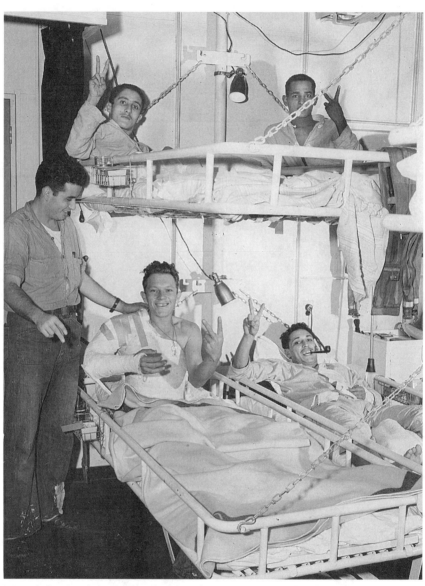

Wounded troops from the Brazilian Expeditionary Force that fought in the Italian campaign in World War II returning home.

Formerly a Swedish passenger ship, the Gripsholm *became one of the principal vessels in transporting Axis nationals and their descendents to Germany and Japan and for internment in the United States.*

Teaching English in a Guatemalan elementary school.

Female students of the Colegio Aleman in Guatemala City marching during an Independence Day parade.

Honduran pilots training with U.S. airplanes.

Tapping rubber. The U.S. Rubber Reserve Corporation encouraged its development across Latin America during World War II.

Loading mahogany lumber for shipment to the United States. Mahogany was used in the construction of PT boats.

II

SOUTH AMERICA DURING WORLD WAR II

SOUTH AMERICA
During World War II

7

Bolivarian Nations: Securing the Northern Frontier

George M. Lauderbaugh

The gathering war clouds in Europe and Asia in the late 1930s presented both challenges and opportunities to the three republics of northern South America: Ecuador, Colombia, and Venezuela. The greatest challenge, of course, was how to preserve their sovereignty and way of life in the face of the overwhelming military power of the Axis (Germany, Italy, and Japan) and the Allies (France and Great Britain, later joined by the Soviet Union and the United States). At first glance, it would appear that Ecuador, Colombia, and Venezuela were of little strategic importance to the belligerents, but such was not the case. All three were in close proximity to the Panama Canal, a strategic waterway whose control by the United States gave the Allies a decided advantage by providing for the rapid deployment of naval forces and war matériel around the globe. In addition, Venezuela was one of the world's largest producers of petroleum and also had the Caribbean possessions of France and the Netherlands close to its shores.[1] These strategic factors meant that the three nations could not avoid some involvement in World War II, especially in the context of the global reach provided by modern aircraft and submarines.

The security challenge was all the more daunting in light of the small defense forces of the three countries, whose weaponry was woefully obsolete. Therefore, the modernization of their armed forces was an immediate objective of all three nations. Nevertheless, the countries lacked the resources to build forces that would be sufficient to deter a direct attack on their territory. At best, the defense forces could be upgraded to patrol national territory and stem any internal threats.

All three employed skillful diplomacy to avoid direct involvement in the war—but with limited success. Ultimately, Ecuador, Colombia, and Venezuela realized that they needed the protection of a Great Power and that the only viable option was the United States. The challenge was to accept U.S. protection while at the same time maintaining sovereignty and achieving their own objectives, which were not necessarily identical to those of the United States. In most instances, the leaders of Ecuador, Colombia, and Venezuela showed remarkable skill and tenacity in accomplishing this goal.

Another security problem for the three nations was posed by the small but influential German populations within their borders. In Ecuador and Colombia, Germans controlled important airlines that were of more than commercial value, and in all three countries, there were active German schools, clubs, political organizations, and commercial enterprises. The host countries did not view these German populations and activities with any particular concern, but the United States did. Ecuador and Colombia faced increasing pressure from the United States to nationalize the German airline companies and expel the German pilots, administrators, and other employees. Later the United States expanded its anti-German program to include the blacklisting of Axis firms and individuals and ultimately the internment of many of the German expatriates in these countries in the United States.

In addition to national security, there were economic problems resulting from World War II confronting the three republics. The loss of some of the European markets for their commodities was particularly troublesome. Here the challenge was to minimize the disruption of their economies and to maintain some control over the price of their exports when the United States became the primary market. The expanding commercial power and influence of the United States became evident when the war removed Germany as an alternative lender and purchaser of commodities for the three countries. Great Britain had already been supplanted by the United States as their most important economic partner, but the war further diminished British commercial influence. "Above all, the wartime experience emphasized the economic and strategic interdependence of the nations of the Western Hemisphere."[2]

World War II also provided the nations with opportunities. Modernization was a top priority, and through adroit bargaining over the use of their territory, war materials, and international political support, all three nations obtained technical expertise and funding to improve their respective societies. In Ecuador and Colombia, the "problem" of German influence was turned into an advantage as airlines were expropriated and reorganized as Ecuadorian and Colombian companies. Despite the protestations made against the "Proclaimed List"—the U.S. blacklist of Axis-owned businesses—the nations took advantage of this situation to eliminate competition from foreign-owned firms and seize their assets. Similarly, the Proclaimed

List was also used as justification to intern troublesome or annoying local community leaders.

In addition to the challenges and opportunities that all three of the nations shared, there were unique circumstances confronting each.

ECUADOR

Because of its strategic location, there was no doubt that Ecuador would be impacted by World War II, especially after the United States was drawn into the conflict in December 1941. Situated on the westernmost point of South America between Peru to the south and east and Colombia to the north, Ecuador also includes the famous Galapagos Islands. The Galapagos, which are situated in the Pacific approximately one thousand miles west of the Panama Canal, offered an excellent location for the forward defense of the canal—or conversely a potential staging area for an attack on it. The United States had long coveted the Galapagos, which it viewed as the Achilles' heel of Panama Canal defenses.[3] U.S. war planners were concerned that Germany might launch a bombing attack on the canal from a secret base in the Amazon region.[4] The United States was also concerned about an attack against the Panama Canal by Japan, either by a carrier task force or by planes launched from the Galapagos. (Indeed, Japan did have plans to destroy the canal through the use of an innovative weapons system—a bomber launched from a submarine.)[5] Although not as well documented, apparently Germany hoped to gain influence in Ecuador by developing commercial airline enterprises and nurturing an intelligence network via German immigrants who resided primarily in Quito.

However, Ecuador's security concerns in 1939–41 were not focused on Germany, Japan, or the United States but were instead directed toward Peru. Ecuador and Peru had long been in territorial dispute over a vast region of the once-remote upper Amazon basin. The area in question was a triangular section east of the Andes referred to by Ecuadorians as the Oriente and bounded roughly on the south by the Marañón and Amazon rivers and on the north and east by the Putumayo. Attempts to resolve the dispute by bilateral or multilateral negotiations since 1830 had reached no resolution. The last serious effort had been the 1936–39 Washington Conference hosted by the United States.

On July 5, 1941, hostilities between the neighboring countries began near the towns of Huaqillas and Charcas on the Zarumilla River. On July 22, Peru opened a major offensive, and the Ecuadorians, outnumbered four to one and with no armor or air support, were quickly overwhelmed. By July 25, a relentless Peruvian air attack, carried out by Italian- and U.S.-supplied fighters and bombers, destroyed the Ecuadorian resistance. The Peruvian

Army poured into Ecuador's El Oro province, while its navy blockaded Guayaquil and shelled the coastal town of Puerto Bolívar. On July 31, Ecuador accepted Peru's terms for a cease-fire.[6] As Ecuador's foreign minister, Dr. Julio Tobar Donoso, wrote, "Disarmed and annihilated, Ecuador resigned herself to this measure which constituted the amputation of her sovereignty."[7]

The Peru-Ecuador War threatened to break hemispheric solidarity that had been so carefully crafted at the Havana and Panama Conferences. Ecuador was confronted not only with the loss of the disputed area but also with the loss of territory that was clearly Ecuadorian. Ecuador wanted the occupation ended, but had no leverage other than diplomacy. Ecuador's situation remained tenuous when the United States entered World War II. Sumner Welles, the U.S. under secretary of state, was determined to present a united hemispheric front against the Axis and sought to quickly resolve the Ecuador question at the January 1942 meeting of foreign ministers in Rio de Janeiro. Welles found support for this initiative from Brazil's foreign minister, Oswaldo Aranha. Ecuador was threatening to abstain from the plenary session if the dispute was not presented.

Welles let Aranha take the lead in convincing Ecuador that its only alternative was to relinquish its land claim to the disputed territory in exchange for a withdrawal of Peruvian troops from its soil. Aranha bluntly told the Ecuadorian foreign minister: "A country that doesn't have borders is like a man without skin. If you do not settle now, Peru will continue the invasion. It is not possible to have preliminary terms, it is better to lose a limb than the whole body."[8] Realizing that neither the United States, Argentina, Brazil, nor Chile would intervene on its behalf, Ecuador reluctantly signed the Protocol of Peace, Friendship, and Boundaries, which became simply known as the Rio Protocol. In exchange for a withdrawal of Peruvian troops from El Oro province, Ecuador agreed to end its claim to most of the disputed area. In addition, Peru and Ecuador agreed to the establishment of boundary commissions monitored by the United States, Argentina, Brazil, and Chile, which had assumed the role of guarantors of the protocol.

The Rio Protocol was clearly the most significant outcome of World War II for Ecuador. In addition to the loss of potential territory and access to the Amazon River, the Rio Protocol became an inflammatory domestic issue used by populist politicians to discredit incumbent governments. When President Carlos Alberto Arroyo del Río was ousted by a coup in 1944, it was largely due to his alleged sellout of Ecuadorian territory to Peru. Ecuador's most controversial politician and five-time president, José María Velasco Ibarra, then declared the protocol null and void and used it to intensify Ecuadorian patriotism and to deepen hatred of Peru.

Nevertheless, the protocol did not deter Ecuador from cooperating with the United States throughout World War II. Ecuadorian collaboration with the United States was the result of a number of factors. The United States provided funding for the modernization of Ecuador's armed forces; the initial Lend-Lease allocation to Ecuador was $17 million. The United States also provided aviation and naval training missions and established training facilities at Quito and Salinas.[9] In addition, Ecuador granted permission to the United States to build air bases at Salinas on the coast and on North Seymour Island in the Galapagos. By permitting the United States to establish bases, Ecuador knew not only that the country was making a positive contribution to hemispheric defense but also that Peru would not renew an attack on Ecuador while U.S. troops were stationed there and that the U.S. military would provide equipment and training to modernize its armed forces.[10]

A secondary security concern was German influence in Ecuador. This issue had surfaced in 1939 and centered on a German-controlled corporation, the Sociedad Ecuatoriana de Transportes Aéreos (SEDTA). When SEDTA began underbidding Pan American-Grace Airways (Panagra) in Ecuador and also sought permission to service the Galapagos, U.S. intelligence was convinced that the company was a thinly disguised front for German agents.[11] Plans were made to provide U.S. military support for the pro-U.S. Ecuadorian president, Arroyo del Río, in case of a German-inspired coup. However, competition from Panagra, U.S. pressure on the Ecuadorian government to deny the desired routes, reduced subsidies from Germany, and the death of SEDTA's founder, Fritz Hammer, in a fiery crash on the Pichincha volcano caused the airline to cease operation in September 1941.[12]

In addition to SEDTA, the United States was suspicious of other firms and individuals residing in Ecuador and began including them on the Proclaimed List. The "Proclaimed List of Certain Blocked Nationals" was initiated in July 1941 as a means of economic warfare against businesses that were deemed pro-Axis by prohibiting U.S. firms and citizens from doing business with them. However, this practice of blacklisting often was extended to include any enterprise, regardless of its national origin, that was found to have engaged in trade with a Proclaimed List entry. Moreover, the list was compiled from the input of U.S. diplomats and intelligence organizations based on little or no evidence. While the Proclaimed List included active supporters of the Axis, it also contained names of legitimate individuals and enterprises. Ecuador objected that it was not consulted when individuals within its jurisdiction were placed on the list and estimated that a significant portion of the list was based on weak or completely unsubstantiated information. Protests from the foreign ministry and even from President Arroyo del Río were firmly rejected by the U.S. embassy.[13]

After the United States entered the war, it requested the deportation of individuals on the Proclaimed List. The U.S. government promised that deportees would eventually be transported to their country of origin, after being interned temporarily in the United States. The United States pressed this issue because it was not comfortable with the ability of the Latin American republics to monitor the activities of list members. In February 1942 President Arroyo del Río raised objections to the U.S. request on the grounds that internment in the United States had no basis in international law. Arroyo continued his obstinacy for another two months before agreeing to the deportation of 188 Axis nationals in April.[14] This contentious issue represented the varying views of the internal Axis threat in Ecuador. While the United States listed all Axis citizens as dangerous, Ecuador found most to be harmless immigrants who had long resided in Ecuador and had merely not gone through the formality of naturalization.

After the 1942 Rio Conference, a comprehensive assistance package was offered to partially compensate Ecuador for war damage suffered at the hands of Peru. The United States provided $20 million for the rehabilitation of El Oro province, including food, tools, and other "necessities of life" to restore the provinces. The water works and other public facilities in Guayaquil received an infusion of $8 million. The Export-Import Bank extended credits of $5 million to the Ecuadorian Development Company, a government organization, to oversee improvements in agriculture, mining, and transportation. Ecuador received another loan of $5 million to stabilize its currency. A further $2 million was designated for health and sanitation projects in other parts of the country. In addition, the United States provided a number of experts to advise on health, sanitation, agricultural experimentation, and economic development.[15]

The U.S. view of Ecuador's wartime policy was stated in a report issued by the Division of American Republics: "The Ecuadorian Government's policy during the present world conflict has been one of cooperation with the United Nations and it has activated this policy through the prosecution of certain measures of an economic, military, political and police nature."[16] The report detailed Ecuadorian actions, including severing relations with the Axis, permitting the United States to construct and operate bases, expelling Axis nationals, freezing funds, confiscating property, and passing decrees that facilitated Allied access to raw materials.

Ecuador, on the other hand, viewed its wartime cooperation as the lesser of two evils. The alternative was to walk out of the Rio Conference, splinter hemispheric unity, and wait to determine if Peru would make further military moves. Instead, Ecuador chose to support the United States in its quest for solidarity and accept the loss of territory and the century-old aspiration to become an Amazon power in exchange for guaranteed security over the area and population that traditionally had been part of Ecuador. By choosing the latter course, it achieved a measure of national integrity, but at a bitter cost.

COLOMBIA

Eduardo Santos became president of Colombia on August 7, 1938. A member of the Liberal Party, Santos had campaigned on a foreign policy that favored improved relations with the United States. There were three reasons for Santos's stance. The first was the Good Neighbor Policy that U.S. president Franklin Delano Roosevelt had implemented in the 1930s to improve relations with Latin America. Santos viewed this policy and the actions of the Roosevelt administration as sincere efforts to change U.S. meddling and military intervention in the hemisphere. Troubling events in Europe provided the second reason. Santos was an unabashed Francophile, and "he looked upon the United States as potentially the strongest defender of democratic values, which to him included both French and Colombian values, in the impending crisis."[17] The third reason was based on Germany's actions, including its treatment of Jews, the Hitler-Stalin Non-Aggression Pact, and ultimately its aggression that resulted in World War II. Santos was able to guide Colombia toward cooperation with the United States despite the opposition of Conservative Party leaders, who initially saw the United States as more of a menace than Germany.

Colombia's greatest challenge was to maintain its national sovereignty in light of its strategic importance to the Axis, which included its proximity to the Panama Canal and its large reserves of platinum, a mineral vital to the production of aircraft instruments. Another concern was potential German use of Colombia's largest commercial airline, the Sociedad Colombo-Alemana de Transportes Aéreos (SCADTA), for military purposes. There were approximately 4,000 Axis citizens residing in Colombia at the outbreak of the war who could support a change in government through a coup. Colombia viewed SCADTA and the Axis resident aliens issue as a minor concern, but the United States felt the threat was real. Finally, World War II presented economic problems for Colombia as the European market for its most important export, coffee, was cut off. At the same time, the war provided Colombia with opportunities to modernize its armed forces and society and to restructure its external debt.

Colombia viewed the Panama Canal as vital to its national interests and was determined that the important waterway be protected from an attack, especially from Colombian territory. President Santos outlined Colombia's policy in an address to Congress in which he indicated that the canal was critical to continental communication and that any interruption would be a blow to Colombia's economy and living standard. Colombia's position was that its "essential interest" was to support "American solidarity" and that "no one will be allowed to menace the Security of the Canal from Colombian territory."[18]

Colombia, however, lacked the military muscle to back up such a bold policy. Therefore, it sought assistance and cooperation from the United States. Colombia's military aviation assistance had been provided previously by Switzerland, while naval support had come from Great Britain. The Swiss equipment had proven to be expensive and also obsolete, and although the British naval mission was more satisfactory, Colombia realized that Britain most likely would not be able to continue its assistance due to its own defense needs. Moreover, British naval officers had actually been in command of Colombian naval units—an arrangement that chafed at national sensitivities. In January 1939, U.S. aviation and naval missions arrived to start a long-standing relationship with the Colombian armed forces.[19]

In addition, Colombia and the United States began a series of consultations on the defense of the Panama Canal. Colombian officers were invited to the Canal Zone to view defensive fortifications and airfields. With the fall of France in June 1940, the need for cooperation became more urgent. In September 1940, the two nations began to work out agreements that became the foundation for military cooperation during the war. Colombia agreed to attempt to prevent an attack on the United States or the Canal Zone from its territory. If Colombia made the request, the United States would come to its aid in the event of an attack by a non-American power. If the United States supported another American republic as a result of an inter-American agreement, Colombia would allow its military and naval facilities to be used by U.S. forces. Other points of agreement included the exchange of technical advisers, cooperation on coastal patrols, and the aerial photographing of strategic areas within Colombia. On the issue of aerial photography, Colombia made it clear that this would be accomplished only from Colombian aircraft with a U.S. cameraman.[20]

While Colombia made clear its intentions to assist the United States, it was equally assertive in limiting the actions of U.S. military operations from its territory. No invitation to establish bases was ever extended, as had been done in Ecuador. The responsibility of Colombia's defense was to be executed by Colombians, albeit at times with U.S. technical assistance and in some cases with steady U.S. pressure, such as in the case of the Colombian airline SCADTA.

SCADTA, which had been established by German expatriates in 1919, had proven to be particularly important to Colombia because of its mountainous terrain and poor ground transportation system. In 1931 Pan American World Airways, a U.S. company, acquired a controlling interest in SCADTA. The company quickly discovered that key administrators, as well many pilots and technicians, were German or Austrian, even though most had lived in Colombia for many years. Some of the pilots even retained reserve commissions in the Luftwaffe. The United States was fearful that SCADTA's German pilots were involved in espionage and could be plotting to convert the commercial aircraft into bombers.[21] SCADTA, for example, had conducted most of the aerial mapping of Colombia and had photographed flight approaches to the Panama Canal.

Colombia, on the other hand, did not harbor suspicions about SCADTA or its German personnel. In fact, SCADTA was the oldest airline in continuous existence in South America and, as such, was a source of national pride.[22] Germans working for the firm were considered to be more Colombian than German. Nevertheless, Colombia passed laws requiring airlines to employ more Colombian citizens and for 51 percent of the stock of these companies to be Colombian held. Dr. Peter von Bauer, SCADTA's president, heeded the new law by becoming a naturalized Colombian citizen. In response to U.S. entreaties, Colombia also placed restrictions on how German pilots could be utilized by the line. For example, at least one pilot on each crew had to be Colombian, and positioning devices were placed on all SCADTA planes so the government could monitor their location.[23] On June 8, 1940, Colombia seized SCADTA's assets, and a new national airline, Aerovias Nacionales de Colombia (Avianca), was formed.[24] Eventually all German personnel, even those who were naturalized Colombian citizens, were purged from the company.

In December 1941 the U.S. government estimated that there were 4,000 Germans living in Colombia. The United States considered the German Colony to be a fifth-column threat—a view that in most instances was not shared by the Colombian government. To be sure, there were some Nazi agitators in Colombia, such as Barranquilla businessman Emil Prufert, but Colombia was not convinced that every German was an agent for the Third Reich. As in Ecuador, the Proclaimed List was often a source of friction between Colombia and the United States because of the differing views of the fifth-column threat. At times, the U.S. ambassador shrewdly used the possibility of provocateurs as reminder to Colombia that if it did not acknowledge the threat, U.S. economic assistance to counter it would not be forthcoming. Colombia initially resisted U.S. pressure to deport Axis nationals on the grounds that, as a neutral country, deportation of aliens to a belligerent nation would be a violation of international law. However, the attractiveness of U.S. economic assistance proved more important than upholding principle, and deportations began while Colombia remained neutral. To soften internal criticism that it had bowed to U.S. pressure, Colombia at first "invited" Germans who were on the U.S. blacklists to leave.[25]

Another strategic issue was Colombia's platinum reserves. Colombia was the only source of platinum for the German and Japanese war industries, and the United States moved quickly to buy out the entire supply through the Metals Reserve Company, an agency of the Reconstruction Finance Corporation.[26] Since the United States also needed additional supplies of platinum, it assisted Colombia with technical advice on increasing production through the Foreign Economic Administration.[27] With platinum being so valuable, even in small quantifies, Axis agents were willing to pay premium prices, and smuggling became a problem. Colombia attempted to control the export of platinum by requiring all producers to sell to the Central Bank. Small producers in remote areas were able to circumvent government control and participate in a flourishing platinum black market, sending the product surreptitiously to Argentina. However, Colombian and U.S. cooperation reduced the flow to a trickle by late 1944.

The economic dislocation caused by World War II impacted Colombia significantly. First, Colombia was cut off from European and Asian markets, leaving the United States as its primary market for exports. Second, Colombia's imports were also dramatically affected, and again the United States was basically the sole source for many commodities such as rayon yarn, steel, machinery, graphite, and lead.[28] One of the primary concerns was the price of coffee, Colombia's largest export and the chief source of its foreign exchange. The U.S. Office of Price Control (OPA) attempted to freeze the maximum price of coffee at the level existing on December 8, 1941. Colombia objected, however, on the basis that the cost of producing and transporting coffee had increased as a result of wartime conditions and, if the price was not adjusted to factor in these conditions, the economy would decline. The OPA relented, agreeing to raise prices immediately and to adjust them in the future based on increased production and transportation costs. This is but one example of how Colombia won concessions by presenting reasonable arguments and how the United States responded quickly and intelligently.

World War II also created opportunities for Colombia to modernize its armed forces and society at large. In addition to the naval and aviation missions that were established in the early years of the war, Colombia later participated in the Lend-Lease program. On March 17, 1942, Colombia and the United States signed an agreement that granted Colombia $16.5 million in military assistance under Lend-Lease. The terms of the agreement were most favorable, as Colombia could purchase military and naval equipment at half the cost and not pay interest on its purchases.[29]

Other favorable development loans and grants soon followed. For example, the Export-Import Bank provided $20 million for highway construction, $10.3 million for agricultural programs, and $3.5 million to build a hydroelectric plant. In addition, U.S. private investment soared to more than $200 million by 1943. Besides stimulating growth in platinum production, U.S. experts worked on programs to increase the production of oil, rubber, and forest products, to list only a few. Another example of the attempt to alleviate economic hardships brought on by restriction on imports from the United States was an Export-Import Bank loan to fund low-cost housing construction.[30]

The main impact of World War II on Colombia was closer cooperation with the United States. On the military and political fronts, Colombia participated fully in hemispheric defense, though it did not actually commit troops to the war. While Colombia had little choice but to accept the trend toward strong economic ties with the United States, it did its best to obtain favorable terms in economic matters. Colombia used its important strategic position and its control of a sizable portion of the world supply of platinum to some advantage. In exchange for cooperation in economic and military matters, Colombia received funding for modernization projects. In the end, Colombia accomplished its primary strategic objective of maintaining its way of life and sovereignty in the face of the overwhelming power of the major actors in World War II.

VENEZUELA

Before and during World War II, Venezuela's abundant supply of oil was of intense interest to both the Axis and the Allies. Thus, Venezuela's greatest strategic challenge from 1938 to 1945 was to protect its most important natural resource from being seized by a belligerent power. Closely related to this objective was the need to market oil, which had become the mainstay of the economy. These objectives put Venezuela in a perilous position. Ideally, the war might prove to be an economic boon if Venezuela could sell petroleum to both sides, but neither the Axis nor the Allies were likely to accept such a situation. In the end, despite attempting a policy of strict neutrality, Venezuela sided with Great Britain and the United States.

As was expected, Germany then attempted to interdict the oil supply by submarine warfare. In addition, Venezuela had nearly 4,000 Germans living within its borders from which a fifth column could emerge and damage oil facilities through sabotage. Venezuela's close proximity to British, Dutch, and French Caribbean colonies also presented security issues; if the French and Dutch possessions fell into the hands of the Third Reich, they could become bases for interdiction of sea lanes that carried Venezuelan crude to market. The colonies could also be used as staging areas for an invasion or commando operations to destroy oil production and storage facilities. At the very least, the capture of Aruba would mean the loss of refineries that refined Venezuelan crude on its way to market.[31]

Like Ecuador and Colombia, Venezuela also saw opportunities to be gained from skillful diplomacy and use of its trump cards—petroleum and its strategic location. Funding was needed to upgrade the armed forces and for modernization projects. Additionally, Venezuela would use the war to gain national territory, as several islands were ceded by Great Britain in exchange for Venezuela's tacit support during the war. Venezuela also sought to limit its dependence on foreign companies for oil production and ship-ment.

Venezuela's vast petroleum reserves gained the attention of the Nazi regime as early as 1933, when Arnold Margerie formed the Grupo Regional de Venezuela del Partido Nazi. Germany launched a diplomatic effort to gain access to Venezuelan oil and began courting the Venezuelan military through its military mission. On the cultural front, one of Hitler's minions, Gen. Wilhelm von Faupel, head of the Ibero-American Institute, attempted to gain influence in Venezuela by sending his wife Edith there to extol the vir-tues of fascism.[32] Germany was also active in countering U.S. economic influence. While the Americans dominated the petroleum industry, the Ger-mans expanded their holdings in mining, agriculture, and railroads. In 1938 Italy sold two cruisers to Venezuela. Moreover, trade with Japan reached an all-time high in 1939. Hence, some observers concluded that Venezuela would side with the Axis in the coming conflict.[33]

Growing German influence set off alarm bells among democratically minded Venezuelans who had only recently experienced the thirty-year dic-tatorship of Vicente Gomez. Venezuela, however, decided upon a different course that would entail remaining outwardly neutral but in reality siding with the United States. This complicated policy was carried out adroitly by the administrations of Eleazar López Contreras (1935–41) and his successor, Isaías Medina Angarita (1941–45). The decidedly pro-U.S. policy was par-tially the result of improved relations with the United States. One issue with the United States was the dominance of Venezuela petroleum by U.S. firms. One alternative available to Venezuela was expropriation, but that option could result in U.S. military intervention. However, when Mexico expropri-ated U.S.-held petroleum assets, the U.S. reaction was reasonable and mea-sured. While Venezuela never seriously considered expropriation, it became more assertive in seeking a larger share of petroleum profits. The United States, eager to have access to Venezuelan oil, agreed to increased revenues for Venezuela. Venezuela supported hemispheric security plans developed at the Lima, Havana, and Panama Conferences.

When the war began in Europe, Venezuela declared its strict neutrality and continued to trade with both the Axis and Allies. However, by early 1941, Venezuela began to strengthen its relationship with the United States and signed executive agreements for the establishment of U.S. bases and an avia-tion mission. Soon U.S. technical advisers were in the country working to improve the capability of the Venezuelan military establishment. The U.S. Navy provided escorts for Venezuelan tankers, while the Army sent planes, instructors, and several battalions to assist in improving the defense of refineries. When the United States entered the war at the end of the year, Venezuela still maintained neutrality, but its actions clearly indicated its sup-port for the Allies. For example, Axis accounts were frozen and their ships impounded, Italy's military mission was expelled, and diplomatic relations were severed.[34]

In February 1942, Germany began submarine attacks by sinking seven Venezuelan tankers. The U-boats soon took their toll, and the flow of Venezuelan oil was sharply curtailed. German submarine warfare again raised the issue of the Dutch and French possessions in the Caribbean. Venezuela was particularly concerned about the Dutch island of Aruba, located only seventy miles from the coast. Venezuela entered into a mutual security pact with Dutch officials and supported a U.S. military takeover of the island to prevent it from falling into German hands.

While protection by the United States and the improvement of Venezuela's own coastal patrols eventually diminished the German naval threat, the potential for sabotage from the Germans, Italians, and Japanese residing in Venezuela was still a troublesome issue. In March the government initiated a program to remove suspicious Axis citizens from important oil districts. Moreover, German schools and homes near ports, power plants, and water mains were placed under surveillance. By July, the program to remove Germans intensified, and many chose to leave voluntarily rather than be subjected to harassment and possible internment. When the Proclaimed List was published in Venezuela, Caracas resisted U.S. pressure to expel all Axis residents. In the end, only diplomats were forced to leave, and German sailors were interned in relatively comfortable confines.[35]

Venezuela's airline had been started by French entrepreneurs and was, therefore, not the problem that those in Ecuador and Colombia were. However, there was a Spanish- and German-owned railway, the Gran Ferrocarril de Venezuela, which, despite its grandiose name, ran but twenty miles, from Valencia on the coast to the capital, Caracas. Pressure was applied by the United States for Venezuela to purge the line of twenty-six employees who were Axis nationals. Venezuela used U.S. allegations as grounds to expropriate the line in November 1943.

As in the other two countries, the war also presented Venezuela with opportunities, and it took full advantage of them. Venezuela gained leverage over Great Britain, which needed its cooperation in the Caribbean as well as its oil. As a result, Venezuela reached an agreement with the British on the ceding of Patos Island and Soldiers Rock, an addition of 2,300 square miles to Venezuela's national domain. By supporting agreements reached through the Pan-American system, Venezuela improved its security without becoming a complete client state of the United States. Moreover, Venezuela increased its prestige by proposing a regional bloc of Bolivarian nations (Venezuela, Colombia, Ecuador, Peru, and Bolivia) to deal with items of common interest.

Economic assistance for modernization was yet another advantage that Venezuela sought. In July 1941 the first Lend-Lease agreement was negotiated. Venezuela cagily requested aid in the construction of airfields and improvements in the navigation of the Orinoco River instead of military assistance. The government had rightly concluded that if an emergency arose, the United States would provide additional aid for military equipment. In July 1942, Venezuela made an urgent plea to Washington for war materials—a request that was filled.

By 1940 the Venezuelan economy began to suffer, as oil production fell 10 percent from its high in 1939 because the war had cut off some European customers. The López Contreras government countered the loss in oil revenues by launching a lawsuit against Gulf Oil for tax evasion between 1927 and 1930. The Division of American Republics studied the situation and concluded that Venezuela had a case against the U.S. oil giant. Realizing the potential impact of the dispute, the State Department put pressure on Gulf Oil to accept a reasonable outcome. Under Secretary of State Sumner Welles had a meeting with Col. J. Frank Drake, Gulf's president. While there is no record of the conversation, within two weeks Gulf reached a settlement with Venezuela that provided for a $10 million payment in back taxes.[36] The deal with Gulf was considered a triumph for López Contreras, who left office shortly after its completion.

The next Venezuelan president, General Medina Angarita, also pursued an aggressive oil policy in an attempt to reduce dependence on U.S. firms. In July 1941, demands were presented to Gulf Oil and Standard Oil of New Jersey for increased royalties, the application of new laws to old concessions, technology upgrades, and the construction of refineries in Venezuela. Gulf and Standard used legal maneuvers to delay negotiations throughout the remainder of 1941. The Medina government was divided on a strategy to deal with the oil giants and did not press for resolution of the issue as oil revenues climbed due to increased U.S. purchases tied to wartime mobilization, which more than replaced the lost European sales. In fact, 1941 was a banner year for Venezuelan oil, as production reached an all-time high.[37]

The following year demonstrated the capricious nature of war and the fragility of Venezuela's oil-based economy. Germany increased submarine warfare in the Caribbean and sank seven tankers loaded with Venezuelan crude. As a result, Venezuela's oil revenues declined by 38 percent, wreaking havoc on the overall economy and forcing Medina to implement austerity measures. However, there was an encouraging development as Mexico and the United States announced a settlement of their long-standing oil expropriation issue. Clearly, the need for Mexican air bases to defend the Panama Canal was an essential factor in the State Department taking a more conciliatory stance in the negotiations. The agreement with Mexico also represented an end to the State Department's unlimited support for U.S. oil corporations.

Medina used the Mexican agreement as an opening salvo in a renewed effort to obtain a better deal for Venezuela. After calling for new petroleum laws to assure Venezuela a greater share in its own wealth, Medina revealed that he expected the same support for his position vis-à-vis the oil giants that the State Department had granted Mexico. In time, Medina's strategy worked. The State Department allowed its oil adviser, Max W. Thornburg, to take the lead in the negotiations between the industry and government. Thornburg was considered by both sides to be a fair man who would work out a reasonable compromise. Standard Oil soon agreed to Thornburg's proposal, and the solidarity of the oil giants was broken. In addition, the U.S. State Department cajoled the British Foreign Office to persuade Shell Oil to also agree to accept new laws governing its Venezuelan operations. On March 13, 1943, the new oil laws went into effect. The impact was immediate and dramatic. Under the laws, Venezuela and the companies were to split the industry's profits on a fifty-fifty basis. In 1944 Venezuela's oil income was 66 percent higher than it was in 1941, and by 1947, total income had increased 358 percent. This largesse allowed Venezuela to be one of the few Latin American countries that could finance significant modernization programs in the postwar period.

CONCLUSION

Ecuador, Colombia, and Venezuela maintained their sovereignty and preserved their way of life despite the global conflict involving the Great Powers raging about them. Each country lacked the military and naval resources to defend its national territory. Nevertheless, through skillful diplomacy and a realistic assessment of their positions in the international system, these three northern South American nations for the most part avoided direct military involvement in the war. This was largely accomplished by policies of cooperation with the United States, which they wisely concluded afforded them the greatest protection at little risk to their national security. Cooperation with the United States did not necessarily mean that their goals always meshed with those of the colossus to the north. As this chapter has demonstrated, Ecuador, Colombia, and Venezuela had agendas of their own and often used the wartime needs of the United States to advance them.

Ecuador was in the most difficult position of the three during World War II. The brief but catastrophic war with Peru in July 1941 might have had a different outcome if the United States and the other American republics had not been preoccupied with the war. There is no question that Ecuador did not receive a fair hearing of its territorial dispute with Peru at the January 1942 Rio Conference, at which the United States and Brazil pushed for hemispheric unity at all costs. The failure to resolve this dispute negatively impacted Ecuador's domestic and international politics for more than five decades. On the other hand, Ecuador was able to gain assistance from the United States to modernize its armed forces. Moreover, it permitted the establishment of U.S. bases in its territory—a policy decision that no doubt inhibited further aggression by Peru. Ecuador also obtained funding for modernization projects for its civilian infrastructure.

The impact of the war on Colombia was less dramatic than was the case of Ecuador, as Colombia faced no significant threat to the loss of its national territory to an aggressive neighbor. By cooperating with the United States, Colombia likewise received funds to modernize its armed forces and to make infrastructure improvements. Although Colombia lost its significant European market for its exports, it proved to be a tough negotiator with the United States over price controls and import quotas. Colombia also used the backdrop of World War II to establish a national airline out of a formerly German-dominated company.

Venezuela came out of World War II a stronger and larger country. Venezuela used the leverage afforded by the war to extract better agreements with U.S. and British oil companies that significantly increased its national wealth and lessened its dependence of foreign companies. In addition, several islands were ceded to Venezuela by Great Britain in exchange for Venezuela's wartime cooperation.

NOTES

1. Frederick Haussmann, "Latin American Oil in War and Peace," *Foreign Affairs* 21, no. 2 (January 1943): 355. Venezuela was the leading producer of Latin American oil and second behind only the United States in worldwide production in 1942.

2. Stephen J. Randall, *Colombia and the United States: Hegemony and Interdependence* (Athens: University of Georgia Press, 1992), 163.

3. "Procurement, Occupation and Use of Air Bases in the Galapagos Islands and at Salinas Ecuador," National Archives and Records Administration of the United States, RG 165, OPD file, 1945, Box 177 580.82 TS. 1.

4. "Necessary Airfield Developments at Manaos, Brazil," January 3, 1942, U.S. Air Force Historical Research Center, file 3 461 08-3.

5. Robert C. Mikesh, *Aichi M6A1 Serian: Japan's Submarine-Launched Panama Canal Bomber* (Boylston, MA: Monogram Aviation Publications, 1975).

6. David H. Zook Jr., *Zarumilla-Marañón: The Ecuador-Peru Dispute* (New York: Bookman Associates, 1964), 155–60.

7. Julio Tobar Donoso, *La invasion peruana y el Protocolo de Rio: Antecedentes y explicación histórica* (Quito: Banco Central del Ecuador, 1982), 216.

8. Tobar Donoso, *La invasion peruana*, 369.

9. "Memorandum: The Status of Measures of Cooperation Which Have Been Agreed Upon Between the Government of Ecuador and the United States," Agreed at the Rio Conference, 1942–1943, Archive of the Ecuadorian Foreign Ministry.

10. Dan Hagedorn, "Lend Lease to Latin America: Part I, Army Aircraft," *Journal of the American Aviation Historical Society* (Summer 1989): 122. Under Lend-Lease, Ecuador eventually received forty-five aircraft from the United States.

11. Melvin Hall and Walter Peck, "Wings for the Trojan Horse," *Foreign Affairs* 19 (January 1941): 360.

12. R. E. G. Davies, *Airlines of Latin America since 1919* (Washington, DC: Smithsonian Institution Press, 1884), 274.

13. Max Paul Friedman, *Nazis and Good Neighbors: The United States Campaign against the Germans of Latin America in World War II* (Cambridge: Cambridge University Press, 2003), 90–91.

14. Friedman, *Nazis and Good Neighbors*, 115.

15. "Memorandum: The Status of Measures."

16. "Action Taken by Ecuador to Implement the War against Germany, Italy, and Japan," October 10, 1944, in *Memorandums Relating to Individual Countries, 2 March 1918–31 December 1947 (Equador [sic])*, Vol. 3, *January 1943–November 1945*, National Archives and Records Administration of the United States, RG 59, File 250-44-7-E-209.

17. David Bushnell, *Eduardo Santos and the Good Neighbor, 1938–1942* (Gainesville: University Press of Florida, 1967), 7.

18. Bushnell, *Eduardo Santos*, 15.

19. "Naval Mission Agreement between the United States of America and Colombia," Executive Agreement Series, no. 140 (Washington, DC: GPO, 1939); "Military Mission Agreement between the United States of America and Colombia," Executive Agreement Series, no. 141 (Washington, DC: GPO, 1939).

20. Bushnell, *Eduardo Santos*, 52–53.

21. "Cooperation and Collaboration of the Republic of Colombia," U.S. Air Force Historical Research Center, file 463.953.2. (9141-1945), p. 1.

22. Davies, *Airlines of Latin America*, 204–5.

23. Friedman, *Nazis and Good Neighbors*, 105–6.

24. U.S. Department of State, *Foreign Relations of the United States: Diplomatic Papers, 1940*, Vol. 5, *The American Republics* (Washington, DC: GPO, 1940), 723–26.

25. Friedman, *Nazis and Good Neighbors*, 114–15.

26. Bushnell, *Eduardo Santos*, 65–66.

27. Randall, *Colombia and the United States*, 181.

28. Randall, *Colombia and the United States*, 182–83.

29. U.S. Department of State, *Foreign Relations of the United States: Diplomatic Papers, 1942*, Vol. 6, *The American Republics* (Washington, DC: GPO, 1942), 189–92.

30. Randall, *Colombia and the United States*, 176–85.

31. Stephen G. Rabe, *The Road to OPEC: United States Relations with Venezuela, 1919–1976* (Austin: University of Texas Press, 1982).

32. Sheldon B. Liss, *Diplomacy and Dependency: Venezuela, the United States, and the Americas* (Salisbury, NC: Documentary Publications, 1978), 107.

33. Liss, *Diplomacy and Dependency*, 108.

34. Liss, *Diplomacy and Dependency*, 114–15.

35. Friedman, *Nazis and Good Neighbors*, 150.

36. Rabe, *The Road to OPEC*, 77.

37. Rabe, *The Road to OPEC*, 79.

8

Peru: International Developments and Local Realities

Daniel M. Masterson and Jorge Ortiz Sotelo

World War II offered Peru many opportunities for nation-building that were unfortunately not realized in the ensuing postwar years. The government of President Manuel Prado y Ugarteche (1939–45) generally lacked the vision to promote policies that would help establish patterns of long-term economic growth and political stability. Yet Peru was a very good ally of the United States during the war. Ironically, its solidarity with the Allied cause created significant disadvantages for Peru's future. Peru was not unique among Latin American nations in this regard. The very short memory of Washington's policy makers, however, over the course of the next half-century regarding what we choose to call "Peruvian exceptionalism" made Peru the target of retaliatory policies that gave little heed to the past wartime loyalty of the Peruvian government. On a broad scale, the decisions made during the war by the Prado government shaped the contours of Peruvian nationalism, domestic politics, civil-military affairs, and economic policy for decades following the war.

In many ways, World War II redefined Peruvian national affairs, since Peru, more than any other country in Latin America except combatants Mexico and Brazil, felt the consequences of the world conflict. Although never a real beneficiary of the Good Neighbor Policy during the 1930s, after hostilities began, Peru became one of Washington's best allies. In accordance with the wishes of the United States, Peru broke diplomatic relations with the Axis powers in January 1942. Three years later, Peru declared war on the Axis nations on a timetable that reflected Washington's desires as well.

During the war, Peru grew nearer to the United States both economically and socially. World War II led to a closer alignment of Peru's economic policies with those of Washington, where they remained for most of the rest of the twentieth century. The war also ended the Peruvian army's long association with the French military. Thereafter, the United States helped train Peru's soldiers until the Velasco era (1968–75). Peru also engaged Ecuador in a brief but decisive border war in July 1941. This conflict had lasting diplomatic and military consequences that were not resolved until the late 1990s.

As was the case in many nations during World War II, innocent civilians suffered terribly as a result of the conflict. Some Peruvian Jews were victims of the Holocaust. Also, Peru's Japanese were especially targeted by the Prado government for arrest and eventual deportation. Fewer numbers of German and Italians were also deported and interned in the United States. In large measure, this was due to Peru's close proximity to the sea approaches to the Panama Canal and its large potential oil reserves in the north near Talara.

PERU'S ECONOMY DURING WARTIME

The Peruvian government during World War II missed the opportunity the war provided to initiate and build a viable domestic industrial and commercial sector. It is possible to point to the desultory efforts in areas such as mining and industry, but it is more important to note that the Peruvian government never devised "a coherent development strategy" when it was auspicious to do so. In the end, as a result of World War II and the cutoff of most of Peru's traditional markets due to maritime restrictions, the nation became more heavily dependent on U.S. public assistance and foreign investment than ever before.

The basis for Peru's lack of success was its decision to maintain price controls on its essential wartime commodities. This laudable economic policy, while supportive of the Allied war effort, effectively deprived Peru of the foreign exchange necessary for investment in such critical economic sectors as mining, manufacturing, and fishing. Consequently, Peru's foreign exchange reserves grew at a much smaller rate than any other major Latin American nation during the war. Peru's reserves rose only 55 percent, while those of Brazil (635 percent), Colombia (540 percent), and Mexico (480 percent) showed far greater gains from higher wartime price levels.[1]

One sector that did benefit significantly was the military. Peru received more than $18 million in Lend-Lease assistance during the war, and a new air force base, El Pato, was constructed at Talara in northern Peru. It should be mentioned, however, that actual disbursements of promised Lend-Lease aid were often not in keeping with the original contracts. As the war progressed and Latin America, especially the Panama Canal, seemed far less likely to be a battleground, U.S. military resources were shifted elsewhere.

In agriculture, cotton was Peru's leading export at the start of the war, with most of its trade directed to England and other European nations. With the restriction of maritime activity, only England was left to buy Peruvian cotton until President Prado signed an agreement with the United States through the Commodity Credit Corporation to buy all of Peru's excess cotton at slightly above the world price. This measure was critical to Peru because at least 120,000 people were employed in the cotton trade. Nevertheless, because the Prado government mistakenly chose to tax cotton exports at a sharply increased rate, while simultaneously encouraging the planting of food crops on previously cotton-growing areas, the number of acres devoted to cotton growing declined by 31 percent during the war years. Ironically, some of the most productive cotton acreage was confiscated from Japanese immigrants who had settled in the Cañete Valley near Lima. Many of the most productive of the Japanese agriculturalists in Peru were deported during the war.

One final aspect of Peru's economic contributions to the war effort needs to be mentioned, because it reflects the critical role this Andean nation played while receiving very little economic benefit in return. Peru, and to a lesser extent Bolivia, provided the Allies with the critical raw materials for the production of quinine, so important to the war effort in the Pacific and South Asia. Processed from cinchona trees, which were originally indigenous only to the eastern slopes of the Andes Mountains, Peru had been supplying the world with life-saving cinchona bark as a highly effective medicine for malaria since the seventeenth century. However, in the mid-nineteenth century, Dutch and British smugglers carried cinchona seeds out of Peru and eventually established highly profitable "quinine" plantations in Java. The quinine industry in the Andes was effectively abandoned until the Japanese occupied Java during World War II. Desperately seeking new sources of quinine, the Allies turned to the Peru and Bolivia. Later in the war, synthetic quinine was developed from cinchona bark, thus lessening the need for large supplies of the plant. Ultimately Peru and Bolivia received little profit from the quinine industry that had been so essential to the war effort.[2] And in the end Peru and Bolivia were stripped clean of their cinchona trees as a result of the frenzied effort to produce quinine. Thus an important component of Peru's biological heritage became a casualty of the war. On the diplomatic front, Peru's cooperation was equally unstinting regarding diplomatic interchange during the early war years.

INTERNATIONAL NEUTRALITY PROVIDES
NATIONAL OPPORTUNITY

Soon after Adolf Hitler's Panzer divisions smashed into Poland on September 1, 1939, the foreign ministers of the American republics met in Panama, proclaimed a "General Declaration of Neutrality," and extended their territorial waters out to 300 miles. Only Canada did not participate in this declaration. In the early months of the war in Europe, Peru was satisfied with its neutrality declaration and took no direct measures against its German, Italian, and Japanese nationals. With the fall of France in June 1940, Peru joined ranks with other nations at the second meeting of foreign ministers in Havana to declare that an attack upon any of the hemispheric powers would be considered by the nations of the Americas as an act of aggression upon all.

Peru vs. Ecuador

By 1939, as a result of potential border conflicts with its neighbors, Peru had built its military into a formidable fighting force, and the pending world war gave Peru an opportunity to use it. Ecuador and Peru had a very long-standing border dispute; if Peru could occupy the territory, the desire of the United States and Brazil for a secure South America in the face of Axis aggression would mean that there would be terrific pressure on Ecuador for a quick settlement. Peru took advantage of the situation created by World War II by occupying the disputed territory, but ultimately the success Peru enjoyed would have some unintended consequences.

Peru and Ecuador had contested the exact location of much of their common border since independence. The 1890 García-Herrera Treaty was negotiated by representatives of Peru and Ecuador, but the Peruvian Congress failed to ratify it. During the opening years of the twentieth century, small detachments of Peruvian and Ecuadorian soldiers skirmished along the Napo and Angosteros rivers northwest of Iquitos. Further attempts to arbitrate the dispute by the king of Spain in the late 1930s once again failed. Meanwhile the Peruvian armed forces suffered a military setback in the 1933–1934 Leticia conflict with Colombia. When Gen. Oscar R. Benavides was appointed president of Peru by the Peruvian Congress after the assassination of President Luis M. Sánchez Cerro in April 1933, he decided to build a modern military force unequaled in the history of Peru. Under Benavides, the Peruvian Army enjoyed an unprecedented increase in manpower. Numbering only 8,000 regular soldiers in 1932, the army grew more than threefold to 25,864 in 1941.[3]

Impressed with the Wehrmacht's rebuilding program, Benavides also replaced the French Army advisory team with Germans in 1937. This was a significant break with the past. Almost without interruption since 1895, the Peruvian army had looked to the French for its educational and training principles, for key leadership roles within the army's command structure, and for a mission that met the reality of Peru. Most importantly, the French training bond forged a professional ethos that linked the Peruvian men-at-arms quite intimately with their French tutors. For example, from the early 1930s on, the Peruvian Army officer corps increasingly saw itself in the same terms as the French colonial army, with a "civilizing" or development mission as a key component of its national defense doctrine.[4] The arrogant attitude of the German advisers so quickly alienated the army's officers, however, that the Prussians were sent packing in less than two years, and the more familiar and *simpatico* French advisers returned to Peru in 1939, where a small contingent would remain until 1944.

Besides bringing in the Germans, Benavides also brought in Italian air force and police training groups in 1937. Seeking to modernize the fledging Peruvian Air Force, the president contracted with the Italian aircraft manufacturer Caproni to build an aircraft factory in Peru in 1937. In addition, Peru's young aviation cadets were sent to Italy's Aviation Academy at Caserta for advanced training. With the European war effectively ending Italian assistance, Peru replaced the Italian air mission with a U.S. Navy aviation advisory team in late July 1940. The replacement of this Italian-Peruvian partnership was a primary component of the Allied hemispheric security plans to eliminate suspected Axis influence in Peru.

Active and retired U.S. naval officers had begun advising and training the Peruvian Navy in the early 1920s, and thus U.S. influence was quite strong in that branch of the armed forces. In the early 1930s, the U.S. Naval Training Mission's contract was allowed to lapse, but the Peruvian Navy resisted Benavides's apparent pro-fascist military rebuilding model and succeeded in having the contract reactivated for a five-year term in 1938 after a five-year hiatus.[5] In 1940 the U.S. Navy's influence heightened when Capt. William M. Quigley was named inspector general of the Peruvian Navy and soon afterward was named naval chief of staff. U.S. Navy officers continued to hold critical command posts in the Peruvian Navy throughout the 1940s.[6]

While it is thus clear that Peru was preparing for armed conflict in the late 1930s, it was not evident that Ecuador, its northern neighbor, was the likely opponent. For decades after its defeat in the 1879–82 War of the Pacific, Peru's general staff anticipated that hostilities would someday be renewed with Chile. The Leticia conflict with Colombia in 1933 also raised the immediate possibility of hostilities with that nation during the 1930s.

When war in Europe began in September 1939, Peru's military leaders knew that the United States would not permit any extended conflict in the Americas to divert Washington's attention from the growing peril in Europe. As Robert L. Scheina has ably concluded regarding the strategy of Peru's military leaders, they knew that Washington would seek a quick diplomatic conclusion to a Latin American conflict, because in June 1941 the Wehrmacht was driving toward Leningrad, Moscow, and Stalingrad on three powerful fronts. Additionally, the Japanese Army was holding vast sections of eastern China, and the United States was frantically trying to buy time while it was rearming. The war in Europe was the Roosevelt administration's overriding concern, and conflict in Latin America could not be allowed to be a major distraction. The Peruvian General Staff's plans for a war within a larger war was exactly on the mark. Using its clearly superior military forces, the Peruvians sought to invade and occupy large sectors of the disputed territory with Ecuador and hold it until diplomatic negotiations validated their military gains.[7]

In July 1941, the disputed territory included a small area bordering the Pacific Ocean and fully 120,000 square miles of territory in the Oriente or eastern provinces of Ecuador and Peru lying between the equator and the Javary River and between the Andes Mountains and Leticia on the Colombian frontier. In the aftermath of a number of border incidents involving Ecuadorian and Peruvian border guards, Peruvian president Manuel Prado adopted a rigid diplomatic stance in negotiations to successfully mediate the issue. Prado felt he could not vacillate on Peru's military posture toward Ecuador, because the Prado family had become very vulnerable to accusations that it was unpatriotic ever since the president's father, President Mariano Ignacio Prado, left Peru in the midst of the War of the Pacific. Peruvian army commanders were unwilling to allow Prado to veto their planned military operations. In fact, the pressure on President Prado was so intense that he negotiated an internal loan to the Defense Ministry of 300 million *soles* from his family's own bank, the Banco Popular, to finance the purchases of small arms and other related military equipment. The loan was never made public and was used throughout the 1940s to supplement the public budget of the armed forces.[8] Thus Peru was as united for war as it had ever been in its history. This proved decisive as Peru sought a quick defeat of its northern neighbor.

When the ongoing negotiations in Washington, D.C., between Peru, Ecuador, and three mediating nations broke down in early June 1941, Peruvian forces situated in the border areas along the Zarumilla and Marañón rivers went on alert. Gen. Eloy G. Ureta of the Peruvian Army commanded the troops in this region, and he was ordered to hold his position. However, he rejected those orders and informed President Prado that if he was not allowed to advance against Ecuadorian positions, he would do so even without presidential permission. This is in fact what occurred, when Peruvian forces under Ureta took advantage of their superior forces and used a sophisticated combination of a naval blockade, motorized infantry, tanks, and even paratroops to launch a highly effective offensive against Ecuadorian units beginning on July 5 and extending to mid-August.

The main theaters of conflict were Ecuador's Pacific coastal region, near the towns of Puerto Bolívar, Santa Rosa, and Machala, and the eastern Selva region, near Corrientes, Cucaray, and Tarqui. By the time these offensives were halted, the Ecuadorian Army had all but disintegrated. Poor leadership, substandard equipment, and a divided civilian population made defeat for Ecuador almost inevitable. Most importantly, the Peruvian Army was poised to advance upon Guayaquil with no opposition. Peruvian military forces had performed as well as at any time in the history of the nation. General Ureta, along with the Selva Division's commander, Gen. Antonio Silva Sanisteban, led campaigns that showed understanding, albeit on a much reduced scale, of modern *Blitzkrieg* and air power tactics then being used in the European and Pacific theaters. Lt. Col. Manuel A. Odría, operating under the command of General Ureta in the Eastern theater, performed exceptionally well in the early stages of the campaign. He, like Ureta and Silva, would gain substantial professional and personal prestige from their war experiences.

By mid-August 1942, the badly outmanned Ecuadorian Army had ceased to be a functioning force. Plagued by desertions on a large scale, Ecuadorian units could engage the Peruvians only in isolated pockets of resistance. Under intense national pressure to end the fighting, the two nations agreed on a cease-fire on October 2, 1941. Peruvian troops remained in place as a powerful negotiating position in the aftermath of the cease-fire. What absolutely assured a rapid resolution of the conflict was the Japanese attack on Pearl Harbor two months after the cease-fire was signed. Between January 15 and 28, 1942, the United States and the other hemispheric nations convened in Rio de Janeiro at the Third Meeting of the Foreign Ministers of the American Republics to plan for war and also to try to resolve the Peru-Ecuador War. Near-unanimity was gained when all Western Hemisphere nations except Argentina and Chile either declared war or broke relations with the Axis powers.

Still, a critically important strategic defense issue needed to be resolved. The United States wanted to build urgently needed bases in Ecuador and Peru to defend the air and sea access routes to the Panama Canal. This could not be accomplished as long as a state of war existed between these two nations. Accordingly, on the last day of the Rio de Janeiro Conference, Peruvian ambassador Alfredo Solf y Muro and his Ecuadorian counterpart, Julio Tobar Donoso, urged on by U.S. under secretary of state Sumner Welles and the foreign ministers of Argentina, Brazil, and Chile, agreed to sign the Peruvian-Ecuadorian Protocol of Peace, Friendship and Limits, also known as the Rio Protocol. The agreement was predictably highly favorable to Peru, but Ecuador's Congress did approve the treaty after Peruvian troops left Ecuadorian soil. Still, Ecuador would later reject the protocol as nonbinding because it was signed under duress. That duress may well have been created as much by the United States, Brazil, and the other Latin American signatory nations as it was by the Peruvian Army.

The Rio Protocol granted Peru most of the territory that had been in dispute for decades—an amount equal to Ecuador's territorial limits that remained after January 1942. Nearly as important, from Ecuador's point of view of itself as a transcontinental nation, Peru's northern neighbor lost its rights to the headwaters of the Amazon basin when it was cut off from the tributaries of the Marañón River. From a more specific geopolitical perspective, Peru's proclaimed rights to provinces of Tumbes, Jaen, and Maynas were confirmed, while it was directed to withdraw from El Oro province and grant recognition to Ecuador's rights of access to the Putumayo River.[9]

An inability to agree on a final demarcation line between the two nations, coupled with Ecuadorian president José María Velasco Ibarra's decision to disavow the Rio Protocol in 1960, opened the entire border question again to dispute. Fighting broke out anew in 1981 and 1995. These continuing border incidents, long after the definitive victory of Peruvian military forces in 1941, meant that Peruvian defense planners were compelled for more than half a century to defend both their northern border and the southern frontier, where Chile loomed as a more likely and more formidable opponent a century after the War of the Pacific. Happily, a final settlement to this old conflict was reached on October 26, 1998.

Aftermath of the Peru–Ecuador Conflict

The border war led to a number of important developments in Peruvian civil-military affairs during World War II that proved problematic for national affairs. The first to emerge was the highly divisive issue of postwar promotions. General Ureta and his other senior commanders, Silva Sanisteban and Odría, all ended the war with the rank of division general. Ureta was also named inspector general of the army. Soon thereafter, Ureta received Peru's highest military rank when he was presented with a marshal's baton. In all, eighty officers of the rank of major or above who served in the northern theater of operations during the border war were promoted by the Peruvian Congress. Many Peruvian Army officers serving in other regions of Peru who were not promoted were dismayed at the blanket promotions of their fellow officers in the north, many of whom had not seen combat but were merely stationed in the right theater. In early 1943, Ureta, who was now competing with Benavides for domination of the armed forces and possibly the election to the presidency in 1945, clashed with Prado over the appointment of a national police general to the Supreme Tribunal of Military Justice. Seeking to name his own man to the post, which would help him gain influence with the national police, Prado held up the routine promotions of senior army officers in late 1943 as a bargaining chip.[10]

Prado was not satisfied with attempting to use the national police as a lever against the increasing power of the army's leaders after the war with Ecuador. The president also sought to gain the allegiance of Peru's army aviation corps. In late 1941, the aviation service was made independent of the Navy Ministry, which had directed its activities since 1929. Prado then named a close associate, Gen. Fernando Melgar, to be minister of aviation in early 1942. To assure the new service's strength, the Prado administration assured that the bulk of the first shipment of $18 million in Lend-Lease equipment from the United States would be directed to the air service. Thirty P-36 fighters, thirteen A-33 bombers, and twenty-five PT-19 trainers were acquired by late 1943. Most importantly, a new air force training facility was established at Las Palmas to expand the pool of air force pilots. The acquisitions came primarily at the expense of the navy, whose capital budget actually declined during the World War II years.[11] Thus, while strengthening and modernizing Peru's armed services, Prado exacerbating existing interservice rivalries. Bitter feelings over promotions and political maneuvering by Prado, Benavides, and Ureta eventually led to open revolt within the Peruvian Army and Navy.

Enlisted men in the army and navy, as well as a militant cadre of junior to middle-grade officers in the army, were particularly disenchanted with their status within the armed forces and what their leaders perceived as a lack of professionalism in the senior command. Despite Peru's dramatic military success against Ecuador, these armed forces personnel viewed the military state of affairs in Peru in the larger context of the world war and found their leaders lacking in professionalism. They were especially distressed with the politicking of Generals Ureta and Benavides as they vied for the presidency in 1945. The generals sought the support of hard-line conservatives such as the Miro Quesada family, owners of Peru's most important newspaper, *El Comercio*. At the same time, they encouraged the outlawed Alianza Popular Revolucionaria Americana (APRA) political party to make concessions in its previously radical program of labor and economic reform.

The founder and leader of a militant group of armed forces personnel formed in 1944 known as the Comité Revolucionario de Oficiales del Ejército (CROE; Committee of Revolutionary Army Officers) authored a manifesto for his group of approximately one hundred army officers below the rank of colonel. Clearly aimed at Generals Benavides, Ureta, and Odría, the manifesto attacked the army's most senior officers, lamenting their political ambition and lack of professionalism. CROE leaders claimed that they were more professional than their leaders because they had a better concept of discipline. The junior officers also asserted that they respected the constitution and opposed the tyrants who for too long had ruled Peruvian national affairs. The manifesto concluded by claiming that the army, excluding its corrupt senior officers, was "of the same flesh and blood as the people and was united with them."[12] Later CROE materials would make reference to Generals George Marshall and Dwight Eisenhower as models of successful military leaders who did not exploit their wartime reputations for immediate postwar political gains.

These militant demands for reforms within the armed forces would not bring a positive response from its leadership until elements of CROE sought to initiate a widespread civil-military rebellion by seizing the air base in

Peru's southern city of Ancón in mid-March 1945. The poorly planned uprising failed, but it established the pattern of conspiracy and betrayal between army and navy dissidents and APRA over the course of the immediate post–World War II years. In October 1948, the most widespread civil-military insurrection in Peru's modern history broke out in Peru's major port city of Callao. Planned and instigated by junior army and naval officers, enlisted personnel, and APRA militants, the Callao revolt was put down quickly. Nevertheless, its ramifications would be felt for a generation afterward as hatred and suspicion of APRA by the military would seem justified. Many talented but militant personnel in the armed forces would be jailed, exiled, or driven out of the armed services. It is important to recognize that this alliance between elements of the APRA party and the lower ranks of the armed forces was forged off and on in Peru from the early 1930s until the immediate postwar years. It reflected both a desperate attempt by APRA to seize power at any cost and the deep disenchantment of professional and class-conscious young military personnel for better lives both in and out of their barracks. But every time the Apristas and their military allies went into the streets, their efforts ended in defeat and much bloodshed.

For the Peruvian military, the twin goals that came out of World War II were the need for democracy and the need for military professionalism. These were the two important legacies of the war, with its long and bloody struggle against fascism and brutal tyranny. Despite efforts to build both professionalism and democracy, however, the subsequent history of Peru suggests that neither was reached.

ALIENS, EXILES, AND
CONCENTRATION CAMPS

As it would elsewhere in Latin America, the FBI after 1940 became the main U.S. counterespionage agency operating in Latin America. Even before Pearl Harbor, the FBI began compiling lists of Axis nationals in the region. Peru was the home to small but vibrant Japanese, Italian, and German immigrant communities. Because of the more immediate threat to the West Coast of the Americas posed by the Japanese, this community was regarded with greatest alarm by U.S. authorities. Accordingly, the United States directed most of its attention at them.

The Japanese in Peru during World War II

It would seem that Japan did not really envision a large-scale espionage network in Peru. Rather, it sought to work through well-established spy rings in Argentina and Chile. Despite many reports to the contrary, FBI dispatches from Peru detail no evidence of any attempt by either the leaders of the Japanese community in Peru or Japan's diplomatic or military personnel associated with Peru to initiate espionage or wide-scale subversion during World War II. Japanese diplomats based in Panama before December 1940 did provide Tokyo with very precise information on ship movements and improvements in the defense of the Panama Canal. After Pearl Harbor, diplomats based in Mexico, acting unilaterally, attempted to put in place a plan to damage the canal, although their efforts came to nothing.[13] It appears that although Tokyo entertained the idea of disabling the canal, it never established a serious plan to do so. This may have reflected the largely defensive mentality of the Japanese military after the "island perimeter" was established by mid-1942. This view is bolstered to some degree by events in Peru in December 1941. In the immediate aftermath of Pearl Harbor, the Japanese ambassador in Lima, before he was expelled from the country, sent a message through the various Japanese-Peruvian associations to remain calm, obey the laws of Peru, and prepare for a protracted time of sacrifice. This is exactly what the more than 25,000 Japanese Peruvians did during the war.

The Japanese immigrants, who first arrived in Peru as contracted sugar workers in 1899, built a highly cohesive and economically successful community largely centered in Lima before World War II.[14] Although small groups of Japanese immigrants settled in northern Peru, in the vicinity of Chiclayo and in communities such as Huaral, south of Lima, most of the Japanese had fled the sugar cane fields early in the century and opened commercial enterprises such as restaurants, bodegas, barber shops, and dry-cleaning establishments.

Helped greatly by their own mutual aid groups, prefectural organizations, and occasional economic support from Tokyo, Peru's Japanese not only survived the Depression but actually substantially improved their economic standing during the 1930s. As one can imagine, Japanese economic success at a time of great economic distress, coupled with the growing and increasingly ominous threat from the Japanese military advance in Asia, contributed to a sharp rise in the ever-present anti-Japanese sentiment within Peru. Japan's brutal military campaigns in Manchuria and China sparked a great deal of anti-Japanese feeling in Peru during the 1930s. The Japanese community's vulnerability to nativist animosity was made worse in 1938 when the Central Japanese Association donated funds to the army and navy of Japan to pay for the construction and delivery of two warplanes for each service. Intended as an act of patriotism, it was viewed by Peruvians as an indication of the loyalty of the Japanese community to Tokyo and the emperor and not to their adopted land.[15]

Sparked by false rumors of a planned military operation against northern Peru, the worst anti-Japanese riots ever to occur in the Western Hemisphere erupted in early May in Lima and other Peruvian cities. Two days of rioting in Lima, Chancay, and Huaral cost the lives of ten Japanese Peruvians and injured hundreds more. When calm was restored, the Japanese embassy in Lima calculated that six hundred businesses and homes had been damaged at a cost of $7 million to the Japanese-Peruvian community. The Lima police did little to protect the Japanese, but most were able to find protection behind the walls of Lima's Japanese School, where they fled during the riots. Facing homelessness or the total loss of their businesses, nearly four hundred Japanese soon left Peru for Japan, abandoning the country which had always grudgingly afforded new opportunity to build successful lives.[16]

The latent anti-Japanese feeling, based primarily on racism and economic rivalries between Peru's insular Japanese community and the nation's struggling working- and middle-class urban dwellers, greatly facilitated Washington's efforts to identify, apprehend, and deport the leaders of Peru's Japanese community in the aftermath of Pearl Harbor. The U.S. Department of State, the Immigration and Naturalization Service, and the FBI cooperated with the government of President Prado and Peruvian police agencies to compile a so-called Proclaimed List of Japanese-Peruvian leaders of prefectural associations, business alliances, schools, and any Japanese Army veterans as potential subversives who would be subject to internment in Peru or deportation to internment camps in the United States. In consultation with U.S. envoy Nelson Rockefeller, Peru planned, and then rejected as too costly, the domestic internment of a least six thousand of its estimated twenty-five thousand Japanese. Meanwhile, Peruvian diplomats in Washington, claiming that Japanese shopkeepers could "set the city of Lima on fire overnight," urged the Roosevelt administration to place as many Japanese Peruvians as possible in concentration camps.[17] And this is in fact exactly what the Prado and Roosevelt administrations did.

From early 1942 until early 1945, more than 1,800 Japanese Peruvians were arrested and detained by the nation's police and military. Since Peru did not have the capability or the willingness to establish domestic internment camps, the United States agreed to ship these detainees—in badly needed transport vessels—to hastily established camps in New Mexico and Texas. Most of the early deportees were males, and many actually were included in the high-priority blacklists. But as families became separated and high-profile Japanese-Peruvian leaders began to flee into the provinces, go underground, or buy their freedom from corrupt police officials, the nature of the deportees changed. By mid-1943, the wives and children of the initial deportees were being allowed to reunite with Japanese-Peruvian family heads, mostly in the "family camp" in Crystal City, Texas. Clearly these women and children were not security threats, nor were the many working-class Japanese Peruvians who had not been included on the original Proclaimed List. These unfortunates were often rounded up in police dragnets that aimed to arrest any Japanese caught on the streets or violating strict curfew or assembly laws. A review of the FBI counterespionage campaign reveals a minimum of legwork by agents, most of whom did not even speak Spanish, much less Japanese. All too often, U.S. officials relied on informants who had little substantive information but a great deal to gain if certain Japanese businessmen were arrested and deported. A U.S. military attaché in Peru confirmed this during the early year when he noted that for every Japanese who was deported, there were three Peruvians waiting to take over his business.[18]

The person best able to assess the validity and effectiveness of the Japanese Peruvian deportation program with regard to the security of Peru and the Allied war effort was John K. Emmerson, third secretary of the U.S. Embassy in Lima during the war. Emmerson was the only U.S. official in Peru during the war who read and spoke Japanese. A competent and humane diplomat, Emmerson did his best to discover Japanese espionage efforts in Peru, but he found none. Additionally, the diplomat sought to supervise and prevent the unauthorized deportation of Japanese he called the "little people"—those that had no real standing within the Japanese community and who were without the means to purchase their safety or freedom from deportation.[19]

The Italians in Peru during World War II

Peru's Italian and German immigrant communities were well established before World War II and did not confront the fierce hostility that marked the first half-century of the Japanese presence. Although Italians were the largest non-Iberian community in Peru at the beginning of the twentieth century, with approximately 13,000 in 1906, outmigration by 1940 had reduced their numbers to only 7,618.[20] With prominent interests in banking (Banco Italiano, Peru's largest), utilities, manufacturing, and other commercial enterprises, Peru's Italian community was well accepted. The threat from Fascism, especially after Italy's invasion of Ethiopia in 1935, made relations more tense. Gen. Oscar Benevides's affinity for some aspects of Fascism and Nazism, and his establishment of ties with Italian and German military training teams during the late 1930s, gave U.S. observers the strong impression that Peru was becoming a Fascist bastion in the Andes as World War II approached. In reality, much of the Mussolini government's aims in Peru were to counteract the strong attacks by the international community against Italy's invasion of Ethiopia.

According to Orazio Ciccarelli, after 1936 the Italian government scaled down its propaganda campaign in Peru because the Italian community in Peru refused to subsidize pro-Fascist propaganda to any significant degree. Rome's policy aims in Peru benefited during the 1930s because of the economic strength of the Italian community; the goodwill of most Peruvians toward Italians, who were ethnically and culturally similar to themselves;

and the strong affinity that members of Peru's elite had with the principles of Italian Fascism. This was particularly true of Carlos Miro Quesada, the owner of Peru's leading newspaper, *El Comercio*. The Lima press's support for the Italian cause in Africa was in sharp contrast to its vociferous opposition to Japanese military operations in Asia and its open animosity toward Peru's Japanese community. This is in part explained by racism, but it also relates to the standing of Italian community leaders, respected businessmen who were born in or were long-term residents of Peru.[21]

In many ways, the Italians in Peru were as well integrated as any other European community in Latin America. Indeed, because of declining Italian immigration to Peru, and the consequent loss of linguistic and cultural bonds with the mother nation, most Italians were very careful to withhold financial and moral support to Mussolini's military ventures in Ethiopia.[22] When World War II began, Italians were never really a serious target of antisubversive activities by the Peruvian government or Allied counterintelligence. Only a small fraction of the Axis nationals deported from Peru during World War II were Italian. Emmerson summarized Washington's view of the Italian community's significance in the war effort when he concluded, "The Italians hardly mattered."[23] The supposed threat from German nationals in Peru and in other Latin American countries was another matter.

The Germans in Peru during World War II

A good deal of high-quality scholarship exists on German nationals and Nazi subversion in Latin America during World War II.[24] But these works focus almost exclusively on Argentina, Brazil, Chile, and Mexico. This is understandable, since the "ABC nations" all contained large or politically significant German populations, and Mexico, because of its close proximity to the United States, provided an ideal venue for espionage or sabotage. The German community in Peru has yet to be researched in depth regarding the World War II experience.

In a very broad sense, the Abwehr (German military intelligence) did not have very ambitious goals for Latin America, and even less for Peru. Agents recruited from among the German nationals in Latin America, who were primarily businessmen and members of the German Clubs in these countries, had the main job: transmitting information obtained by radio from agents in the United States. Since East–West radio transmissions were often impeded across the North Atlantic, the Latin American nations became the radio relay link between spies in the United States and Germany.[25] Therefore, three main issues weighed against the efficacy of establishing a working Abwehr cell in Peru:

1. Peru's geographic position on the Pacific, which precluded the observance of general shipping traffic to Germany

2. a very small German population of 2,122 (1940)
3. the willingness of the Prado administration to cooperate fully with U.S. counterintelligence operations

Moreover, Peru's German community, like the nation's Japanese community, was concentrated in the Lima metropolitan area, especially in the exclusive suburb of Miraflores.

Peru's Germans did not confront the open hatred that the Japanese faced even after the war in Europe began in September 1939. Perhaps this was because the German community was only one-tenth the size of the Japanese population. It was also very likely that the Germans' contact with Peruvians was with members of the Peruvian upper-middle and upper classes through business interchange. Much like the Italians, the Germans had little contact with the "street people" on an everyday basis as the Japanese did. This made them far less visible to the general populace and less likely to suffer the effects of wartime xenophobia.

The low profile of the German community in Peru did not prevent the arrest and deportation of many of its members to internment camps in the United States during World War II. Most ended up in the same "family" internment camp at Crystal City, Texas, where a number remained until 1946 along with the 346 Japanese detainees. One of the last shipments of these deportees from Peru arrived at the temporary internment camp in the Panama Canal Zone on March 21, 1944. The vessel carried 7 Italians, 165 Germans, and 368 Japanese. These numbers accurately reflect the ratio of internments of Axis nationals from Peru during the war. Of the 165 Germans, only 42 were female and a very few were children. The youngest of the group was four months and the oldest 65. It appears that German males either could not or chose not to bring their wives, as was the case with the later detainees among the Japanese.[26]

Like their Japanese internee counterparts, a significant number of the Germans deported from Peru applied for repatriation to Germany during the war. This almost insured that they would be deported to Germany after the war when their cases were reviewed by the Alien Control Board of the Department of State. The record of the hearings on these cases is instructive regarding the prevailing attitudes and legal conduct of these cases. The State Department officials conducting the reviews warned German nationals from Peru that they would "probably" be breaking the law if they did not testify completely truthfully even though they were not testifying under oath. The lawyers hired by these detainees protested that the proceedings were not in keeping with the constitutional right of the German internees and were therefore not valid. The questioning was done in a highly prosecutorial manner that left the internees, who often spoke only poor English, clearly at a disadvantage. On the other hand, these internees professed to remember very little about the involvement in the Nazi Party while in Peru, their activities when they returned to Germany on visits, or their views on politics in general.

One of the most notable of these internees was Hermann Niebuhr, who came to Peru in 1937 for business reasons after serving from 1932 to 1937 as a Nazi storm trooper and participating in many street brawls. He was member of the Peruvian Nazi Party until it was dissolved in 1939, serving as its "cultural director." Like all former members of the Nazi Party in Peru, Niebuhr was on the blacklist that was employed by the State Department and FBI to facilitate their deportation. Niebuhr was ultimately deported to the United States and spent most war in the Crystal City camp. He was eventually ordered deported to Germany in 1946, largely on the basis of his activities before coming to Peru.[27]

CONCLUSION

Any analysis of Peru's relationship with the Allies during World War II must conclude that this Andean nation was one of the most ardent supporters of the Allied cause. Even though Peru did not send combatants to fight in the war as Brazil and Mexico did, it cooperated fully with the United States, economically, commercially, and diplomatically.

The Prado administration felt that cooperation was necessary to avoid any accusation of pro-Axis feeling or lack of patriotism. Additionally, Peru's military, especially its navy, was now forced to establish even closer ties to the United States because of the rupture of military and diplomatic ties with traditional European partners, particularly France. The July 1941 border war with Ecuador and the subsequent settlement at the January 1942 Rio Conference cemented the relationship between Washington and Lima and ensured future Lend-Lease supplies and development loans from the Export-Import Bank.

All this would seem to point to close diplomatic and military ties between Peru and the United States that would last for generations to come. This did not happen. Washington seems to have played a game of Peruvian exceptionalism with regard to policy on petroleum contracts, arms purchases, fishing rights, and development policy in general. In other words, Peru was made an example for issues of arms sales by France (Mirage jets in 1967) and the Soviet Union (T-55 tanks in 1971) and of petroleum policy (IPC dispute, 1963–68). The goodwill that was won during World War II, at the cost of many ruptured lives among the Japanese, Italian, and German communities in Peru, was quickly squandered for reasons that were largely due to the Cold War and the often misplaced priorities in the post–World War II years.

NOTES

1. Rosemary Thorp and Geoff Bertram, *Peru, 1890–1977: Growth and Policy in an Open Economy* (New York: Columbia University Press, 1978), 182–87.

2. Leslie Taylor, *The Healing Power of Rainforest Herbs: A Guide to Understanding and Using Herbal Medicinals* (Garden City Park, NY: Square One, 2004).

3. Robert L. Scheina, *Latin American Wars: The Age of the Professional Soldier, 1900–2001* (Washington, DC: Brassey's, 2001), 118.

4. One of the best examples of this thinking expressed by the Peruvian army is the article by Lt. Col. E. P. Manuel Morla Concha, "Función social del ejército en la organización de la nacionalidad," *Revista Militar del Perú* (October 1933): 843–72.

5. An assessment of Peru's military buildup is offered in the U.S. State Department document Dreyfus to Secretary of State, September 8, 1938, National Archives and Records Administration of the United States (hereafter cited as NARA), RG 59, 823.00/1315. For a thorough discussion of Fascist influence in Peru during this period, see Orazio Ciccarelli, "Fascism and Politics in Peru during the Benavides Era, 1933–1939: The Italian Perspective," *Hispanic American Historical Review* 70, no. 3 (August 1990): 413–32.

6. Scheina, *Latin American Wars*, 117.

7. Scheina, *Latin American Wars*, 118.

8. U.S. military attaché to War Department, G-2 Report No. 385333, June 30, 1947, NARA, RG 319.

9. Ministerio de Relaciones Exteriores, *Acuerdos suscritos entre el Peru y el Ecuador en Brasilia el 26 de Octubre 1998* (Lima: 1998).

10. U.S. Ambassador John Campbell White, to Secretary of State, 3 April 1945, "Escalafón general del Ejército Peruano, 1941," NARA, RG 59, 823.00/4–345, pp. 21–69; U.S. military attaché to War Department, G-2 Report No. 5857, NARA, RG 319.

11. U.S. Department of State, *Foreign Relations of the United States: Diplomatic Papers, 1944*, Vol. 7, *The American Republics* (Washington, DC: GPO, 1944), 1508; U.S. military attaché to War Department, G-2 Report No. 352, April 1, 1944, NARA, RG 319.

12. White to Secretary of State, February 2, 1945, NARA, RG 59, 823.00/2–245; personal interview with Victor Villanueva Valencia, July 27, 1974, Lima, Peru.

13. U.S. Department of Defense, *The MAGIC Background of Pearl Harbor* (Washington, DC: GPO, 1946), 2:98–100 (document summaries 110 and 113). The diplomatic cable intercepts, which were codenamed MAGIC, are provided in summary form rather than the complete text document.

14. For an overview of the Japanese immigration patterns to Latin America, see Daniel M. Masterson, with Sayaka Funada Classen, *The Japanese in Latin America* (Urbana: University of Illinois Press, 2004). A particularly valuable analysis of the Japanese-Peruvian experience is Alejandro Sakuda's *El futuro era el Perú: Cien años o más de inmigración* (Lima: Esicos, 1999).

15. Peruvian Japanese Association, *The Centennial of the Japanese Immigration to Peru* (Lima: JICA, 1999), 79.

16. For a description of the riots, see Masterson, *Japanese in Latin America*, 156–57, and Sakuda, *El futuro era el Perú*, 229–37.

17. Masterson, *Japanese in Latin America*, 160–61.

18. The now-classic study of Japanese-Peruvian deportation and internment during World War II is C. Harvey Gardiner's *Pawns in a Triangle of Hate: The Peruvian Japanese and the United States* (Seattle: University of Washington Press, 1981). Also useful are Sakuda, *El futuro era el Perú*, 261–88, and Masterson, *Japanese in Latin America*, 161–70.

19. John Emmerson, *The Japanese Thread* (New York: Holt, Rinehart and Winston, 1978), 144–45.

20. Janet Worrall, "Italian Migration to Peru, 1860–1914," Ph.D. diss., Indiana University, 1972. The population figure for Italians in 1940 was undoubtedly derived from the Peruvian census of that year. It was quoted in an FBI memorandum to President Roosevelt entitled "Totalitarian Activities in Peru Today." The memorandum is dated May 1942 and is directed from J. Edgar Hoover to the president and his advisors, most prominently Harry Hopkins. Harry Hopkins Papers, Box 143, Franklin D. Roosevelt Presidential Library, Hyde Park, New York.

21. Orazio A. Ciccarelli, "Fascist Propaganda and the Italian Community in Peru during the Benavides Regime, 1933–1939," *Journal of Latin American Studies* 20, no. 2 (November 1988), 368–71.

22. Ciccarelli, "Fascist Propaganda," 374–75.

23. Emmerson, *Japanese Thread*, 174.

24. See for example, Leslie B. Rout Jr. and John F. Bratzel, *The Shadow War: German Espionage and United States Counterespionage in Latin America during World War II* (Lanham, MD: University Publications of America, 1986); Max Paul Friedman, *Nazis and Good Neighbors: The United States Campaign against the Germans of Latin America in World War II* (Cambridge: Cambridge University Press, 2003); Stanley E. Hilton, *Hitler's Secret War in South America, 1939–1945: German Espionage and Allied Counterespionage in Brazil* (Baton Rouge: Louisiana State University Press, 1981); and Ronald C. Newton, *The "Nazi Menace" in Argentina, 1931–1947* (Stanford, CA: Stanford University Press, 1992).

25. Rout and Bratzel, *Shadow War*, 9; Friedman, *Nazis and Good Neighbors*, 65.

26. U.S. Department of State, "German and Japanese Nationals from Peru," March 21, 1944, NARA, RG 59, Special War Problems Division Records, Box 105.

27. Department of State, "German and Japanese Nationals from Peru"; "Alien Enemy Internees from Peru," NARA, RG 59, Box 44.

9

Brazil: Benefits of Cooperation

Joseph Smith

THE FASCIST IMAGE OF BRAZIL AT THE BEGINNING OF THE WAR

In 1939 the Brazilian political system could be described as a personal dictatorship that in some respects had much more in common with the fascist states of Germany, Italy, and Portugal than with the democracies of the United States and Western Europe. The federal president of Brazil, Getúlio Dornelles Vargas, ruled the country as a dictator. After rising to political power in 1930 with the aid of an armed revolt and a military coup, Vargas had engineered a constitutional election in 1934 that confirmed him as president.

Although the 1934 Constitution contained a provision making Vargas ineligible for reelection in 1938, this problem was resolved by another military coup in November 1937 that resulted in a declaration of a state of national emergency and the cancellation of the scheduled presidential election.[1] At the same time, Vargas also announced the imposition of a new constitution for what he called the "Estado Nôvo" (New State), a term borrowed from the authoritarian regime of Antonio de Oliveira Salazar that had seized power in Portugal in 1933. According to the 1937 Constitution, the federal president possessed virtual dictatorial powers. In addition, the presidential term of office was extended from four to six years so that Vargas would remain as president until 1943.

Vargas publicly stated that his goal was the creation of a "corporate state" that would bring economic and social benefits to all citizens. The concept of corporatism owed much to European fascist models. It sought to build not

144

only a prosperous and stable Brazil but also a country that was both economically and militarily strong, two objectives that particularly appealed to
the nationalism of the military and the urban middle classes—the same institutional and social forces that provided significant support for the fascist
regimes in Europe. Another feature of the corporate state was the bureaucratic growth of the federal government, a development that increased the
number of officials and expanded the patronage available to those politicians
who supported Vargas and the Estado Nôvo.[2]

During the 1930s, the political history of Brazil differed from the United
States and was more similar to Europe in that the Right gained political
ascendancy at the expense of the other political parties. The foremost right-
wing movement was Brazilian Integralist Action (Acão Integralista Brasileira, or AIB), which was formed in 1932 as a deliberate imitation of the Fascist parties of Benito Mussolini in Italy and Salazar in Portugal. Dressed in
a uniform conspicuous for its green shirt and jackboots, the paramilitary
forces of the Integralists were a prominent feature at massive public rallies
and demonstrations that declared support for the "integral" moral and traditional values summed up in the motto of "God, Country, Family." The
largest rallies usually took place in cities and frequently erupted into violent
clashes on the streets with members of the "Popular Front" of left-wing
organizations known as the National Liberation Alliance (Aliança Nacional
Libertadora, or ANL), which was supported by the Brazilian Communist
Party (Partido Communista Brasileiro, or PCB).

Vargas did not become directly involved in the political battles fought
between the Integralists and the Popular Front. He differed from European
authoritarian leaders such as Italy's Mussolini and Germany's Adolf Hitler
in his reluctance to form his own political party machine or to create and
lead a popular national movement that would reflect and propagate his personal views and ideology. While Vargas remained something of a political
enigma in this respect, he was prepared to be ruthless in his repression in
order to hold onto the presidency and to defeat all challenges to his authority. For example, an abortive Communist uprising in April 1935 presented
an opportunity to launch a vigorous and brutal anti-Communist campaign.
Furthermore, at the beginning of the Estado Nôvo, Vargas ensured that there
would be no effective opposition to his dictatorship by decreeing the disso-
lution of Congress, the imposition of strict censorship of the press, and the
abolition of all political parties—including the Integralists, whom he
denounced as Nazis. During the Estado Nôvo from 1937 to 1945, thousands
of political opponents of the regime were placed under police surveillance
and suffered arrest, torture, and imprisonment. The resort to repression and
censorship was explained and justified on the grounds that it was necessary
to preserve the country from internal and external enemies and especially
from the danger of Communism.

The political importance and heavy investment in the military was another feature that Brazil shared with contemporary European fascist states. In the years preceding the war, Vargas had offered the military generous financial appropriations so that the amount allocated in the federal budget for the federal army increased from 12 percent in the years 1910–30 to more than 20 percent in 1937.[3] Indeed, the 1937 coup required surrounding the Congress in Rio de Janeiro with federal troops, and the success of that operation was based upon Vargas's close relationship and collaboration with senior generals such as Army Chief of Staff Pedro Aurélio de Góes Monteiro and Minister of War Eurico Gaspar Dutra. While they agreed with Vargas that the nation faced a serious Communist threat, they were also sympathetic to his continuance in power due to his nationalist policies and especially his careful cultivation of the military ever since he had come to office in 1930.

BRAZILIAN FOREIGN POLICY

In his relations with the wider world, Vargas pursued a pragmatic and reactive foreign policy. The cornerstone was the maintenance of close and friendly relations with the United States, the preeminent nation in the Western Hemisphere and a traditional friend of Brazil. Moreover, the United States was Brazil's single largest export market and the source of new capital investment; friendly relations with that country were vital to bringing about Brazil's recovery from the Great Depression that had struck Brazil and the world economy in 1929. The Brazilian government also placed considerable importance on the country's long-standing economic relationship with Great Britain. The most notable growth in Brazil's overseas trade during the 1930s, however, was with Germany. In fact, Brazil doubled its exports to Germany between 1933 and 1938. Germany not only purchased large quantities of coffee and rubber but also became the largest market for Brazilian cotton and cacao. During the same period, Germany's share of Brazil's import trade more than doubled from 12 to almost 25 percent.[4]

The visible growth of German interest in Brazil was not just limited to commercial activities. The National Socialist Party's foreign organization, the Auslands organization, spread pro-Nazi propaganda through the establishment and subsidy of German cultural and sporting clubs and societies. In fact, Brazil was only one of a number of Latin American countries that the Nazi government of Adolf Hitler wished to cultivate because the local population contained a substantial number of immigrants of German extraction who were regarded as a potential "fifth column" that would assist the international objectives of their fatherland.[5] In Brazil, ethnic Germans numbered more than one million and were concentrated in communities mostly located in the southern states of Paraná, Santa Catarina, and especially Rio

Grande do Sul.⁶ In addition, Germany sought to revive its pre–World War I influence over the Brazilian Army by supplying armaments and issuing invitations to senior officers to attend German military maneuvers. Prominent generals such as Góes Monteiro and Dutra accepted German decorations and were known to be admirers of German military skill and accomplishments.

U.S. diplomats anxiously observed the advance of German influence, which they regarded as serious competition and also a challenge to their country's well-established political and economic standing in Brazil. Their concern was further heightened by the creation of the Estado Nôvo in 1937 and its close association with the ideas and practices of European fascism. As a result, when Vargas sought to purchase military equipment from the United States in 1939, his officials encountered a negative response in Washington. U.S. diplomats not only were disturbed at the clear signs of fascist developments in Brazil but were also aware that assisting the emergence of a powerful Brazilian military would alarm Argentina and thereby upset the existing balance of power in South America.

In 1938 the Brazilian government had signed a $55 million order for artillery from the German armaments manufacturer Krupp. Vargas showed his annoyance with U.S. rebuffs by making further overtures to German companies to supply weapons and by his determination to maintain friendly diplomatic relations with the Nazi government even after the beginning of the war in 1939. In fact, Germany's proactive Latin American diplomacy possessed real advantages for Brazil. Indeed, the Vargas administration welcomed the increase of trade with Germany and even entered into discussions over possible German loans for Brazilian industrial development such as the building of the steelworks at Volta Redonda. This was a massive project to promote self-sufficiency in steel production that would contribute to "economic independence" and was greatly desired by the Brazilian military and nationalists.⁷

Nazi Germany's prestige was also greatly enhanced by its stunning military victory over France in the spring of 1940, which led some Brazilian generals, notably Góes Monteiro, to believe that a Nazi victory over Great Britain would be achieved by September. The uncertainty of the military outcome in Europe reinforced Vargas's diplomatic pragmatism and was exemplified in his sending on May Day 1940 a message of personal greetings to Hitler and best wishes to the German people. In June the German ambassador in Rio gladly reported to Berlin the president's comment that Brazil was "the bulwark against the inclusion of South America in Roosevelt's anti-German policy."⁸ The tilt toward the fascist powers was noted in the United States, where the administration of President Franklin D. Roosevelt began to contemplate the possibility that Brazil might align with Germany and Italy.

Despite its acknowledged links with European fascism, the Estado Nôvo pursued a nationalist policy of "Brazilianization" (*brasilidade*) that directly clashed with ideas of German racial superiority and cultural uniqueness promoted by the Auslands organization. Vargas publicly emphasized to Brazilians of German extraction that it was their patriotic duty to be Brazilian first, and German second. Pro-German political and cultural activities were, therefore, vigorously repressed in Brazil. Many German schools were closed and teaching in the German language was prohibited. Army garrisons were reinforced in areas where large German communities were resident. Moreover, Brazilian diplomacy carefully avoided becoming identified with the international ambitions of Nazi Germany or Italy and continued to seek close relations with the United States. For example, Oswaldo Aranha, who served as Brazilian ambassador in Washington from 1933 to 1938 and minister of foreign affairs from 1938 to 1944, constantly stressed the importance of pursuing the traditional strategy of seeking a friendly, if not a special, relationship with the United States.[9]

When war broke out in Europe in September 1939, Brazil declared its neutrality in the conflict and followed a policy very similar to that of the United States and the other Latin American nations. Brazil attended the Pan-American conference of foreign ministers held at Panama City and subscribed to the adoption of a 300-mile neutrality zone, which, it was hoped, would protect and insulate all the American republics from the war in Europe.

The attitude of the Brazilian public toward World War II was very similar to that shown at the outbreak of World War I in 1914. The educated elite generally favored Britain and France and viewed the struggle as one of democracy versus barbarism. Some ethnic Germans, Italians, and Japanese undoubtedly were sympathetic to their countries of origin, but fear of nationalist reprisals meant that they refrained from making their views public. "In my opinion," stated the U.S. ambassador to Brazil, Jefferson Caffery, "70% of the Brazilian population, which has any opinion on the European war, is pro-Ally; 30% which has an opinion on the war is pro-Germany or Italian."[10] In fact, there was no great diplomatic or public pressure for the federal government to abandon neutrality and enter the war. Vargas and the senior military leaders were only too well aware that the country was relatively weak militarily and extremely ill-prepared for a war involving European powers. Nevertheless, Brazilian national security was directly affected, if not threatened, by the expanding world conflict. A major security concern was the perceived inadequacy of the navy to protect the huge "bulge" of the northeastern coastline from an external attack. There was also anxiety that the disaffection of pro-German elements in the south might induce civil unrest or even encourage an opportunistic Argentine military invasion across the border states of Misiones and Corrientes.

WARTIME COOPERATION WITH
THE UNITED STATES

Prior to 1939, U.S. diplomats had regarded the emergence of a powerful Brazilian military as a danger to the political and military stability of South America. But this view was considerably altered by the outbreak of war in Europe. "If the Germans furnish the arms and finance the steel project," warned Ambassador Caffery in July 1940, Brazil would fall within "the German orbit."[11] Furthermore, the geopolitical reality was that Brazil's large size and extended coastline made it extremely vulnerable to external aggression. Indeed, after the dramatic military collapse of France in 1940, there was anxiety in the United States that Germany might be tempted to use the French colonies in West Africa as a base to launch an invasion of northeastern Brazil. "A small force in initial occupation," noted U.S. Army chief of staff George C. Marshall, "will compel a major effort to expel it."[12] Not only could this lead to the cutting of the shipping lanes to and from the South Atlantic but, for Americans, it also posed the nightmare scenario of falling dominoes, in which German forces first established a beachhead in Brazil and then made a military advance to Central America, Mexico, and eventually reached the border of the United States.

Moreover, the onset of war and the resulting disruption of trade with Europe heightened Brazil's value as a vital source of foodstuffs, strategic raw materials, and minerals, especially rubber, iron ore, and quartz crystals, a vital element in radio transmitters. Consequently, in his dealings with the United States, Vargas now found himself in a stronger bargaining position than before the war. He was therefore able to conclude a series of beneficial arrangements in which Brazil agreed to supply raw materials and allow the use of naval bases in the northeast in return for U.S. arms and financial assistance. The latter included a substantial loan, initially of $20 million and later increased to $45 million, from the U.S. Export-Import Bank toward the cost of the construction of the steelworks at Volta Redonda. Furthermore, Lend-Lease aid amounting to $100 million in credits mainly for the purchase of armaments was formally extended to Brazil in October 1941.[13]

After the United States joined the war in December 1941, Brazil abandoned neutrality and agreed to host the Pan-American meeting of foreign ministers at Rio de Janeiro in January 1942 that recommended the breaking of diplomatic relations with Germany and Italy.[14] Brazil duly broke off relations on January 28, 1942. While Vargas declared Brazil's solidarity with the United States, he delayed joining the war until August 22, 1942. The actual sequence of events leading to Brazil's declaration of war was influenced as much by the German submarine threat as U.S. pressure or blandishment. Even though Brazil was not formally at war, the increase in trade between

Brazil and the Allied powers and the use of land and naval bases on Brazilian territory by U.S. military personnel signified to the German government that Brazil was effectively on the side of the Allied powers. From February 1942 onward, Brazilian merchant ships were attacked by German U-boats operating in Atlantic waters. A major German submarine offensive in the South Atlantic was launched in August 1942, resulting in the sinking of six Brazilian ships within a period of less than a week; four were passenger liners, with heavy loss of civilian life. Mass demonstrations erupted throughout the country demanding retaliation. German- and Italian-owned businesses were singled out for attack. Vargas responded by issuing a declaration of war against Germany and Italy on August 22. A few days later, in an Independence Day speech, the president indicated the vital role of public opinion in influencing the decision to go to war: "You asked by every form of expression of the popular will that the Government should declare war on the aggressors, and this was done."[15]

BRAZIL AT WAR

Close cooperation bordering on subordination to the United States became the principal characteristic of Brazil's diplomacy and military policy in World War II. For the first time since the brief period of Foreign Minister Rio Branco's policy of "approximation" at the beginning of the twentieth century, Brazil enjoyed appearing as the favored South American ally of the United States.[16] Not only did this enhance Brazil's regional status ahead of Argentina but there were also immediate and substantial financial and military benefits. By breaking off diplomatic relations with Germany and Italy in January 1942, Brazil was rewarded by the Roosevelt administration with a doubling of the amount of the Lend-Lease aid that had been initially allocated in October 1941. American assistance was further increased after Brazil's formal declaration of war in August 1942 and grew to such an extent that Brazil received almost $350 million or around 75 percent of the total Lend-Lease aid given by the United States to all the Latin American nations during World War II.[17] The aid was not limited to just weapons and munitions. One highly visible and controversial element was the arrival in Brazil of substantial numbers of U.S. military and civilian officials. Many were assigned to the "bulge" of the northeast, where they worked to construct and improve local air and sea defenses against possible German attack. The naval bases of the northeast soon became an important staging post for the preparation and dispatch of U.S. troops, equipment, and supplies for the Allied invasion of North Africa in 1942.

In terms of actual military contribution to the war effort, it was assumed by both Allied and Brazilian commanders that Brazil would fulfill limited naval duties, but would not be able to commit troops to an overseas combat role. In 1942 the army numbered less than 100,000 soldiers and was mostly stationed in the center-south region to protect Rio de Janeiro and São Paulo.[18] It was also deployed to counter potentially pro-Nazi activities and the possibility of a military incursion from Argentina. "We did not have an organization and a mobilization [plan] to fight overseas," recalled Col. Humberto de Alencar Castelo Branco, "only for combat in South America and internally."[19]

President Vargas, however, wanted the army to undertake an overseas combat mission. He was mindful that the success of the Allied landing in North Africa in November 1942 had reduced the strategic significance of northeastern Brazil. Vargas reckoned that an overseas mission would not only assure the continuation of U.S. military aid but would also boost Brazil's hemispheric and international prestige and thereby its potential for influence after the world war had been concluded. Consequently, against the advice of some senior generals, he ordered the creation of an expeditionary force, the Força Expeditionária Brasileira (FEB), that would be sent to participate in the Allied invasion of Italy. The FEB was equipped, transported, and supplied by the U.S. government and served under U.S. military commanders. In July 1944 the first contingent left Rio de Janeiro for Italy, where it joined the U.S. Fifth Army, commanded by Gen. Mark Clark. A fighter squadron was also dispatched to Italy to serve with the Twelfth U.S. Army Air Force.

Around 25,000 Brazilian troops were sent to Italy and were on active service between September 6, 1944, and May 2, 1945. The exploits of the FEB, notably its significant contribution to the hard-fought Allied victory at Monte Castello in March 1945, evoked great pride and patriotism in Brazil. Vargas's decision to send troops overseas was therefore vindicated and brought him considerable political popularity. The FEB was also significant in stimulating close professional and personal cooperation between the Brazilian and U.S. militaries and established an enduring relationship that would be a prominent feature of the postwar period. Many Brazilian officers acquired considerable respect and admiration for the United States— especially its military and technological skills. "In the War the United States had to give us everything: food, clothes, equipment," summed up one ex-FEB officer, adding: "After the War, we were less afraid of United States imperialism than other officers because we saw the United States really helped us without strings attached."[20]

Participation in World War II led to Brazil surpassing Argentina to become the leading military power in South America. In addition to the resulting revival of pretensions to regional leadership, there was also the belief that Brazil should acquire an influential role in the new international councils such as the United Nations that were being formed to shape the postwar world. Indeed, there were high hopes among the Brazilian elite that more diplomatic success would be forthcoming in 1945 than at the end of World War I, because Brazil had gained considerable prestige as the first South American nation to join the war and for being the only Latin American country to have actually sent combat troops to Europe. Brazilian officials made much of the fact that their country's new regional and international status had been underlined at a meeting between the two presidents in Natal in January 1943, when Roosevelt had stated that the United States and Brazil were equal partners in the war and that Vargas would be invited to attend the peace conference that the victors would hold at the end of the war. Later at the Dumbarton Oaks conference at Washington in 1944, Secretary of State Cordell Hull implied that Brazil might even be assigned a permanent seat on the Security Council of the new United Nations.

However, U.S. support proved more uncertain after Roosevelt's sudden death in April 1945.[21] The first peace conference to meet after the end of the war was held at Potsdam in July 1945 and was monopolized by the leaders of the "Big Three" powers: the United States, the Soviet Union, and Great Britain. The Big Three were preoccupied with settling the political boundaries of Europe and displayed an attitude of indifference toward minor powers such as Brazil. Nevertheless, Brazil was able to play an active part in the subsequent formation of the United Nations and was given membership on the Security Council, though on a temporary two-year basis.[22]

During the years immediately following the end of World War II, Brazilian diplomacy stressed the continuation of close relations with the United States. Brazil was gratified to host the Inter-American Conference at Petrópolis in 1947 and to receive a personal visit from President Harry Truman to close the meeting. Brazilian delegates worked effectively with U.S. officials to secure the smooth negotiation of the Inter-American Treaty of Reciprocal Assistance, a collective security arrangement more popularly known as the "Rio Pact."

Although it served to gratify Brazilian diplomatic pretensions to regional leadership, postwar cooperation with the United States resulted in relatively few tangible benefits simply because Brazil no longer received preferential treatment. During World War II, the United States had treated Brazil as its most valued ally among the Latin American nations. At the same time, however, the United States had risen from isolationism to globalism. Consequently, its geopolitical priorities were significantly altered, and all the countries of Latin America, including Brazil, were generally neglected after 1945. "We fought in the last war and were entirely forgotten and rejected in the division of the spoils," summed up Vargas in 1951.[23]

BRAZILIAN ECONOMY DURING
WORLD WAR II

The significant influence of external factors on Brazil's economy was again underscored by World War II. The economic impact of the outbreak of war in Europe in 1939 was similar to that of 1914 in stimulating a substantial increase in the quantities of exports of Brazilian raw materials and minerals. A new development, however, was the marked overseas demand for Brazilian manufactured goods, especially cotton textiles, which rose to become the country's principal export earner during the war. Indeed, the trade balance moved decisively in Brazil's favor, not only on account of the boom in exports but also because of the coincident decrease in foreign imports caused by the severe wartime dislocation of shipping and the switch in the belligerent countries from civilian consumer goods to war production. The resulting interruption of traditional patterns of trade encouraged and necessitated the development of the policy of import substitution. Brazilian manufacturing particularly gained from the decline of foreign competition, although its growth was restricted by the relatively small size of the domestic market and especially the lack of capital investment, foreign machinery, and a skilled labor force. Consequently, in comparison with the late 1930s, when annual industrial growth averaged more than 10 percent, the rate of increase for the period from 1940 to 1945 was more modest and actually fell to just over 5 percent.[24]

An interesting aspect of World War II was the strengthening of economic ties between Brazil and the other countries of the Western Hemisphere. In what might be considered an early precursor of Mercosul, Brazil attended a regional economic conference of the River Plate countries held at Montevideo in 1941 to discuss the dismantling of tariff barriers. Indeed, trade with Argentina noticeably increased during the war. Brazil's exports to Argentina more than doubled in value, while imports from that country rose from 12 percent to 17 percent of Brazil's total imports during the period from 1938 to 1943. The biggest commercial gains for Brazil, however, were in trade with the United States. During the period of the war, U.S. goods made up more than 50 percent of Brazil's foreign imports. In addition, the United States purchased almost 50 percent of Brazil's exports.[25] American Lend-Lease aid in the form of military equipment was also substantial and was designed to cultivate a close economic, political, and military relationship between the United States and Brazil. Technical advice on developing the country's natural resources and industry was notably provided by an economic mission headed by Morris Cooke, which visited the country in 1942.[26]

World War II contributed further to the expansion of the economic role and activities of the Brazilian federal government. Central planning was increased by the creation of a national mobilization board to allocate economic resources for the war effort. The economic power of the government was most keenly felt in the imposition of rationing of strategic goods such as oil, the levying of direct taxes on consumer products to compensate for the loss of customs revenue, and in 1942 the issue of a new currency, the cruzeiro, to replace the milréis. However, the increased spending of the government, combined with a persistent shortage of capital and consumer goods, resulted in inflationary pressures that drove up the cost of living. During the 1930s, prices had risen on average by 6 percent annually. This figure rose to almost 20 percent from 1941 to 1945.[27] Far from being a temporary aberration, the rapid increase in inflation soon became a regular feature of Brazil's economic life.

In real monetary terms, Brazilian workers suffered a decline in their standard of living because wages rose at a slower rate than prices. This resulted in 1945 in hundreds of strikes to secure wage increases. For most of the wartime period, however, industrial discontent was restrained by appeals to patriotism and also by the inclusion of employers organizations and labor unions within the corporate state. In the case of labor unions (*sindicatos*) of skilled workers, the Ministry of Labor possessed veto power over the selection of union officials and set up government-appointed tribunals to deal with disputes between employers and organized labor.[28]

Despite the outbreak of industrial militancy in 1945, Brazil appeared economically prosperous at the end of the war. A succession of wartime trade surpluses in the annual balance of payments meant that the country had built up considerable reserves of foreign exchange amounting to $708 million. This position of economic strength resulted in the dismantling of the wartime interventionist policy in favor of a return to the economic liberalism of the First Republic (1889–1930), in which prosperity once again relied on the export of staple goods led by coffee while a policy of laissez-faire was adopted toward domestic industry. Like 1919, however, the sudden ending of wartime economic restrictions in 1945 was followed by the similar release of pent-up consumer demand for foreign imports, which quickly depleted Brazil's foreign exchange reserves to less than $100 million and provoked a balance-of-payments crisis. In 1947 the administration of President Eurico Dutra attempted to restrict imports and to introduce complex foreign exchange controls designed to defend the value of the cruzeiro in terms of the U.S. dollar.[29] It was a response to economic crisis that would be repeated on many future occasions by his successors.

POLITICAL TRANSITION IN 1945

World War II accelerated the centralizing tendencies of government in Brazil. It also justified emergency powers and consequently helped to strengthen

Vargas's position as dictator. Criticism of Vargas and the Estado Nôvo was stifled by the prohibition on political parties and the enforcement of strict censorship of the press. However, Brazil's participation in the war underscored the ironic contradiction of a country under an authoritarian regime sending an army to liberate people in Western Europe from the tyranny of similarly repressive political systems.

But political protest could not be permanently stifled. A manifesto published in Minas Gerais in October 1943 was the first public indication of unrest. It was signed by ninety prominent citizens of that state and appealed to the rest of the nation to press for the abolition of dictatorship and the restoration of political rights. "If we fight against fascism at the side of the United Nations so that liberty and democracy may be restored to all people," the Mineiros argued, "certainly we are not asking too much in demanding for ourselves such rights and guarantees."[30] Vargas vigorously denounced the manifesto as not only unpatriotic but also divisive and therefore damaging to the national war effort. Indeed, he cleverly used the fact that the country was at war to justify the cancellation of the presidential election due in 1943 when his six-year term expired. Shortly afterward, however, Vargas felt compelled to state that elections would be held after the war had ended, a concession implying his recognition that a return to constitutional government could not be perpetually postponed.

The prospect of elections occurring sooner rather than later was further enhanced by the course of the war in Europe when it became clear at the end of 1944 that the democracies were certain to achieve a smashing victory over their fascist enemies. Consequently, the public pressure for the adoption of democratic forms of government and an end to discredited fascist-style dictatorships swelled in Brazil and throughout Latin America. Ominously for Vargas, the Brazilian military was in favor of a move toward democracy. To a considerable extent, this reflected the growing admiration for the democratic political system and values of the United States that had resulted from the close wartime cooperation between Brazilian and American officers. Leading generals such as Góes Monteiro and Dutra, who had been primarily instrumental in ensuring the success of the 1937 coup, privately informed Vargas that his period of dictatorial rule would have to end.

The question became not whether elections would be allowed, but when exactly they would be held. Indeed, Vargas himself appeared to be making advance preparations for his own future presidential campaign. In marked contrast to his political behavior before the war, he began to exploit the patronage of the presidency and the resources of the federal government in order to present himself not as an authoritarian ruler but as "a man of the people." This populist strategy was strikingly similar to that of Juan Perón in Argentina, especially in seeking to cultivate a close relationship with labor unions and their working-class members. Information was disseminated placing particular emphasis on the many benefits industrial workers and their families had gained under the Estado Nôvo, such as the introduction of the minimum wage in 1941, improved pensions, and medical care.

The momentum in favor of holding elections was stepped up in February 1945 by the publication in the daily press of an interview with leading politician and former presidential candidate José Américo de Almeida, who argued that the presidential election must be held shortly and that Vargas's candidacy should not be permitted. The fact that the interview actually escaped censorship was interpreted as a sign that the period of political repression—and also the era of Vargas's long personal rule—was finally drawing to a close. In March, Eduardo Gomes, an air force brigadier and survivor of the celebrated 1922 revolt of the "tenentes," publicly announced that he would be a candidate for the presidency. Gomes enjoyed wide support from junior military officers. His criticism of the 1937 coup also made him popular among the various political factions that opposed Vargas and wanted to see the dictator overthrown and constitutional government restored. Furthermore, Gomes was a beneficiary of the fact that Brazil was still at war, which meant that a military candidate was likely to be better known to the public and stood a better chance of success of winning a presidential election than a civilian.

Meanwhile, Vargas hinted that he was ineligible to be a candidate and that he intended to go into retirement after the elections. The war minister, Gen. Eurico Dutra, subsequently emerged as the "official" candidate and was assumed to be the president's chosen successor. In May, Vargas confirmed that elections for president and for the National Congress would be held on December 2, 1945. A new political party, the Social Democratic Party (Partido Social Democrático, or PSD), which had been formed in April, endorsed Dutra's candidacy. The PSD had the backing of the majority of state interventors (individuals appointed by Vargas to govern the states) who remained loyal to Vargas. The liberal constitutionalists and anti-Vargas forces pledged to support Gomes and formed the National Democratic Union (União Democrática Nacional, or UDN) to organize his national campaign for the presidency.

Despite the fact that an official electoral campaign was under way between Gomes and Dutra, the behavior and intentions of Vargas soon became the principal topic of discussion and speculation in the press. Rumors abounded that he would attempt another coup to hold onto his position of power, just as he had done previously in 1937. Corroborating evidence for this was found in his studiously ambiguous attitude as to whether or not he would actually be a candidate. The confusion was increased rather than diminished by the creation of the Brazilian Labor Party (Partido Trabalhista Brasileiro, or PTB), a new political party that was actually organized within the Ministry of Labor and had named Vargas as its "honorary president." There was also the sudden appearance of a group of private citizens known as the "Queremistas," who adopted the slogan "Queremos Getúlio" (We Want Getúlio). The Queremistas organized a mass rally that paraded outside the presidential palace in Rio de Janeiro on October 3 to mark the fifteenth anniversary of the start of the armed revolt that had brought Vargas to power in 1930. Their proclaimed object was the cancellation of the presidential election so that Vargas would remain president.

The attempt by Vargas to manipulate the political process in 1945 proved unsuccessful and ultimately self-defeating. Statements that he intended to retire clashed with rumors of an imminent coup, the formation of the PTB, and the emergence of the Queremistas. The result was a mood of increasing confusion and distrust. The U.S. ambassador to Brazil, Adolf Berle, who regarded Vargas as a staunch ally in the war, expected the presidential election to take place on schedule. "As long as Brazil travels towards democracy with a definite date on 2 December," Berle noted early in September, "we are happy." He added: "We will be happier still when the job is complete."[31] By the end of September, however, Berle felt it necessary to make a speech to the press in Petrópolis stating that any interference in the timetable for election or "continuance of the dictatorship" would be regarded by the United States as "tragic."[32]

Senior military commanders were increasingly concerned about the drift of political events in 1945. "If President Vargas loses the support of any substantial portion of the Army," a U.S. diplomat predicted in January 1945, "his government is not likely to survive."[33] In 1937 the military and Vargas had been united in their alarm over what they regarded as a serious Communist threat to the nation. In 1945, senior army officers thus expressed dismay over his decision to establish diplomatic relations with the Soviet Union in April of that year and especially the granting of political amnesty to imprisoned Communists and the subsequent legalization of the Communist Party. There was even suspicion that the president had entered into a secret accord with the Communist leader, Luís Carlos Prestes. After his release from prison in April 1945, Prestes had made a number of public speeches in which he often expressed the opinion that Vargas should remain as president.

The generals were also perturbed by current political events in Argentina and feared that Vargas intended to imitate Argentine leader Perón and establish a populist regime that would deliberately stir up class conflict and social unrest in Brazil. Perón's triumphant return to political office in Argentina on October 17 was widely attributed to the weakness and prevarication of the Argentine military. The lesson was not lost upon the Brazilian generals, who concluded that quick and timely action was necessary to overthrow Vargas.

On October 29, troops surrounded the presidential palace and an ultimatum was presented to Vargas to resign. Taken by surprise, Vargas recognized that resistance was futile. A bloodless coup took place in which he formally resigned the office of president and left Rio de Janeiro to return as a private citizen to his ranch in Rio Grande do Sul. The intervention of the military in 1945 once again confirmed their role as arbiters of the political process— but it was quite different from the action taken in 1937 in that the intention was to *ensure* rather than *prevent* the forthcoming presidential election from taking place on schedule. The ending of the world war had stimulated a demand for democratization that could not be ignored. The 1945 coup was highly significant because it not only overthrew the personal dictatorship of Vargas but also marked the end of the Estado Nôvo and the inauguration of a Fourth Republic, whose political system would be based upon a demo-cratic and not a fascist model.[34]

The presidential and congressional elections that took place in December 1945 were the first national elections to be held in Brazil since 1934. More than six million voters voted in the 1945 presidential election, a record figure more than three times higher than the number that had voted in 1930. For the first time, urban workers participated fully in the electoral process. In addition, the election was regarded as having been fairly conducted. While the operation of the secret ballot reduced intimidation and corruption, the manipulative influence of the state political machines and the local political bosses known as the *coronéis* remained powerful especially in rural areas. This factor undoubtedly aided Dutra, who was the "official" candidate and possessed the patronage of the federal government and most of the state interventors who had been appointed during the Estado Nôvo. Dutra polled just over three million votes, against two million for Gomes. The margin of victory was considered narrow, even though Dutra had gained 55 percent and an absolute majority of the popular vote.

The third candidate in the election had been Yedo Fiúza, the former mayor of Petrópolis. Though a non-Communist, he was sponsored principally by the PCB, the Brazilian Communist Party, as an antimilitary candidate. Fiúza surprised political commentators by gaining more than half a million votes. In fact, the political party that made the most striking advance in 1945 was the PCB. Even though its presidential candidate had entered the campaign only two weeks before the election, he still achieved a very respectable half-million vote total. Furthermore, in the congressional elections, PCB leader Prestes was elected to the Senate from the Federal District and fourteen other Communists were chosen as deputies, giving the PCB the best elec-toral results of any Communist party in Latin America. Its success was mostly attributed to the personal popularity of Prestes, who was, after Vargas, the second best-known political figure in Brazil. In addition, as in Western Europe just after the end of World War II, Communist parties throughout Latin America benefited from the improved international image of the Soviet Union as a brave wartime ally in the fight for freedom against fascism. While suspicion of Communism remained well entrenched in Brazil, the war had helped the PCB to begin to recover from the stigma attached to its leading role in the abortive and violent 1935 revolt.[35]

In 1939 the fascist political systems of Germany and Italy had attracted admiration and imitation in Brazil. World War II, however, brought about the collapse and destruction of those regimes in 1945 and pointed to the superiority of democracy. For Brazil, the result was a growing public demand for an end to dictatorship and its replacement by a democratic political system. Guided by the military, a transitional process was effected in which Vargas was removed from office and the Estado Nôvo brought to an end. But the change was hardly revolutionary. The emergency of war had increased the centralization of government and justified more state interventionism and planning in the economy. Most of all, it had enhanced the prestige and resources available to the military, a development that would have enormous significance for postwar Brazil. In terms of foreign relations, World War II had considerably strengthened Brazil's ties with the United States while loosening political and economic links with Great Britain and Germany. For Getúlio Vargas, the military coup in 1945 was a personal blow, but only a temporary setback. The war had evidently not diminished his prestige or popularity because he soon returned to active politics and won the popular vote in the 1950 presidential election. The former fascist dictator, therefore, became a democratically elected president.

NOTES

1. For an expert analysis of political and ideological developments in Brazil during the 1930s, see Robert M. Levine, *The Vargas Regime: The Critical Years, 1934–1938* (New York: Columbia University Press, 1974). For a shorter and very readable study by the same author, see *Father of the Poor? Vargas and His Era* (Cambridge: Cambridge University Press, 1998).

2. A notable example of the growth of bureaucracy was the creation in 1938 of the Administrative Department for Public Service (Departamento Administrativo do Serviço Público, or DASP)

3. See Joseph L. Love, *Rio Grande do Sul and Brazilian Regionalism, 1822–1930* (Stanford, CA: Stanford University Press, 1971), 254.

4. For trade statistics, see Stanley E. Hilton, *Brazil and the Great Powers, 1930–1939: The Politics of Trade Rivalry* (Austin: University of Texas Press, 1975), 137.

5. A separate Brazilian organization was established in 1936. It was called the Federation of the 25th of July (Federação 25 de Julho) in honor of the first German immigrants who had arrived in Brazil on July 25, 1824. See Frank D. McCann, *The Brazilian-American Alliance, 1937–1945* (Princeton, NJ: Princeton University Press, 1973), 81.

6. The difficulties experienced by the ethnic German community in Brazil during

an earlier period of international tension are expertly examined in Frederick C. Luebke, *Germans in Brazil: A Comparative History of Cultural Conflict during World War I* (Baton Rouge: Louisiana State University Press, 1987).

7. For the political background to the Volta Redonda project, see John D. Wirth, *The Politics of Brazilian Development, 1930–1954* (Stanford, CA: Stanford University Press, 1969).

8. Quoted in McCann, *Brazilian-American Alliance*, 227.

9. Aranha openly admired the United States and described the country as "incredible" and a "land without equal." See Hilton, *Brazil and the Great Powers*, 52. Toward the close of World War II, Aranha began to distrust the intentions of the United States; see Frank D. McCann, "Brazil, the United States, and World War II: A Commentary," *Diplomatic History* 3 (1979): 75.

10. Caffery to Cordell Hull, June 17, 1940, in U.S. Department of State, *Foreign Relations of the United States: Diplomatic Papers, 1940*, Vol. 5, *The American Republics* (Washington, DC: GPO, 1940), 623.

11. Caffery to Hull, July 16, 1940, quoted in Hilton, *Brazil and the Great Powers*, 219.

12. Marshall to Sumner Welles, June 17, 1941, in U.S. Department of State, *Foreign Relations of the United States: Diplomatic Papers, 1941*, Vol. 6, *The American Republics* (Washington, DC: GPO, 1940), 499.

13. For details of the Lend-Lease Agreement, see Department of State, *Foreign Relations of the United States, 1941*, 6:528–38.

14. On the diplomatic controversy surrounding the conference, see Michael J. Francis, "The United States at Rio, 1942: The Strains of Pan-Americanism," *Journal of Latin American Studies* 6 (1974): 77–95.

15. Speech dated September 7, 1942, quoted in Robin A. Humphreys, *Latin America and the Second World War* (London: Athlone Press, 1982), 2:67.

16. An informative examination of the historical relationship is Luiz Alberto Moniz Bandeira's *Brasil, Argentina e Estados Unidos: Conflito e integração na América do Sul (Da Tríplice Aliança ao Mercosul, 1870–2003)* (Rio de Janeiro: Editora Revan, 2003).

17. See J. Lloyd Mecham, *A Survey of United States–Latin American Relations* (Boston: Houghton Mifflin, 1965), 152.

18. Between 1939 and 1942, the estimated strength of the army ranged from 66,000 to 95,000 soldiers. See Frank D. McCann, "The Brazilian Army and the Problem of Mission, 1939–1964," *Journal of Latin American Studies* 12 (1980): 108.

19. Quoted in McCann, "The Brazilian Army," 118.

20. Interview with Gen. Edson de Figueiredo, September 24, 1968, quoted in Alfred Stepan, *The Military in Politics: Changing Patterns in Brazil* (Princeton, NJ: Princeton University Press, 1971), 242. Gen. Mark Clark visited Brazil in July 1945 and conferred medals on senior officers of the FEB, and in 1950 Clark was made a general in the Brazilian Army; see Gerald K. Haines, *The Americanization of Brazil: A Study of U.S. Cold War Diplomacy in the Third World, 1945–1954* (Wilmington, DE: SR Books, 1984), 41.

21. For the view that Roosevelt's death "did not adversely affect Brazil's status in Washington," see Stanley E. Hilton, "Brazilian Diplomacy and the Washington–Rio

de Janeiro 'Axis' during the World War II Era," *Hispanic American Historical Review* 59 (1979): 223–28.

22. Oswaldo Aranha served as president of the General Assembly of the United Nations.

23. Vargas to Lourival Fontes, July 1951, quoted in Stanley E. Hilton, "The United States, Brazil, and the Cold War, 1945–1960: End of the Special Relationship," *Journal of American History* 68 (1981): 611.

24. See Ronald M. Schneider, *"Order and Progress": A Political History of Brazil* (Boulder, CO: Westview Press, 1991), 143–44, and Werner Baer, *The Brazilian Economy: Growth and Development*, 3rd ed. (Westport, CT: Praeger, 1989), 39.

25. On the inter-American trade, see table 2 in Gabriel Porcile, "The Challenge of Cooperation: Argentina and Brazil, 1939–1955," *Journal of Latin American Studies* 27 (1995): 140.

26. The findings of the U.S. experts were published in Morris Llewellyn Cooke, *Brazil on the March, a Study in International Cooperation: Reflections on the Report of the American Technical Mission to Brazil* (New York: Whittlesey House, 1944).

27. See Richard Bourne, *Getulio Vargas of Brazil, 1883–1954: Sphinx of the Pampas* (London: Charles Knight, 1974), 108.

28. A perceptive analysis on labor relations is Joel W. Wolfe's "The Faustian Bargain Not Made: Getúlio Vargas and Brazil's Industrial Workers, 1930–1945," *Luso-Brazilian Review* 31 (1994): 77–96.

29. See Thomas E. Skidmore, *Politics in Brazil, 1930–1964: An Experiment in Democracy* (New York: Oxford University Press, 1967), 70.

30. Quoted in E. Bradford Burns, *A History of Brazil* (New York: Columbia University Press, 1980), 436.

31. Berle to President Truman, September 4, 1945, quoted in Leslie Bethell and Ian Roxborough, eds., *Latin America between World War and the Cold War, 1944–1948* (Cambridge: Cambridge University Press, 1992), 52.

32. Berle to Truman, October 1, 1945, quoted in Bethell and Roxborough, *Latin America*, 53.

33. Randolph Harrison to Philip Chalmers, January 27, 1945, quoted in McCann, *Brazilian-American Alliance*, 448.

34. See Stanley E. Hilton, "The Overthrow of Getúlio Vargas in 1945: Diplomatic Intervention, Defense of Democracy or Political Retribution?" *Hispanic American Historical Review* 67 (1987): 1–37.

35. For the history of the PCB, see Ronald H. Chilcote, *The Brazilian Communist Party: Conflict and Integration, 1922–1972* (New York: Oxford University Press, 1974).

10

Chile: An Effort at Neutrality

Graeme S. Mount

Until January 1942, Chileans assumed that their country would be neutral throughout World War II, just as it had been throughout World War I. Geography separated Chile from most of the action, and there were strong political considerations, buoyed by key personalities in strategic positions, for not choosing sides. At the same time, Chile had a significant German ethnic population who voted in elections. Moreover, the fact that Chileans had a number of historic grievances against the United States encouraged a Chilean foreign policy that remained aloof from the lead of the United States. Another factor that determined Chile's policy during World War II was economics. Copper was a critical commodity for a wartime United States, while Chile needed oil and other manufactured goods. The mutual need to trade became a serious wartime issue between the two countries.

Yet, it must be remembered that Chile—like all countries—is a product of its history, and in Chile's case that history included the War of the Pacific against Bolivia and Peru. In the end, the aftermath of the War of the Pacific appears to have proved the most decisive factor in ending Chilean neutrality. While Allied victories on the battlefields pushed Chilean policy makers to support the Allies, a more pressing argument for cooperation was the fear that Bolivian and Peruvian support for the United States would lead to U.S. military assistance and diplomatic backing of those two rivals' claims against Chile.

In the end, the suspension of diplomatic relations by Chile proved a minor setback to the Axis but certainly not a decisive factor in losing the war. Through agents left behind in Chile, through Spanish diplomats, and through Argentina (until it terminated diplomatic relations with the Axis powers in January 1944), Axis governments continued to gather potentially useful information. Ultimately, the heroic men and women of the Allied armies, navies, and air forces deserve the credit for ridding the planet of Hitler's Germany, Mussolini's Italy, and Imperial Japan.

CHILEAN POLICY CONSIDERATIONS, 1939–1945

The Legacy of the War of the Pacific

Critical to an understanding of Chilean behavior during World War II is the 1879–83 War of the Pacific between Chile on the one hand, Bolivia and Peru on the other. The war had its roots in the failure of Spanish authorities to define boundaries separating its colonies from each other, especially through such sparsely populated regions as the Pacific coast north of the 24th parallel. This ambiguity was not a serious problem—until the discovery in the region of nitrates, which are critical for the production of fertilizer and gunpowder.

In 1874, Bolivian and Chilean authorities concluded a treaty which recognized the 24th parallel as their boundary and also guaranteed a freeze on the rates of taxation Bolivia would impose on Chilean nitrate companies located north of that line. Four years later, however, the Bolivian government repudiated the accord, and in 1879, the Chilean government of President Anibal Pinto declared war on Bolivia. Because Peru was an ally of Bolivia, it too entered the conflict. The Chilean Army and Navy ultimately triumphed, and Chile annexed Bolivia's coastal strip as well as mineral-rich land in what had been southern Peru.

To this day, Bolivians and Peruvians feel strongly about the loss of their territory and have been working to regain some or all of it. Chile, meanwhile, remains vigilant to ward off each Bolivian or Peruvian gambit. In late 1942, Chilean authorities became increasingly concerned about the likelihood of rising U.S. Lend-Lease arms shipments to their nation's erstwhile enemies. This fear was exacerbated by a series of boundary disputes with Argentina and the daunting possibility of war on two fronts.[1]

The German Population in Chile Prior to the War

One of the factors that determined Chilean views of the war was that country's large German population. Germans had been migrating to Chile since the mid-1840s, when the Chilean Army defeated the Araucanians and opened the area south of the Bío Bío River to European settlement. Germans were particularly desirable as immigrants to Chilean authorities because, like other Western Europeans, they had a strong work ethic but, unlike the British and the French, lacked a strong government of their own that might conceivably exert pressure on the government of Chile. The Immigrants to Chile included German liberals disillusioned with the failure of the 1848 revolutions in their homeland, pragmatists for whom migration to Chile was an opportunity for upward mobility, and nationalists disgusted at Germany's defeat in 1918 and what they perceived as the effeminate nature of the Weimar Republic. Chilean censuses do not distinguish the Chilean-born according to ethnicity, so it is difficult to determine how many residents of Chile in the early 1940s had German ancestors, but the number was significant. More importantly, the high educational achievements of this group gave German-Chileans influence disproportionate to their actual numbers.

In 1885, officers of the army of Imperial Germany began to train Chilean officers. German officers went to Chile, and Chilean officers-in-training went to Germany. This arrangement survived World War I, during which Chile remained neutral. In the Hitler era, some officers formed the Asociación de los Amigos de Alemania (AAA). The FBI discovered in 1942 that one AAA leader, Francisco Xavier Diaz, was translating German books into Spanish so that Chilean soldiers could read them.[2]

Chilean Relations with the United States Prior to the War

In the early twentieth century, the image of the United States in Chile was dismal. For one thing, despite the Monroe Doctrine, the administration of President Andrew Johnson had failed to lift a finger when the Spanish Navy bombarded Valparaiso in 1866. Given his unpopularity in his own country and the fact that the U.S. Civil War had just ended, it is understandable that Johnson did not go looking for another war, but not all Chileans were prepared to be magnanimous. Fifteen years later, secretaries of state James G. Blaine (1881) and Frederick Frelinghuysen (1881–1885) opposed the Chilean annexation of Bolivian and Peruvian territory. Despite their own country's seizure of Mexican lands in the 1840s, they were aware that German annexation of Alsace-Lorraine in the aftermath of the 1870 Franco-Prussian War had destabilized Europe, and they feared for the future of South America. To complicate matters, in 1891, when Blaine was serving a second term as secretary of state, the administration of President Benjamin Harrison appeared to support what became the losing side in a Chilean civil war.

Perhaps the most discordant event marring the relationship between Chile and the United States occurred in 1891 when sailors off the USS *Baltimore* were involved in a riot in Valparaiso, in which two died and others suffered injuries. An apparent war threat from Blaine forced a reluctant Chilean apology, from which sprang the widely believed—although untrue—legend of Lt. Carlos Peña. The story was that Peña volunteered to lower the Chilean flag as an act of contrition, and then immediately committed suicide. Chileans perceived the United States as a bully.

Finally, in 1930, the U.S. Congress and the Herbert Hoover administration adopted the Hawley-Smoot Tariff. This tariff, intended as a Depression-fighting measure to protect U.S. jobs from foreign competition, effectively excluded Chilean products from the U.S. market and worsened the unemployment situation in Chile.[3]

It was against this backdrop that Chileans read about the Japanese attack on Pearl Harbor of December 7, 1941, and the subsequent declarations of war between the United States and the Axis belligerents Japan, Germany, and Italy. At this point, none of the Western Hemisphere republics had yet entered World War II. In January 1942, their foreign ministers met in Rio de Janeiro and recommended that all countries in the region suspend diplomatic relations with Nazi Germany, Fascist Italy, and Imperial Japan. All complied, except Chile and Argentina.

CHILE CONSIDERS BREAKING
RELATIONS WITH THE AXIS

The Immediate Aftermath of Pearl Harbor

There were several immediate reasons for the Chilean refusal to break relations with the Axis countries after the attack on Pearl Harbor. First, Chile was in the midst of a presidential election campaign, and the governing Popular Front did not want to alienate voters of German extraction. Moreover, Chilean territory included a long coastline as well as many islands, including distant Easter Island. Until the United States started to win naval battles in mid-1942, the government of Chile feared attacks from Japanese and German submarines against Chilean ships and lands. When Under Secretary of State Sumner Welles, who represented the United States at the Rio Conference, tried to assure Chilean foreign minister Juan Bautista Rossetti that the U.S. fleet would come to the rescue, Rossetti callously responded, "What fleet? The one sunk at Pearl Harbor?" FBI sources indicate that Rossetti—who was of Italian extraction—was clearly partial to the Axis.[4] As long as Chile maintained diplomatic relations with Germany, it had little reason to terminate them with Italy or Japan.

In February 1942, the Popular Front, led by the Radical Party's Juan Antonio Ríos, defeated Conservative Carlos Ibáñez by a vote of 257,980–202,235.[5] Ibáñez had received substantial support from the Japanese government and the Abwehr, Germany's military spy service. On January 12, 1942, an Abwehr agent in Santiago also sought authorization to provide between $100,000 and $150,000 to the Ibáñez campaign. Ríos and the Popular Front politicians could not have known this, but they must have known that they owed no favors to the Axis. Indeed, the Popular Front had received money from British sources.[6]

Once the election was behind them, the Nazi provocations offered members of the outgoing government justification for a diplomatic rupture, had they wanted it. In the heavily German southern Chilean city of Osorno, Nazis had maintained such a high profile over the Christmas season of 1941 that Chilean police invaded the German vice-consulate there, arrested Vice-Consul Richard von Conta, and seized documents from the vice-consular archives. Rossetti returned the documents to German ambassador Wilhelm von Schön,[7] but first took the opportunity to read them, evidently believing that prudence dictated that all such groups be watched. Finally, in March 1942, a German submarine sank the Chilean merchant ship _Toltén_ off the U.S. coast, apparently by mistake.[8] Despite these provocations, Rossetti left diplomatic relations in place.

The Presidency of Juan Antonio Rios

Juan Antonio Ríos assumed the presidency on April 2, 1942, with Ernesto Barros as his foreign minister. The foreign minister's cousin, Tobias Barros, was Chile's ambassador in Berlin, and he sent Ernesto a steady stream of pro-Nazi commentary. As an officer-in-training, Tobias Barros had lived in Germany from 1926 to 1929, where, according to his memoirs, one of his friends was Alfred Jodl, who became one of Hitler's top generals.[9] While advising his cousin the foreign minister, Ambassador Barros received the Order of the German Eagle from Hitler's government for his role in promoting German–Chilean friendship.[10]

Ambassador Barros saw World War II as a clash of rival imperialists. That the British and Americans would ally themselves with the despicable Soviet Union, he thought, confirmed the irrelevance of ideology or morality. Barros chose not to discuss the reasons behind the Anglo-American-Soviet alliance. Those who spoke English, he thought, had little respect for Spanish-speaking people. Reports of German setbacks on the Soviet front, the ambassador reported, were exaggerations. He also forwarded as fact Axis propaganda of an RAF bombing raid on Paris, which was supposed to have killed six hundred and wounded one thousand. Tobias Barros was indignant at the British and American air raids on German cities, but full of praise for Ernesto Barros because he had refused to condemn German atrocities on the Soviet front. Tobias poured scorn on the United States for losing Kiska and Attu in the Aleutians to Japan on June 17, 1942, but ignored the U.S. victory of June 4–5 at the Battle of Midway. The U.S. victories of November 1942 in North Africa he dismissed as a sideshow. If the United States really had strength, he said, it would have attacked German positions in Europe.[11]

In his memoirs, Foreign Minister Ernesto Barros depicted himself as a Chilean nationalist. Chile, he wrote, had as much right to maintain diplomatic relations with the Axis even though the United States was at war as the

United States had had the right to maintain diplomatic relations with those countries when the United Kingdom had been at war.[12] In addition, he rejected as preposterous the idea that Axis diplomats were sponsoring Chilean-based spy rings that endangered Allied shipping. There had been no sinkings south of the Panama Canal, he observed. Chile could not accept the blame for more distant sinkings.[13]

The U.S. ambassador to Chile, Claude Bowers, tried in vain to persuade Ernesto Barros otherwise. Historian Irwin F. Gellman has identified Bowers as "the most vocal and influential critic of nazism in South America throughout the war."[14] Bowers told Foreign Minister Barros about the case of Johannes Szeraws, a commercial sailor who had supposedly deserted a ship named the *Frankfurt*, illegally entered Chile, and become the key person in the operation of a clandestine radio station with the call letters PYL. Bowers reminded Barros that the Chilean government had ordered Szeraws's deportation, but so vital was Szeraws to PYL that the German embassy had intervened on his behalf and requested Chilean authorities to let him stay.[15]

Chile as an Axis Spy Center

Captured German documents confirm Bowers's suspicions. On February 16, 1942, Ambassador von Schön reported to Berlin that he had found a reliable radio operator, one Pedro del Campo, who owned a shortwave transmitter and was ready to be useful if Chile and Germany severed diplomatic relations.

Having failed to persuade Ernesto Barros to close the Axis diplomatic and consular posts, on July 28 Bowers provided further documentation on German espionage to the Chilean foreign minister. Someone at the Foreign Office, not necessarily Barros himself, provided copies of these intercepts to an agent of the Abwehr named Brücke. Brücke realized at once that U.S. counterintelligence could "read" German radio mail. Brücke lamented that the Americans knew about "Bach" (a German spy whose real name was Ludwig von Bohlen), a radio operator at Antofagasta named Pedro, a contact person in Valparaiso, and others. Szeraws had disappeared. It was also unfortunate, thought Brücke, that the Americans had conclusive evidence that the Spanish diplomatic courier carried sensitive German documents in his pouch. Von Schön forwarded Brücke's observations to Berlin.

Further revelations confirmed that the Nazi espionage network based in Santiago extended thousands of kilometers beyond Chile's borders. Von Schön mentioned a payment to a spy named Leiser in the Brazilian capital. He also mentioned the arrest of another agent, Luni, in Havana. Von Schön had little doubt that intercepted telegrams were responsible, and Brücke added that following his arrest in September, Luni had been condemned to death.[16] Further details about this case are provided in a detailed FBI report on Enrique Augusto Luni, whose German name was Heinz August Luning. German businessmen in Chile—identified in the FBI report—had sent him funds and communicated with him by radio. So overwhelming was the evidence that Chilean authorities made several arrests in October 1942. On November 10, Luni himself died on the gallows in a Cuban jail.[17]

Yet, diplomatic relations between Chile and Germany continued. Moreover, in a letter endorsed by von Schön, Brücke sent the Abwehr a precise map on a scale of 1:25,000 of Ecuador's Santa Elena Peninsula. The map indicated locations for harbors, munitions depots, destroyers, and submarines. The Japanese military attaché in Santiago had managed to obtain the map, and Brücke forwarded it to Berlin with the Spanish courier, deeming it "too sensitive" for ordinary mail. Included with the map was a letter from the Ecuadorian president to his foreign minister.[18] So valuable was Chile as an Axis listening post that on July 9, 1942, von Schön asked Berlin for 100,000 Reichmarks to be used as bribes to keep Chile neutral.[19] This money may have delayed a rupture, but in the end did not prevent it.

Japan, too, used its diplomatic post in Santiago for purposes of espionage. On October 12, 1942, Japanese leader Hideki Tojo wanted a spy, identified only as "MO . . ." in Canadian intercepts, to study shipbuilding in the United States. (The FBI identified MO . . . as Rafael Moreno, a Conservative deputy in the Chilean Congress.) As Japanese could not travel to the United States in 1942, it was useful to find a sympathetic Chilean. So important was this information to Tojo that Keyoshi Yamagata, the head of Japan's Legation in Chile, gave MO . . . $5,000 and told him to ask for more if he found that he needed it "for his living expenses in the US and Canada." U.S. ambassador Bowers—apparently unaware that MO . . . was a spy—wrote a letter of introduction so that he could meet Under Secretary of State Welles. Finally, Yamagata instructed MO . . . not to return directly to Chile, should Chile sever diplomatic relations with Japan before he returned, but to file his report at the Japanese embassy in Buenos Aires.[20]

Chile Begins to Align Itself with the Allies

Several factors during the third quarter of 1942 persuaded President Ríos that Chile ought to align itself with the rest of the Western Hemisphere and close the diplomatic and consular posts of the Axis belligerents. Not the least was the series of Allied victories in the Pacific and North Africa, which strengthened the possibility that the United States might ultimately be on the winning side.

Little by little, Chilean foreign policy became less neutral and more favorable to the Allies. In August 1942, the Chilean government publicly protested when hundreds died after German submarines sank five Brazilian merchant ships near the South American coastline. The German action, said

Chile, was contrary to "international law and the rules of humanity."[21] Brazil declared war against Germany and Italy soon afterward, and the Chilean government softened the laws of neutrality for Brazil as it already had for the United States and Mexico. Brazilian ships could stay in Chilean ports for more than twenty-four hours and take on supplies. Their cargoes would not be considered contraband of war. They could acquire unlimited quantities of petroleum, not simply what was needed to go to the nearest Allied port.[22]

On October 1, the Chilean Foreign Office threatened to arrest Axis diplomats who continued to transfer large sums of money from Germany to Chile via the Banco Alemán Transatlántico in violation of Chile's foreign exchange laws.

Early in October the Chilean government also ordered the deportation of three Germans who confessed to operating clandestine radio transmitters and maintaining contact with Luni, the German spy in Cuba. One of the three, Alfredo Kleiber, had a rather high profile as manager of that same German bank (the Banco Alemán Transatlántico) in Chile. Von Schön's correspondence confirms FBI intelligence that Kleiber headed a valuable espionage ring. After all, he had subordinates throughout his bank's Chilean branches who could (and, according to the FBI, did) engage in espionage throughout the country. Unfortunately for the Allied cause, any helpful intentions on the part of the Ríos government proved of minimal value. Because Argentina refused transit rights so that the three Germans could board a ship for Spain, the Chilean government simply interned them at Zapallar, a resort town near Valparaiso. There they had minimal surveillance and extensive personal contact with German embassy officials, including the ambassador himself.[23]

U.S. Policy and Perceptions of Chile

Just as Chile was debating a break in relations with the Axis, U.S. authorities were debating whether Chile *should* break relations. The U.S. War Department was less than enthusiastic about a rupture. On August 1, the acting secretary of war, Robert T. Patterson, questioned the advantages of a diplomatic rupture between Chile and the Axis. The War Department needed Chilean copper, and Chile was providing it. Chilean shipping was "now immune from Axis attack," but after a rupture it "would be subject to hostile submarine action." These points, thought Patterson, more than outweighed the advantages of the diplomatic rupture, namely, an end to Chilean–Japanese trade, the elimination of Axis influence in Chile, and the setting of a good example for the rest of Latin America.[24]

Sumner Welles was dumbfounded by this line of reasoning. Despite Chilean obstinacy, he wrote President Roosevelt, the United States had sent Chilean authorities "four batteries and a few airplanes" in order that Chile might defend herself from a sudden Japanese attack. Certainly the Chileans wanted more, and the State Department would consider more after a rupture. However, continued Welles, there had been no commercial trade of any description between Chile and Japan since December 7, 1941, and most of the Chilean copper transported to the United States went in ships of Allied belligerents. The Japanese were not sinking those ships because they lacked the capacity to do so, not for reasons of goodwill. The rupture must come, said Welles, because of the Axis diplomats' role in "directing subversive activities" and in espionage, particularly with regard to shipping. The process of persuading Chileans to make the break was long and difficult—but if Welles was right, success could also force Argentina to do likewise. Hence, aggressive pursuit of the diplomatic rupture was highly worthwhile.[25]

Because of his conviction that Foreign Minister Barros was misleading President Ríos, Bowers requested—and received—an audience with Ríos early in September. Bowers discovered that Barros had indeed been withholding information from the president, "information regarding the use of telecommunications by the Axis." When Bowers presented his evidence, Ríos, he thought, "seemed stunned." Ríos appeared appalled that Barros had not forwarded the information provided to him by Ambassador Bowers, and Bowers "then showed the President a number of intercepts, in substance, which shocked him." Ríos also displayed amazement "that the German Embassy's telegrams had increased 216 per cent since 1941" given that there was no trade between Chile and Germany.[26]

There were other pressures as well. Bowers told Welles, his immediate superior in Washington, that the Peruvian ambassador had pleaded with Barros to make the break, but that Barros thought it essential that "some South American countries [have] contact with Berlin and Tokyo."[27] Then in mid-September, Nelson Rockefeller, the head of the Office of the Coordinator of Inter-American Affairs, paid a visit to Santiago. Bowers commented that Rockefeller had been able to do much that a diplomat would not do. The government of Chile had received him on the assumption that all economic aid to Chile depended on him. Rockefeller used the opportunity to convey the impression that unless Chile sided with the Allies, she would come to regret her situation. With his projected trip to Washington in mind, President Ríos told Rockefeller that he could not break with the Axis before visiting the United States "because of internal matters." Rockefeller replied that "in that case [it would] be better if he broke and did not go."[28]

Ambassador Bowers mounted a public relations campaign of his own, taking high-profile action to preserve a historic church in Santiago so that he might win some goodwill for the United States. When the priest had told him that the parish could not afford the taxes and would have to level and sell part of the property, Bowers spoke to Ernesto Barros, "as an individual, not as an Ambassador, as an historian with a reference for historic things."

Barros expressed interest, and the government reduced the taxes to a level the parish could afford to pay. The foreign minister then released to the media correspondence between himself and Barros on the subject. Said Bowers, "The press has been filled with fulsome praise of me." Bowers thought that he had won goodwill among Chilean Roman Catholics, whom the Spanish ambassador was lobbying on behalf of the Axis.[29]

U.S. Demands

The U.S. government, however, worried less about its image than about results. It wanted action. The first confrontation came over telecommunications. On September 5, Bowers sent a memorandum to Ernesto Barros saying that the U.S. government was "deeply disturbed" at Chile's ongoing communications links with the Axis countries. These links, said Bowers, were a threat to shipping, and therefore to human lives. Allied cryptographers, said Bowers, could read but a fraction of the messages, which were numerous. The German government was spending $6,000 per month to send telecommunications from Chile, said Bowers, despite the total absence of trade or tourism. To the memo, Bowers attached decrypted German messages about shipping and the impact of submarine warfare. One decrypt of June 12, 1942, dealt with a Chile-based German spy and his contact in Rio de Janeiro. Bowers sarcastically commented to Barros that Brazil must be pleased to discover that arrangements for German spies in Rio had been organized through the German embassy in Santiago.[30]

On September 24, Bowers discussed the issue personally with President Ríos, and the next day, Bowers repeated some of his points to Foreign Minister Barros. Despite the lack of commercial, financial, or travel arrangements with Chile, the German embassy, he said, was spending twenty-eight times—and the Japanese Legation in excess of thirty times—more for cipher telecommunications as they had before the war. This in itself should be grounds for suspicion. Even the operator of a clandestine Axis radio station in Cuba, charged Bowers, received ciphered instructions from Transradio Chilena, Chile's telecommunications authority.[31]

On October 16, Barros wrote Bowers that the Chilean government would no longer allow Axis diplomats to send ciphered cables to their capitals. The message from Transradio Chilena (written in English) to von Schön was somewhat less blunt but still to the point.[32] Bowers was pleased,[33] but some Chileans were not.

To his cousin Tobias Barros, still Chile's ambassador in Berlin, the foreign minister explained that Transradio Chilena had informed the government that it would no longer accept ciphered messages for transmission between Axis diplomats in Chile and Axis capitals. "The US Embassy was pushing for this, but we did not think it wise," said the foreign minister. However, as foreigners from Allied countries controlled a majority of Transradio Chilena's shares, they had been able to force a decision. Faced with a fait accompli on the eve of a scheduled visit by President Ríos to Washington (scheduled for September 22–29, although it did not actually take place because of ongoing political difficulties for President Ríos), the cabinet did not want a confrontation with the company, especially as many in Allied countries thought that the ciphered messages were costing them lives and property losses.[34]

The Italian government regarded retaliation as pointless, as did Yamagata, the Japanese head of legation. Communications, he realized, were far more important to himself than to Chile's minister (head of legation) in Tokyo.[35] Furthermore, von Schön and Yamagata already had a solution. From that point on, they sent their ciphered messages to the German and Japanese embassies in Buenos Aires, which faced no such restrictions and could forward them to Berlin or Tokyo. Effectiveness or results counted for more than dignity or strict neutrality. In a tit-for-tat reprisal, Chilean diplomats in Berlin and Rome lost the right to send ciphered messages to Santiago, but this also proved of little consequence. They simply sent their messages to Chile's embassy in Bern, Switzerland, which then forwarded them to Santiago.[36] Only Armando Labra, head of the Chilean legation in Tokyo, could not communicate confidentially, but it is doubtful that he had much to say. Cutting the ciphered telecommunications links with Berlin, Rome, and Tokyo was a step toward the curtailment of sensitive information to the Axis, but only a diplomatic rupture could make a significant difference.

The second confrontation came in Boston, where on October 8, 1942, Under Secretary Welles launched a blistering attack on the foreign policies of Argentina and Chile. Welles told his audience, people interested in foreign trade, that the United States was "profoundly grateful" for the assistance it had received from the other Latin American republics, eleven of which had become belligerents on the Allied side, and seven more of which had at least terminated diplomatic relations with Germany, Italy, and Japan. Argentina and Chile, by contrast, were acting in defiance of the Rio Conference and allowing their territory to be used for hostile activities against their neighbors. Because of such Argentine-Chilean noncompliance, Axis diplomats were in a position to send messages to submarine commanders. Axis submarines had then sunk without warning ships of several Latin American countries while they tried to carry goods from one republic to another. Those same Argentine-Chilean policies had cost many Latin Americans their lives. Thereupon Welles expressed optimism that Argentina and Chile would soon mend their evil ways.[37]

U.S. Pressure Builds

Bowers initially regarded the speech as a "heroic" pressure tactic.[38] At the same time, three past presidents rallied behind President Ríos against the "ugly American" who was providing their country with unsolicited advice. Santiago's most prestigious newspaper, *El Mercurio*, editorialized that the speech challenged Chilean dignity and ignored Chile's efforts to assist the Allies' cause.[39] Individual Chilean senators also expressed disapproval.[40]

Two days later, Ríos announced a further postponement of his already delayed trip to Washington, citing the speech as the reason. However, ten days later, he had a major cabinet shuffle. Interior Minister Raúl Morales and Industry Minister Oscar Schnake, both of whom favored rupture with the Axis, retained their positions within the cabinet. Foreign Minister Barros did not. Joaquín Fernández became Chile's new foreign minister.

As he reorganized his cabinet on October 21, President Ríos issued a public statement. Its essence was that each individual minister had made a worthy contribution to his administration. However, he needed a team, not a group of rugged individualists each headed in the direction of his own choice at any given moment. His goal, said Ríos, was to align Chile on the side of the rest of the Western Hemisphere, in defense of liberty and democracy.[41] *El Llanquihue* of Puerto Montt thought that the statement made good sense, and *El Correo de Valdivia* expressed optimism that with a more harmonious cabinet than the one he formerly had, President Ríos could cope with the foreign and domestic challenges facing him.[42]

Some people in Santiago had no doubt as to what the cabinet shuffle meant. Bowers told President Roosevelt that Ríos had decided that his failure to break with the Axis had been a mistake and that his foreign minister had become a political liability.[43] On October 21, von Schön reported a verbal duel between Interior Minister Morales, who favored the break, and Foreign Minister Barros, who did not. Ernesto Barros told cousin Tobias that his departure would be the prelude to a change in policy and the diplomatic rupture, and he sent a similar message to the government of Argentina.[44] While *El Mercurio* provided extensive coverage of the cabinet shuffle in its issues of October 21 and 22, it did not mention the question of diplomatic relations with the Axis as an issue. However, the *Times* of London saw that the departure of Ernesto Barros might well foreshadow a change in Chilean policy toward the Axis.[45]

CHILE SIDES WITH THE ALLIES

Trying to Reach a Consensus

It may well be that Ernesto Barros's successor, Joaquín Fernández, wanted a rupture as soon as he could find a plausible pretext. Yet because Chile was a democracy and the cabinet would need Senate support for what it was planning, Fernández chose to move cautiously. Fernández knew that despite the Allied victories of 1942, he could not achieve a consensus if he appeared overly subservient to U.S. pressure. He believed that the Welles speech had been a mistake. As late as November 24, President Ríos himself said that Chile would need military and financial guarantees before it could agree to such an "extreme" step as a diplomatic rupture.[46]

Of greater significance, however, was that the United States was supplying weapons to other Latin American countries, including Peru and Bolivia. These two countries had, of course, never fully reconciled themselves to their military defeat by Chile during the nineteenth-century War of the Pacific and to their subsequent territorial cessions. With the accretion of arms by Bolivia and Peru, the military balance of power in South America was changing, a matter of significant concern to strategists in Santiago. They feared that weapons provided to Bolivia and Peru for use against the Axis might sooner or later point in the direction of Chile. Chile could not afford to be in a militarily weak position relative to its neighbors to the north and northeast. Chilean officials in Washington therefore requested more weapons.

The reply from Secretary of State Cordell Hull was blunt. "The [State] Department," he said, "does not feel that it can accede to the request of the Chilean authorities that certain of the armament set forth in a list handed to the Chilean Ambassador by the Under Secretary last August be made available to Chile prior to Chile's rupture of relations with the Axis." Given Chile's limited support for the Allied cause, other Latin American governments would fail to understand why the United States was sending the weapons to Chile rather than to other, more loyal republics. Finally, as long as Chile maintained relations with the Axis, Axis agents would quickly acquire detailed knowledge of whatever arms and munitions the United States might send to Chile, as well as their location and intended use. The value of the weapons for hemispheric defense would accordingly diminish.[47]

Fernández told a secret session of the Chilean Senate that Chile could not afford to antagonize the United States at a time when Peru was strengthening its armed forces. Nor could it ignore Bolivia. Bolivia's president refused to accept the outcome of the War of the Pacific as final and claimed that his country's "just aspiration" for a port on the Pacific was "permanent" and "unshakeable." Bolivian authorities, Fernández reported, were also taking advantage of Chile's lack of cooperation to lobby other countries for support against Chile.[48]

On January 19, 1943, the Chilean Senate voted 30–10, with two abstentions, to support the diplomatic rupture with the Axis.[49] Most of the dissenters did not have German or Italian surnames, and they came from all parts of the country. The following day, President Ríos explained in a radio broadcast that Chile had a long-standing moral obligation to break with the Axis and had delayed only to establish a national consensus on the matter. Following the break in relations, Spain became the official protector of German and Italian interests in Chile, while Sweden assumed responsibility for those of Japan.[50]

The Spanish Connection

When Chilean authorities were on the verge of breaking with the Axis, Spain's foreign minister, Count Francisco Gómez Jordana, wrote to the governments of Portugal and Argentina expressing concern that the Latin bloc of "neutral countries"—Spain, Portugal, Argentina, Chile—which might mediate the dispute between the Anglo-Americans and the Germans, was disintegrating.[51] Furthermore, he asked Spain's ambassador to Chile, Juan Ignacio Luca de Tena, to use whatever influence he had to persuade the Ríos government not to make the break. Luca replied to Jordana that the rupture was inevitable. Bolivia and Peru had irredentist land claims against Chile dating back to the War of the Pacific, said Luca. If Chile remained out of step with the rest of the Western Hemisphere, Luca continued, the Ríos government feared that other countries would ally themselves beside Bolivia and Peru, against Chile.[52]

Spanish interests were far from neutral, of course. Spanish diplomats assisted German as well as Japanese diplomats throughout the Western Hemisphere. They were able to report on ship movements, as they did in April 1942 when nationals from Axis countries sailed from Arica in northern Chile.[53] On May 10, 1943, Bowers reported that the Spanish embassy in Santiago was organizing an Indo-American Society to continue the work of the AAA. On February 1, 1944, Bowers asked Washington to use its influence to pressure Francisco Franco to "cease using Spanish missions in Latin America in such a manner as to serve the Axis and create prejudices against the United States."[54]

For their part, because they abided the sham Spanish neutrality to avoid active Spanish military collaboration with Germany and Italy, there were limits to what the Allies could do to restrain Franco and his representatives.[55] If they could not stop them within the United States and the United Kingdom, they could hardly ask other countries to sever diplomatic relations with Spain.

Fortunately, such a rupture proved unnecessary. Franco and his diplomats had a series of confrontations with Japan, and, as a pragmatist, Franco began to distance himself from Hitler as an Axis defeat appeared increasingly likely. There is no evidence in the archives of Spain's Foreign Office, the Ministerio de Asuntos Exteriores in Madrid, that the Spanish embassy used its role as protector of German interests in any inappropriate manner. What documents there are show that in January 1944 Spain's embassy, under a new ambassador, the Marqués de los Arcos, became involved when the Chilean government placed restrictions on German financial institutions such as the

Banco Alemán Transatlántico and the Banco Germánica de América del Sur. De los Arcos reported what was happening to his superiors in Madrid, who undoubtedly relayed the news to Berlin. Whatever evidence there may have been of Spanish espionage on behalf of Germany has disappeared.[56]

Chile: 1943 to 1945

The rupture with Germany, Italy, and Japan was certainly not a panacea; Axis espionage was not suddenly halted. According to U.S. intelligence sources, on January 20, 1943—hours before the rupture took effect—Yamagata advised: "We have a simple means for communication between Chile and Argentina, which can be safely used following the break in relations." Nor was Yamagata bluffing. As late as March 7, Yamagata—still in Chile—sent ciphered messages to Japan's embassy in Buenos Aires for forwarding to Tokyo.[57]

Nor did the diplomatic rupture silence clandestine German radio stations that operated in Chile. Radio station PYL remained on the air until its discovery at Quilpué on October 27, 1943.[58] Action by the Chilean police, not the closure of the German embassy, terminated PYL. Moreover, PYL was not the only outlet of its kind in Chile. PQZ continued to function for an additional sixteen months. Indeed, there is strong evidence that it forwarded to Germany "plans or blueprints dealing with the Panama Canal defenses built in 1940–41."[59]

Bolivian foreign policy, which had influenced Ríos and Fernández in their decision to break with the Axis, continued to concern Fernández throughout 1943. At the end of March, Bolivia decided to declare war on the Axis, and its government suggested that the other four nations liberated by Bolívar—Venezuela, Colombia, Ecuador, and Peru—do likewise. Fernández thought that such declarations of war would not strengthen the Allied cause militarily, and he charged that Bolivia planned to declare war only as a means of winning U.S. support for its claims to a seaport and of gaining weapons for another war against Chile.[60]

Bowers regarded Allied military victories as more important than the rupture itself in winning Chilean goodwill and minimizing Axis influence. The liberation of North Africa in the first half of 1943 was a first step. On June 9, 1944, Bowers told President Roosevelt that the United States had won considerable support in Chile "by taking Rome . . . without destroying any of the religious or historic buildings." Two and a half months later, he reported pro-U.S. demonstrations following the liberation of Paris. The demonstrators ignored the British, Bowers noted.[61]

Chile did not actually enter the war until February 1945, by which time the U.S. State Department was threatening that failure to do so would mean Chile's exclusion from the United Nations. Fernández found the pressure from Washington "meaningless and possibly embarrassing." Members of the Ríos administration regretted that it came at a time when there was no obvious reason for a declaration of war and feared that senators and others would think that the Ríos administration lacked the will or the ability to protect Chilean interests.[62]

Even then, German espionage continued, headed by the veteran spy Albert Julius von Appen, aka "Apfel," until his arrest in March 1945. Von Appen was a businessman with the Hamburg-American Line for South America, not a diplomat, and his network extended into Peru, Argentina, Brazil, Colombia, and Venezuela. Chilean authorities first arrested him in October 1942 when they smashed PYL, then released him. After Chile's declaration of war and subsequent "ship disasters," they arrested him again. With the war in Europe almost over, von Appen confessed that he had studied sabotage in Germany, then traveled with explosives and codes to South America, where he organized activities in the aforementioned countries. Concluded J. Edgar Hoover, "Von Appen's confession reveals the scope of German plans for sabotage in South America, and also reflects that these plans have not been effective."[63]

ECONOMIC AND MILITARY CONCERNS

Economic Issues

Despite prolonged neutrality and nonbelligerence, Chile was in a position to assist the Allied cause and did so through the sale of copper and nitrates. Secretary of State Hull thought that the United States was "paying . . . unusually high prices for Chilean copper concentrates and copper ores" and discouraged Chilean exports of that precious mineral to other Latin American republics for the duration of the war. By July 1943, the U.S. and Chilean governments had reached an agreement on copper. In exchange for an inflated price which the United States government agreed to pay, Chile accepted controls on exports to other Latin American republics. By 1944, however, the U.S. copper shortage was not as acute, and the State Department sought to terminate the agreement. Bowers warned that if this were to happen, Chile would find itself under increased pressure to supply copper to Argentina, whose government's sympathy toward the Axis remained a concern even after Buenos Aires severed diplomatic relations with Germany and Japan in January 1944. In a worst-case scenario, Axis agents in Argentina might even stage a coup d'état in Chile. Eventually, U.S. and Chilean authorities found a way to lower the price the United States would pay for Chilean copper without increasing sales to Argentina,[64] and Chile in the end did not experience an Axis-inspired coup.

Because of the war, Chile lost some of its export markets for nitrates and asked whether the U.S. government might compensate by buying more. Rodolfo Michels, the Chilean ambassador in Washington, complained that the U.S. government, by purchasing vast quantities of Chilean copper and nitrate for the war effort, had distorted the Chilean economy but now refused to accept responsibility for what it had done.[65] By the end of 1943, the two countries managed to arrange a trade agreement.[66]

In June 1943, the Chilean government permitted the sale of three ships belonging to the Compañía Sud Americana de Vapores (based in Valparaiso) to the government of the United States, but this happened over the objections of Chile's minister of defense, who feared that Chile might be caught without appropriate means to defend itself in the event of war against Bolivia or Peru. How would Chile transport its soldiers to the battlefront?[67] By 1944, Chile's energy crisis was acute, and the United States agreed to increase that country's share of petroleum products.[68]

Military Issues

Supplies for the Chilean Army remained a problem. Since the late nineteenth century, that army had depended on German equipment, but with the suspension of diplomatic relations, the army had to look to the United States. With World War II in full swing and its own global commitments, U.S. authorities could not spare for Chile as much as the Chilean generals wanted. A coup d'état of December 20, 1943, in Bolivia rendered the situation more serious, as it was not clear whether the new Bolivian government might pursue an irredentist agenda.[69]

CONCLUSION

Chile had managed to avoid World War I, and Chilean authorities hoped that history would repeat itself. However, the world had changed, and geography no longer offered a guarantee against involvement in distant wars. Despite a Chilean desire for neutrality, pressure from both the Allied and Axis belligerents proved overwhelming. The substantial German community in Chile and a history of bad relations with the United States notwithstanding, the administration of President Juan Antonio Ríos could not ignore the possibility that Bolivia and Peru would acquire weapons and pounce on Chile. Moreover, by 1942, all of Chile's trade was with the United States and other Allied countries. Finally, as the Allies began to win victories, it seemed foolish not to be on the victorious side.

In the end, the war had negative repercussions for Chile in both the short and long terms. Chilean neutrality cost the country in terms of weapons, finances, and goodwill. It also left Germanophile politicians and military officers in place with their reputations intact. Carlos Ibáñez won the presidential election of 1952, and Tobias Barros served him both as foreign minister and defense minister. That, however, is another story.[70]

NOTES

Much of the material in this chapter originally appeared in my book *Chile and the Nazis*, published in 2001 by Black Rose Press of Montreal. The editors and I are grateful to Black Rose for permission to extract from that work here.

1. As recently as September 2, 2003, a U.S. State Department travel advisory was warning of "credible reports that land mines [might] pose a danger to hikers in remote sections . . . near northern border areas," near Punta Arenas at the southern tip of the mainland, and on Tierra del Fuego; U.S. Department of State, Bureau of Consular Affairs, *Consular Information Sheet*, September 3, 2003.

2. "FBI Reports, Chile," Franklin Delano Roosevelt Presidential Archive, 85–89; J. Edgar Hoover to Adolf Berle, September 24, 1942, National Archives and Records Administration of the United States (NARA), RG 38, Box 211.

3. Dexter Perkins, *The Monroe Doctrine, 1826–1867* (Gloucester, MA: Peter Smith, 1966), 539–45; James G. Blaine, Washington, to Judson Kilpatrick, Santiago, June 15, 1881, in U.S. Department of State, *Foreign Relations of the United States: Diplomatic Papers* (Washington, DC: GPO, 1861– ; hereafter cited as *FRUS*), *1881*, 131–33; Blaine to William Henry Trescot, December 1, 1881, *FRUS, 1881*, 146; Frederick Frelinghuysen to Trescot, February 24, 1882, *FRUS, 1882*, 75–76. For a more thorough review of U.S.–Chilean relations, see William F. Sater, *Chile and the United States* (Athens: University of Georgia Press, 1990). See also Philip Marshall Brown, "Frederick Theodore Frelinghuysen," in Samuel Flagg Bemis, ed., *American Secretaries of State and Their Diplomacy* (New York: Pageant, 1958), 8:9–17; and Joseph B. Lockey, "James Gillespie Blaine," in Bemis, *American Secretaries of State*, 8:146–63. For more extensive accounts of Chilean foreign relations to 1933, see Mario Barros Van Buren, *Historia diplomática de Chile, 1541–1938* (Santiago: Andrés Bello) and Sater, *Chile and the United States*. See also Ricardo Couyoumdjian, "En torno a la neutralidad de Chile durante la primera guerra mundial," in Walter Sánchez G. and Teresa Pereira L., *Cientocincuenta años de política exterior chilena* (Santiago: Editorial Universitaria, 1977), 180–222.

4. Sater, *Chile and the United States*, 114; Hoover to Berle, June 26, 1942, NARA, RG 38, Box 211.

5. *El Mercurio* (Santiago), February 2, 1942.

6. MAGIC summary no. 329, February 18, 1943, NARA, RG 457, Box 3; John Bratzel, "The Limits of Power: Chilean Neutrality during WWII," paper presented at the Grand Valley State University Historical Conference, 1993.

7. Von Schön to Rossetti, December 23, 1941; Judge Humberto Mewes to Rossetti, January 19, 1942; Rossetti to von Schön, March 9, 1942; Von Schön to Rossetti, March 11, 1942—all in Archivos del Departmento de Relaciones Exteriores, Santiago, Chile, Boveda 14 (hereafter cited as ADRE), vol. 13.

8. Rossetti to Tobias Barros, March 15–27, 1942, ADRE, vol. 1968, nos. 44, 46,

49, 50, 52–54; Tobias Barros to Rossetti, March 16–27, 1942, ADRE, vol. 1969, nos. 70, 77, 78, 81, 84.

9. Tobias Barros Ortiz, *Recogiendo los pasos: Testigo militar y político del siglo XX* (Santiago: Planeta Chilena, 1988), 2:159, 297–98.

10. Tobias Barros to Ernesto Barros, July 31, 1942, ADRE, vol. 1969, no. 172. There is no evidence in the appropriate volume, 1968, that the foreign minister responded. See also Weizäcker to von Ribbentrop, July 30, 1942, NARA, RG 242, Series t-120, Reel 183 (hereafter cited as AA), frame 88697.

11. Barros Ortiz, *Recogiendo los pasos*, 2:351. Also Tobias Barros to President-Elect Ríos, February 4, 1942, unnumbered; Tobias Barros to the acting foreign minister, January 19, 1942, no. 25; Tobias Barros to Rossetti, March 9–10, 1942, nos. 63 and 65; Tobias Barros to Rossetti, March 7, 1942, no. 61; Tobias Barros to Ernesto Barros, August 5, August 17, and June 28, 1942, nos. 177, 186, 146; Tobias Barros to Fernández, November 12, 1942, no. 259—all in ADRE, vol. 1969.

12. Ernesto Barros Jarpa, "Historia para olvidar: ruptura con el Eje (1942–1943)," in Neville Blanc Renard (ed.), *Homenaje al Profesor Guillermo Feliú Cruz* (Santiago: Editorial Andrés Bello, 1973), 31–96.

13. Ernesto Barros to Ríos, October 9, 1942, ADRE, vol. 9, no. 297.

14. Irwin F. Gellman, *Good Neighbor Diplomacy: United States Policies in Latin America, 1933–1945* (Baltimore: Johns Hopkins University Press, 1979), 112.

15. Bowers to Barros, July 9, 1942, with Bowers's Memorandum "German Espionage Agents in Chile," plus selected intercepts, ADRE, vol. 2012.

16. Von Schön to Auswärtiges Amt (Foreign Office), February 16, 1942, AA, frame 88469; Brücke via von Schön to the supreme commanders of the Abwehr, Busch and Stiege, Berlin, August 5, 1942, AA, frames 88703–88704; von Schön to Auswärtiges Amt, September 23, 1942, AA, frames 88760–88761; von Schön to Berlin, with a postscript from Brücke, September 25, 1942, AA, frame 88762.

17. "FBI Reports, Chile," 151–53.

18. The letter from the president to the foreign minister was dated December 26, 1941; Brücke via von Schön to the Abwehr, Berlin, June 3 1942, AA, frames 88643–88645.

19. Von Schön to Berlin, July 9, 1942, AA, frame 88680.

20. Foreign Office, Tokyo, to Japanese Embassy, Buenos Aires, October 12, 1942, National Archives of Canada, RG 24, vol. 20307 (hereafter cited as NAC), no. 965; "FBI Reports, Chile," 222; Yamagata to Buenos Aires, November 10, 1942, NAC, no. 1106.

21. Ernesto Barros to Tobias Barros, August 19, 1942, ADRE, vol. 1968, no. 130.

22. *El Llanquihue* (Puerto Montt), August 24, 1942; *La Prensa* (Osorno), August 24, 1942, quoting a United Press International report of the previous day from Santiago.

23. Von Schön to Auswärtiges Amt, October 1, 1942, AA, frame 88763; Ernesto Barros to Tobias Barros, October 7, 1942, ADRE, vol. 1968, no. 155; Bowers to Welles, October 15, 1942, PSF, Hyde Park; von Schön to Berlin, September 23, 1942, AA, frames 88760–88761. See also "FBI Reports, Chile," 73, 79, 126–27, 152–53, 170.

24. Patterson to Hull, August 1, 1942, PSF.

25. Welles to FDR, August 3, 1942, PSF.

26. Bowers to Welles, September 4, 1942, in Sumner Welles Papers Official Correspondence, 1920–1946, Franklin Delano Roosevelt Presidential Archive, Box 46 (hereafter cited as SWP).

27. Bowers to Welles, September 4, 1942, SWP.

28. Bowers to Welles, September 17 and 18, 1942, SWP.

29. Bowers to FDR, September 10, 1942, PSF.

30. Bowers to Barros, September 5, 1942, ADRE, vol. 2012.

31. Bowers's summary of his talk with Ríos is attached to a letter from Bowers to Barros, October 2, 1942, ADRE, vol. 2012; see also Bowers to Barros, September 25, 1942, ADRE, vol. 2012.

32. Transradio Chilena to von Schön, October 9, 1942, AA, frame 88789.

33. Bowers to Barros, October 20, 1942, ADRE, vol. 2012.

34. Ernesto Barros to Tobias Barros, September 14 and October 7, 1943, ADRE, vol. 1968, nos. 141, 154. See also the message sent by Ernesto Barros to Conrado Ríos, Chilean ambassador in Buenos Aires, October 6, 1942, ADRE, vol. 9, no. 292.

35. Yamagata to Buenos Aires, November 2, 1942, NAC, no. 1125.

36. The file on outgoing messages from the Chilean Embassy in Berlin is ADRE, vol. 1969, while that on outgoing messages from the Chilean Embassy in Rome is vol. 2044. To see the Japanese diplomatic traffic, examine the file of Canadian intercepts, National Archives of Canada, RG 24, vol. 20307.

37. Welles's speech appeared in full in *El Correo de Valdivia*, October 9, 1942.

38. Bowers to FDR, October 15, 1942, PSF.

39. *El Mercurio* (Santiago), October 10, 1942.

40. *El Llanquihue* (Puerto Montt), October 10, 1942.

41. A copy of Ríos's letter of October 11, 1942 to President Roosevelt appeared on the front page of *El Llanquihue* (Puerto Montt), October 12, 1942. The statement of the president appeared in *El Llanquihue* (Puerto Montt), October 22, 1942.

42. *El Llanquihue*, October 22, 1942; *El Correo de Valdivia*, October 23, 1942.

43. Bowers to FDR, October 19, 1942, PSF.

44. Ernesto Barros to Tobias Barros, October 21, 1942, ADRE, vol. 1968, no. 162; Ernesto Barros to Conrado Ríos, October 21, 1942, ADRE, vol. 9, no. 303.

45. *Times* (London), October 22 and 23, 1942.

46. Associated Press report from *Le Devoir* (Montreal), November 24, 1942.

47. Hull to Bowers, November 23, 1942, *FRUS, 1942*, 6:39–40.

48. Weekly Political Intelligence Summary No. 191, Foreign Office (Research Department), June 2, 1943, Series A 989/1, Item 43/145/411, Australian Archives, Canberra.

49. *El Diario Ilustrado* (Santiago), January 20, 1943.

50. Bowers to FDR, February 1, 1943, PSF.

51. Jordana to Spanish ambassador, Lisbon, January 15, 1943; Jordana to Spanish ambassador, Buenos Aires, January 15, 1943—both in Ministerio de Asuntos Exteriores, Madrid (MAE), Leg.R., Caja 1372, Exp. 1.

52. Luca de Tena to Jordana, January 16, 1943, MAE, Leg.R., Caja 1372, Exp. 1.

53. Madrid to Tokyo, April 24, 1942, NAC, nos. 168, 169.

54. Bowers to FDR, May 10, 1943, PSF; Bowers to State Department, February 1, 1944, PSF.

55. Carlton J. H. Hayes, *Wartime Mission in Spain, 1942–1945* (New York: Macmillan, 1945); Templewood, *Ambassador on Special Mission* (London: Collins, 1946), 15–16.

56. De los Arcos to the foreign minister, Madrid, January 24, February 17, and April 24, 1944, MAE, Leg.R., Caja 5749, Exp. 25.

57. MAGIC summary no. 358, March 19, 1943, NARA, RG 457, Box 4.

58. Bowers to Fernández, January 18, 1944, *FRUS, 1944*, 7:789.

59. See *FRUS, 1944*, 7:789–802. See also Leslie B. Rout Jr. and John F. Bratzel, *The Shadow War: German Espionage and United States Counterespionage in Latin America during World War II* (Frederick, MD: University Publications of America, 1986), 279.

60. MAGIC summary no. 386, April 16, 1943, NARA, RG 457, Box 4.

61. Bowers to Welles, May 10, 1943, PSF; Bowers to FDR, June 9 and August 24, 1944, PSF.

62. Bowers to Hull, December 5, 1944, *FRUS, 1944*, 7:691; Bowers to FDR, December 12, 1944, *FRUS, 1944*, 7:697. See also *FRUS, 1945*, 9:755–70.

63. Hoover to presidential adviser Harry Hopkins, March 31, 1945, Papers of Harry L. Hopkins, Franklin Delano Roosevelt Presidential Archive, Box 141.

64. The Secretary of State to the Ambassador in Chile (Bowers), January 28, 1943, *FRUS, 1943*, 5:827. See also *FRUS, 1943*, 5:827–44, and, in particular, the correspondence between Bowers and the State Department in *FRUS, 1944*, 7:705–35.

65. The Chilean Embassy to the Department of State, July 10, 1943, *FRUS, 1943*, 5:844–48; Memorandum of Conversation, by the Adviser on Political Relations (Duggan), August 31, 1943, *FRUS, 1943*, 854–57.

66. The Ambassador in Chile (Bowers) to the Secretary of State, November 24, 1943, *FRUS, 1943*, 5:857–59.

67. The Ambassador in Chile (Bowers) to the Secretary of State, July 9, 1943, *FRUS, 1943*, 5:881–82.

68. See the correspondence in *FRUS, 1944*, 7:738–52.

69. See the correspondence in *FRUS, 1944*, 7:673–91, especially Memorandum of Conversation, by the Adviser on Political Relations (Laurence Duggan), December 30, 1943, 673–75. For more information on the Bolivian revolution, see Bryce Wood, *The Dismantling of the Good Neighbor Policy* (Austin: University of Texas Press, 1985), 9; and Max Paul Friedman, *Nazis and Good Neighbors: The United States Campaign against the Germans of Latin America in World War II* (Cambridge: Cambridge University Press, 2003), 124–34.

70. For that story, see Graeme S. Mount, "Chile and the Nazis," in Marjorie Agosin, *Memory and Oblivion: Modern Jewish Culture in Latin America* (Austin: University of Texas Press, 2005), 77–89.

11

Argentina: The Closet Ally

David Scheinin

To judge by the contents of *Leoplán*, Argentina's most popular magazine of the day, a month after the Japanese attack on Pearl Harbor Argentines were not particularly concerned with World War II. The December 31, 1941, issue included only one report with some minimal relevance to the war: Leandro Pita Romero wrote an inconsequential piece on French diplomacy between the Treaty of Versailles and the beginning of the (unnamed) current war. The author sympathized vaguely with victims of Nazi aggression, but there was no commentary on events after August 1939. There were articles on women in Argentine society and a visit to Buenos Aires by Lord Carnarvon, advertisements for Palmolive soap and how to learn to dance by mail, a Georges Simenon mystery, and Charles Dickens's "A Christmas Carol." The formulaic contents of *Leoplán*, *Para Tí* (a periodical specifically targeted at women), and other popular publications remained unchanged through the mid-1940s, despite the conflagration abroad and revolutionary political change at home.

Through the war years, *Leoplán*'s editorial policy combined a mild nationalism—reflected in pieces on nineteenth-century *caudillo* Juan Manuel Rosas and the publication in Hungarian of the epic Argentine poem *Martín Fierro*—with a celebration of Hollywood celebrity, as seen in puff pieces on Shirley Temple and Joan Crawford. The works of Simenon and Dickens were complemented by those of other international literary greats, including Mark Twain, Guy de Maupassant, and Fyodor Dostoyevsky (German authors were inconspicuously absent from the magazine's pages). The "good life" was espoused in brief notes on and advertisements for health and beauty care. On the back of some issues were commercial pitches similar to those on equivalent publications in the United States; readers were instructed on how easy it might be to become an accountant, a cartoonist, a clothing designer, or a radio technician by correspondence course.[1]

For many U.S. and other foreign observers, Argentina's wartime history is one of, at best, stubborn refusal to support the Allied cause and, at worst, closeted and sometimes open sympathy for the Nazis. By and large, most histories of Argentina during the 1940s represent Argentines as having been dragged kicking and screaming into the war at the last minute, in a cynical effort to take advantage of postwar commercial opportunities and to play a role in the newly formed United Nations. Historians have approached the war years defending or lambasting Argentina's neutrality. Some have attacked Argentina's Nazi sympathies while others have worked to disprove them. But before 1946, most Argentines had little knowledge of the mounting overseas hostility toward them as "pro-Nazi." As Americans became increasingly impatient with what they viewed as an Argentine embrace of fascism, Argentines continued to admire Americans through authors such as Twain and, more important, through their fascination with Hollywood. In part, this explains President Juan Domingo Perón's success in generating anti-U.S. hostility at the end of the war. Argentines felt betrayed by what seemed for them an inexplicable American hostility; Argentines simply did not view their wartime neutrality as anything other than that—neutrality.

ARGENTINA'S VIEW OF NEUTRALITY

Leoplán's contents reflect the character of that neutrality. The absence of the war from its pages did not mark disinterest, but rather that, politically and culturally, the conflict simply did not have an impact on Argentina anything close to that experienced in belligerent nations, despite a powerful economic shock in South America as a result of international trade disruptions. Where Argentines did react to the war, they did so in a manner that favored the Allies. Argentine political and military leaders did not march in lockstep with the Nazis, as some Americans believed. While some in the Argentine Congress, diplomat corps, and military did favor close ties with Germany and Italy, and while some (though not all) Argentines of German descent sympathized with Nazism, most Argentines favored the Allied cause. This was evident not only in massive pro-Allied demonstrations in Buenos Aires and the ongoing popularity of Hollywood as the foremost foreign cultural import, but in Argentina's tacit support for the Allied cause through food and other exports throughout the war. As a major supplier of food to the Allies, Argentina was a closet Ally.

Beyond popular pro-Allied sentiment, life went on with relatively few changes for most Argentines, despite the profound historical shift occurring during those same years for reasons only indirectly related to the war. The most important of these changes was the armed forces' seizure of the Argentine government in 1943, which paved the way for the emergence of Perón, Argentina's dominant political leader of the last half of the twentieth century. Despite Perón's enormous popularity, he was never able to imbue Argentines with a lasting anti-Americanism in the late 1940s. The reason for Perón's failure is found in the pages of *Leoplán*. The fascination with Hollywood among Argentines in the early 1940s grew at the end of the decade and in the early 1950s. One important legacy of World War II was that in early Cold War Argentina, as in many Latin American countries, political anti-Americanism coexisted with a fascination for American popular culture.

The Argentine Economy and Neutrality

As had been the case in 1914, the outbreak of world war in 1939 quickly shook Argentina's economy. Argentina's declared neutrality, which lasted until March 1945, became essential to a series of economic plans to address changes brought by war. Argentine leaders set out to guide the economy toward firmer ties with the United States, without closing the door on trade with the other Great Powers during and after the war. Five years before the war began, Argentina had recovered from the Great Depression far faster than most Latin American countries. By 1935, agricultural production and exports had bounced back to pre-Depression values; in 1936–37, for example, grain exports reached new heights. Import substitution policies led to a boom in manufacturing, though by and large this did not include heavy industry. Textile production surged, as did a renewed wave of European immigration and, more important, massive migration from the provinces to Buenos Aires and a handful of other Argentine cities. Despite the growing importance of industrial production and the presence in the cities of hundreds of thousands of workers from the Argentine interior, neither of these dramatic changes had had any impact on political power in Argentina by mid-1939. The federal government remained in the hands of the Conservative Party, whose primary objective in economic growth and recovery after the outbreak of war was a return to agricultural production as an engine for growth, as had been the case a generation earlier.

Argentine Politics and Neutrality

With the outbreak of war, most political leaders regarded neutrality as the only logical path as they mulled over what to do in the face of a sharp decline in imports from Great Britain and other European countries. Shipping-lane disruptions emphasized the need for new and better trade deals with one or more of the Great Powers to offset this sort of catastrophic disruption in trade. While some Argentine leaders considered working on improving ties to Germany and Great Britain, neither was ever viewed as a serious or practical alternative to the United States. Argentine leaders saw Great Britain as being in decline and Germany as unstable. Finance Minister Federico Pinedo and Central Bank president Raúl Prebisch identified the United States as the only reasonable target for a new and comprehensive Argentine trade. Pinedo considered the United States crucial to ongoing Argentine economic expansion and argued that any Argentine material support for the Allies should be contingent on guaranteed contracts for Argentine exports.[2]

Through mid-1940, the Argentine government worked diligently for an elusive trade pact with the United States as a solution to Argentina's worsening economy, but also as a means of salvaging President Roberto Ortiz's democratizing political project in the face of the mounting political power of the armed forces. As the war depressed commerce with the other Great Powers, trade with the United States soared. In 1940, for example, the United States overtook Great Britain as Argentina's principal supplier of imports. American imports of Argentine products, including hides, quebracho wood, and wool, were primed by the war. They amounted to $166,618,000 in 1941, twice the import value for 1940 and the highest level of Argentine imports since 1930.[3]

Inaugurated in February 1938, Ortiz faced an almost nonstop series of political and economic crises that made it impossible for his government to hold back the growing influence of the military in politics. After 1938, the sharpening polarization between political support for and opposition to Ortiz stressed competing views among Argentine political and military elites over whether the government should tend toward Great Britain or Germany.

Ortiz had emerged as a democratic candidate backed by political conservatives and some supporters of the Unión Cívica Radical (UCR). He won the presidency on a fraudulent election but set about trying to build a viable democracy as an antidote to authoritarianism. As Ortiz pressed for a return to open electoral politics following the more restrictive, military-dominated politics of the 1930s, Argentines understood that such a move would favor the UCR, proscribed from full political activity since a coup d'état in 1930. Because the UCR openly favored strong ties with the British, those who backed strong relations with Germany, particularly within the military, tried to undermine Ortiz.

Once World War II was under way, the pro-Allied foreign minister, José María Cantilo, joined Ortiz in expressing support for the Allied cause. But their position within Argentina's foreign policy-making structure quickly became untenable. In the Foreign Ministry, within the military, and in government more generally—in a context of the growing association in the minds of many Argentines between the Allied cause and U.S. policies for hemisphere control—there was growing disdain for the Allies, even though popular sentiment remained consistently, if mildly, supportive of the Allied cause.[4]

ARGENTINA, ANTI-SEMITISM, AND JEWISH IMMIGRATION

In reference to Argentina's stand on Nazism, Argentine author Uki Goñi has attached tremendous significance to a July 12, 1938, message from Cantilo to all Argentine consulates. "Directive 11" instructed consuls to refuse Argentine entry visas to anyone leaving their home country as "undesirables."[5] With no corroborating evidence other than the assurances of his father—a World War II–era diplomat in Bolivia—Goñi concludes that by "undesirables" Cantilo meant "Jews." He argues further that every Argentine diplomat understood the coded language, which led to a shameful Argentine record on the admission of Jewish refugees from Nazi Europe during the war.

If Cantilo meant to exclude Jews from Argentina, as Goñi maintains, and if his directive did lead directly to Argentina's large-scale refusal of Jewish refugees during the war, the documentation Goñi offers simply does not demonstrate the case. Still, Goñi's analysis does make clear that Argentina's underlying support for the Allied cause was tempered by widespread anti-Semitism in its bureaucratic and political structures, as well as by the presence of significant numbers of pro-Nazi officials in government.

It is likely that the refusal of Jewish refugees during the war was no more or less orchestrated than it was in other countries in the Americas.[6] That is to say, while thousands of Jews were turned away from Argentina, this was the result of the same sort of decision making that led to equivalent patterns of rejection in (and numbers of Jews turned away from) Canada, the United States, and Brazil. Dozens of high- and mid-level officials in the Argentine Immigration Department, the Foreign Ministry, and a variety of diplomatic posts did what they could to turn back Jews, partly because of pro-Nazi sympathies and partly because of their own anti-Semitic tendencies. This did not mean that Argentina was pro-Nazi, but rather that anti-Semitism, a weak record on Jewish refugees, and stronger pro-German sympathies in some sectors of government than among the population at large could all coexist with a weak democratic government that tended toward the Allied cause in both its economic and strategic policies.

The fact that disproportionate numbers of military and government officials sympathized with the Nazi cause and represented a domestic political threat to the Ortiz government had little to do with German propaganda and other German initiatives in Argentina before and during the war. That sympathy drew in the first instance on a resurgence in conservative Catholicism during the 1930s, which featured a nostalgia for past linkages between the Catholic Church and the state. It fostered ambiguous notions of a Christian "social order" on questions of education, family, and the intersection between supposed Catholic morality and the law. It was also fiercely anti-Semitic, which elite Argentines found particularly appealing. As in the case of the rejection of Jewish refugees, while appalling, the virulent anti-Semitism in Argentine Catholicism was hardly unique in the Americas.[7] Conservative Catholicism was particularly strong among those army officers committed to overturning the Ortiz government, which the military viewed as secular and morally weak.

At no time during the war were the Axis powers able to capitalize on the anti-Semitism and pro-Nazi sentiment of some Argentines. Unlike trade with the United States, Argentine–German commerce dropped drastically once the war began and continued to fall for the duration of the conflict. In 1936, pro-German officers in the armed forces had established an arms-purchasing commission in Germany that functioned through 1944, but once the war began, there was no significant traffic of weapons between the two countries. To no avail, Germany pressed repeatedly for Argentina to relax its neutrality rules, particularly with regard to the presence of German naval vessels in Argentine waters.

ARGENTINA SHIFTS TOWARD
THE UNITED STATES

Whereas German officials found that Argentina could not be budged on its neutrality policy, the war marked a more complex period for relations between Argentina and the Allies. There were successive misunderstandings between Argentines and the Americans. While U.S. diplomats mistrusted Raúl Prebisch as "anti-American," the Central Bank president, like other Argentine democrats at the time, saw the fate of Argentine democracy as being inevitably bound to closer economic ties with the United States and a distancing of the country from Germany—whose supporters tended to back a stronger role for the military in Argentine politics.

In June 1940, Prebisch secretly contacted the U.S. embassy in Buenos Aires for help. War shortages had forced Argentine power plants to use corn for fuel. Prebisch wanted the Americans to send a representative incognito to Buenos Aires to help the government find a way out of this and other supply difficulties. He asked Washington to finance a substantial portion of rising Argentine imports from the United States through the Export-Import Bank. Prebisch tugged at U.S. diplomatic sensibilities. Such assistance would have "a very beneficial psychological effect upon the Argentine people who are disturbed by intelligent Nazi-Fascist propaganda," he noted. "The

Argentine government," he went on, "is now probably better disposed towards the United States and sees more nearly eye to eye with the United States with respect to the European situation than any other American Republic."[8] This and other appeals failed. While Argentina saw the United States as an obvious wartime partner, and while there no equivalent approaches to Germany, Americans saw no clear value in strengthening economic ties with Argentina.

Even so, Argentina's strategic and diplomatic policies continued to shift toward the United States. German propaganda in Argentina after September 1939 was strong and drew on the expertise and interest of a large German community in Argentina. But it was largely ineffectual until Pearl Harbor and the subsequent U.S. initiative to exclude Argentina and Chile from a Pan-American alliance. During the 1930s, Argentina had repeatedly refused to join a collective, U.S.-led, Pan-American defense initiative. But on war-related issues, Argentina's position varied little from that of the United States. At the First Pan-American Consultative Meeting of Foreign Ministers in 1939, Argentina backed the United States in approving the adoption of a 300-mile neutrality zone around the hemisphere. At the end of 1939, that zone was tested. After a firefight with the British warships *Achilles, Exeter,* and *Ajax,* the German pocket battleship *Graf Von Spee* limped into Montevideo badly damaged. Argentine authorities joined Uruguay and other Latin American nations in protesting the violation of the neutrality of Uruguayan territorial waters. Despite Germany's private diplomacy against such a move, Argentina then argued for a Pan-American declaration prohibiting belligerent ships from entering Latin American waters.[9]

In 1940 persistent domestic crises accounted for Argentina's interest in finding a united Pan-American position on the war. A quickly worsening foreign debt load and political unrest in a handful of provinces that led to federal interventions left the Ortiz administration shaken and divided. Partly as an effort to reassert control in an increasingly uncertain political climate, Ortiz encouraged Foreign Minister Cantilo to advance the position that the American republics set neutrality aside in favor of nonbelligerency. While in fact little different than neutrality, nonbelligerency suggested a less passive international response.

On April 19, Cantilo presented the argument that neutrality was too meek a stand for the American republics. He proposed nonbelligerency as a means for individual and joint action among the American republics to confront the belligerents on a range of military and economic matters. Historian Joseph Tulchin reasons that Cantilo timed the announcement of the nonbelligerency proposal to coincide with the worst of a series of crises unfolding in his now-shaky government. When the federal government intervened against the province of Buenos Aires in March, two cabinet ministers resigned. Foreign governments knew Ortiz was weak. The president was looking for a way to shore up his political position and sent Cantilo to the Pan-American Union with his nonbelligerency plan to do just that.[10]

The Argentine Navy, Army, Foreign Ministry, and other branches of government saw U.S. neutrality as a tacit but strong link with the Allies. In keeping with his goal of an overarching trade agreement with the United States as an avenue to Argentine economic prosperity, Ortiz's government wanted to push Washington away from Great Britain toward a more truly neutral position. In so doing, Ortiz hoped to disarm his pro-Axis political enemies and possibly dislodge the Americans from their leadership in the Americas on neutrality.[11] In addition, Argentine leaders continued to expect the United States to complement neutrality or nonbelligerency with an aggressive set of trade and financial guarantees to Argentina.[12]

The nonbelligerency initiative had the desired effect, but only very briefly. Signals of interest in nonbelligerency from Washington and some Latin American countries were matched in May with some popular support in Argentina for Ortiz's pro-Allied group in response to the German invasion of the Netherlands. But unwilling to give Argentina a diplomatic or strategic edge in the hemisphere and overwhelmed with news from Europe of Nazi advances, the American republics let Argentina's nonbelligerency proposal die.

The nonbelligerency idea had not prompted a U.S. government policy shift favorable to Argentina, and it also drew a rebuke from Germany. In May the German government accused Argentina of favoring the Allies. Germany was concerned that the Argentine initiative on nonbelligerency was in fact an attempt to assert Argentine diplomatic leadership in South America. According to the German foreign minister, the Argentines were trying to trade neutrality for "an active belligerency against Germany."[13]

Ortiz continued to lose political ground through 1940. With the German occupation of Scandinavia, Belgium, the Netherlands, and France and the British naval blockade of Europe, wartime disruptions decimated Argentina's grain exports.[14] Working with Raúl Prebisch, Finance Minister Federico Pinedo devised the Plan de Reactivación Económica or "Plan Pinedo." Its goals were to keep inflation down, employment up, and labor unrest at a minimum. Pinedo channeled funds into agricultural financing, tried to stimulate manufacturing, and promoted a South American free trade zone. The plan tied Argentina's economy still further to that of the United States. American importers, for example, would have to do their share to boost Argentine exports. The Ford Motor Company branch office in Argentina might have to export Argentine dairy products to earn exchange for car imports beyond a limited importation quota.

As it turned out, Ortiz's government fell before the Plan Pinedo could be implemented. The finance minister's earlier ideal of Argentina supplying the

Allies with food in return for a trade pact with Washington went up in smoke.[15]

Physically exhausted and ill, Ortiz left office in July 1940, and Cantilo followed him in August. Vice President Ramón Castillo took over the reins of government and in June 1941 named Enrique Ruiz Guiñazú as foreign minister. Under these two men, Argentine government policy became more sympathetic toward the Axis powers in the face of what seemed U.S. unwillingness to sign a bilateral trade pact. Argentine authorities left negotiated loan agreements with Washington unapproved. They criticized American intentions to establish military bases in Uruguay and made no effort to revive now-lapsed bilateral high-ranking military staff conversations.

American scholars have frequently attributed the hardening Argentine position toward the United States as a reflection of pro-Nazi sentiment both within government and among Argentines more generally. In fact, for Argentines, the circumstances were similar to those that governed policy during World War I. Many Argentines continued to believe that their government should stake out an international position clearly at odds with Germany and closer to the United States. But through 1941, many more believed that relations with the United States were much as they had been during the First World War. While Argentina traded actively with the United States under unfavorable conditions, the Americans pressed unreasonably for diplomatic and military leadership over the Argentines, demanding at the same time that Argentina rupture its neutral cordiality with Germany, a country on which the Argentines pinned strong current and future expectations for trade.[16]

THE UNITED STATES CONFRONTS
ARGENTINE NEUTRALITY

After Pearl Harbor, Argentine hopes were dashed for a friendly and productive relationship with the United States through shared neutrality. Always concerned over Nazi activities in South America, the Americans now saw Nazis everywhere in Argentina and quickly came to view Argentine neutrality as an excuse for tacit support for Germany. This was nonsense. According to historian Ronald C. Newton, there was never a Nazi menace in Argentina.[17]

To be sure, the Nazis did their best to generate support and establish a strong base in Argentina. In the 1930s, organizers arrived to proselytize in German-speaking communities. Others spread the word more broadly in Argentina, while some German diplomats made the case to political leaders, then worked hard to help ensure Argentine neutrality during the war. Between 1942 and 1944, Argentina became Germany's primary intelligence and covert warfare base in the Americas. There were many powerful Argentines, particularly in the armed forces, who sympathized with the Axis cause or were simply indifferent to the outcome of the war except as it affected the Argentine economy.

Nevertheless, as in World War I, Argentina maintained a neutrality that was increasingly pro-Allied as a function of the value of goods shipped to the Allies. And as in that earlier war, the U.S. government after Pearl Harbor viewed anything short of a military ally as suspect. Beginning in 1942, the United States began to curtail exports of dozens of categories of goods to Argentina, in part as punishment for Argentina's ongoing neutrality but also as a stockpiling measure for Washington's war effort. As trade with England, Germany, and the rest of Europe halted, only the United States remained as a source of manufactured goods, and because there was no alternative, the U.S. decision to spurn Argentine trade had a truly profound impact on Argentina during the war.

One area of spectacular impact that marked the connection of the war to the growing strength of U.S. influence in Argentina was in film production. During the 1930s, the United States had had a dramatic influence on Argentine film production in three ways. First, Argentine audiences loved Hollywood films. At the start of the Great Depression, with the exception of Australia, there was no greater market than Argentina for Hollywood movies. Second, Argentine producers looked to Hollywood film formulas as models for their own movies. Commenting on Mario Soffici's 1939 film *Prisioneros de la tierra*, critic Domingo di Núbila noted the influence of John Ford.[18] Frank Capra's impact was evident in Manuel Romero's comedy *La rubia del camino* (1938). Romero also made the first Hollywood-style Argentine gangster film, *Fuera de la ley* (1937). Third, American technology transformed how Argentines themselves made films and helped usher in the first great era of Argentine movie production in the 1930s.[19] The leading Argentine production company Lumiton, for example, built a massive studio on the Hollywood model of multiple sound sets on one location and brought in lighting expert John Alton from the United States to direct filming.[20]

Beginning in 1942, the Argentine film sector went into a long period of decline that came, in large measure, as a result of U.S. economic and political pressures. The United States included raw film stock among the items it embargoed for Argentine export. Without access to film in other markets, Argentine filmmaking simply ground to a halt. From fifty-six films in 1942, production fell to only twenty-three in 1945. As in many other areas, the U.S. government accused both the Argentine government and the national film industry of having pro-Axis sympathies. In fact, during the 1930s and 1940s, Argentine film culture was profoundly prodemocratic and antiauthoritarian. And although they banned Charlie Chaplin's *The Great Dictator* in 1940, even had Argentine authorities been pro-Axis, they would have had no means at their disposal to shape a national ideology through film. At the same time, the three largest U.S. film companies with subsidiaries in Buenos Aires earned strong profits—$300,000 in 1941 alone.[21] In conjunction with the embargo and the decline of Argentina's film industry, U.S. producers stepped in to fill the vacuum. By 1943, twenty-five films with Latin American themes were in production in Hollywood. U.S. producers brought Carmen Miranda and other South American film stars to Hollywood to "latinize" production and to fill the void left in the Americas by the declining Argentine output.

As the U.S. embargo shook the Argentine economy and helped to promote political turmoil, Washington financed a 1942 South American trip for author Waldo Frank in the hope that he might help bring Argentina into the war on the side of the Allies. Frank was an odd choice. Although he made some sense in an Argentine context, he was no favorite of the Roosevelt administration. Frank had won a following in Argentina as a result of his call for a "new American," an American who would combine what he called the mysticism and precapitalist ideals of Latin America with the grasping, aggressive drive of the United States. These notions, coupled with his assertion that Latin American elites should lead, gained him many adherents in the Americas. In the United States, though, Frank was not nearly as popular. His membership in the Communist Party, a writing style that was very difficult to read, and his lyrical ideas inspired by Ralph Waldo Emerson that seemed irrelevant in a United States at war, all served to diminish his standing and define him as a gadfly.

But in his lecture tours, Frank came alive as a pro-Allied propagandist. In one lecture, "Hacía la derrota del hombre," he urged Latin American young people not to join fascist gangs and accused fascism of humiliating mankind. In his speech "Llegado a Buenos Aires," Frank called on Latin Americans to abandon their World War II neutrality, to join the fight against the Axis, and to bear in mind that the political choice was a stark one, for death or for birth. Both the pro-Allied and pro-Nazi press in Buenos Aires knew of and publicized Frank's visit. Struck by the threat of military rule that he found, and in consultation with Argentine friends and colleagues, Frank agreed to speak at a prodemocracy, antigovernment rally at the Luna Park arena in Buenos Aires.

On July 30, 1942, the Buenos Aires newspapers *Crítica* and *La Razón* published Frank's "Mensaje de despedida a la Argentina," in which the American lamented a moral and political decline in Argentina tied to the nation's unwillingness to join the fight against Hitler. Two days later the Argentine government declared Frank persona non grata and on the morning of August 2, five men identifying themselves as police officers appeared at the apartment where Frank was staying. Once inside, all five beat Frank on the head with sidearms, while shouting pro-Nazi, anti-Semitic epithets.

When Frank yelled out, neighbors came running and the attackers fled. Argentine author Victoria Ocampo arrived shortly afterward to find the walls bloodied and Frank lying on the bed with a gash on his head.

Frank's beating was front-page news in several countries. An article Frank wrote for *Collier's* in September 1942 not only underlined his dismay over the political and cultural repression in Argentina but also focused public attention on the ugly side of Argentine "primitivism" that Frank had celebrated on previous trips to South America in the 1930s. One photograph that accompanied the essay showed a bandaged Frank lying in an Argentine hospital bed recovering from the beating.[22] Ironically for Frank, it was the press reports of the violence he had suffered—not his own chronicle of the trip, *South American Journey*,[23] or his other efforts to popularize Latin America in the United States—that had the greatest impact on American public opinion. Coverage of the attack in the *New York Times* and in dozens of other newspapers helped generate a popular sense in the United States that Argentina was inherently repressive and pro-Nazi, a popular view that would linger in one form or another through most of the Cold War. The attack on Frank and its coverage in both countries also heralded unprecedented tensions between the United States and Argentina over World War II and what the U.S. government had already concluded was a dangerous Nazi threat in the Southern Cone of South America.

In January 1942, the United States used the Third Meeting of Foreign Ministers in Rio de Janeiro to confront Argentina. Were Argentina to refuse a break in diplomatic ties with Germany, there would be no more U.S. military aid at precisely the moment when such assistance to Brazil was on the rise. Argentine president Ramón Castillo faced a dilemma: the United States demanded a diplomatic break with the Axis before it would resume aid, but the Argentine military had demanded of him that new U.S. military aid be agreed upon before any new diplomatic or strategic arrangement was negotiated with the Americans or through the Pan-American Union. There would be no break with Germany until the United States agreed to new weapons sales, now an impossibility.

Through 1943, the Roosevelt administration continued to press Argentina for a break with the Nazis. The Americans persisted wrongly in seeing Argentine neutrality as sympathy for Nazism. As in World War I, the British had a more sensible approach than the Americans to Argentina's wartime position—an approach that better reflected Argentina's contribution and potential contribution to the war effort. By early 1942, Argentina was already fulfilling a wartime role similar to that which it had undertaken after 1914: supplying the Allies with crucial foodstuffs and raw materials. The British believed that Argentine neutrality would, in fact, enhance its ability to continue to ship goods to the Allies. While the British joined the Americans in condemning what they viewed as Argentine wartime stands that favored Germany, they accepted Argentine neutrality and generally felt that the Americans were harsh in their insistence that Argentina join the Allied war effort. The British had a better appreciation than the Americans for the domestic and international pressures on Argentina that made marching in lockstep with the Allies impossible.[24]

THE ARGENTINE MILITARY SEIZES POWER

The Argentine military wanted to turn to Germany for weapons, particularly in light of traditional rival Brazil's growing power and its close ties with the Americans. Cut off from U.S. Lend-Lease matériel, Argentina entered into discussions with Germany for arms purchases, above and beyond the work of the languishing Argentine military commission in Germany. The Americans could not understand this move.

While Washington vilified Argentina as pro-Nazi, Argentine military authorities saw the government as weak and not up to the task of maintaining order, progress, and a strong military apparatus. On June 4, 1943, officers staged a successful coup d'état to topple Castillo. The United States feared this would quickly lead to an open alliance with the Nazis. In fact, the new junta hoped at first for better relations with Washington. The officers believed that military cooperation with the Americans would help chart the most effective path toward Argentine military modernization. The new, pro-Ally foreign minister, Adm. Segundo N. Storni, spoke publicly of Argentina's commitment to Pan-American military cooperation and told U.S. ambassador Norman Armour that Argentina would break ties with the Axis. However, U.S. secretary of state Cordell Hull wanted quick results that the Argentine government could not provide. A letter to Storni from Hull blasting the Argentine government was made public in Argentina and prompted Storni's resignation. Fallout from what Argentines regarded as a hardening anti-Argentine position in Washington strengthened the position of the nationalist Grupo de Oficiales Unidos (GOU), a secret officers' club unsympathetic to the Allies.[25]

The long-anticipated military coup d'état had come, but like Argentine society in general, the officers who came to power represented a mix of ideas on what direction Argentina should take with regard to the war. All were agreed on what they viewed as the need for an end to what they saw as capricious, irresponsible, and corrupt government masquerading as democracy. A majority of officers backed the sort of government that Ortiz had cobbled together—a loose grouping of parties in the political center that would move the country toward an eventual alliance with the Allies. The GOU represented a competing set of officers characterized by their conservative Catholic nationalism, their antipathy to U.S. influence, and their willingness to contemplate closer ties to the Axis powers.

It was the GOU that consolidated control of the military government by early 1944. The new government reversed Pinedo's position on economic strength through closer ties with the United States. There were no further discussions with Washington on new trade agreements. Economic policy shifted toward a plan for growth through massive industrial expansion and closer ties to neighboring countries, which Argentina's leaders planned to dominate. Argentine diplomats quickly and aggressively negotiated new trade agreements with Paraguay, Chile, and Bolivia. Relations with the Bolivian military were particularly strong, and when a military government came to power in that country late in 1943 with a pro-Argentine, anti-U.S. political agenda, the United States accused the Argentines of having sponsored the Bolivian coup as part of a pro-Nazi South American plot.[26]

Part of what the military understood as its purpose in governing was the suppression of growing unrest on the part of both students who were agitating for political reform and working Argentines who were demanding improved wages and better working conditions. The military government responded with growing brutality. As they had in the past, foreigners (particularly Americans) wrongly equated this with Argentine Nazism and a growing danger that Argentina would throw its lot in with the Axis powers. In October 1943, for example, after violently repressing a university student strike, the government imposed widespread curricular reforms in the nation's schools that included a return to Catholic religious education. A strike by meatpacking workers at the same time was also met with government violence.

But despite these authoritarian acts, the military also appealed to Argentines who felt disenfranchised by previous governments. The junta effected legislative firsts by reducing rural rents by 20 percent while freezing rent payments in the city of Buenos Aires. Tramway fares were slashed, and the military began to negotiate with the British government to allow the Argentine government's sterling reserves in British banks to be repatriated. While Argentina continued to ship foodstuffs to Britain, the British were unwilling to transfer payments for those goods out of the country during wartime. British officials quietly acknowledged that this represented a major Argentine contribution to the Allied war effort, but the Americans did not. For most U.S. observers, a repressive military government with a plan for state intervention in the economy and politics on behalf of the workers meant fascism with Nazi tendencies.

Though crop production had entered a long-term slide, through 1942 the Argentine economic situation began to improve dramatically, leading to formidable export earnings surpluses that would help prime social reform and other significant government spending projects through the decade. Construction in the cities thrived, unemployment dipped, salaries and bank savings rose, and Argentina experienced a new round of industrialization. Wartime export-led growth now made neutrality more popular, not less.

Argentines continued to see the Americans as those most determined to end Argentine neutrality, but the persistence of some popular anti-U.S. sentiment had little to do with pro-German sympathies and everything to do with what was seen as a U.S. threat to Argentine economic stability and growth.[27] Through late 1943 and early 1944, U.S. officials cut still more exports to Argentina, augmented arms sales to Brazil, and denounced the military government as fascist.

The British were horrified over the U.S. position. They appreciated Argentina's shipments of meat and found Hull's hard-line position both irrational and potentially damaging to Argentina's closet cooperation with the Allies. When the U.S. secretary of state suggested to Churchill that the British cancel their meat contract with the Argentines, Churchill angrily insisted to Roosevelt that this was impossible.

By early 1944 unrelenting U.S. diplomatic pressure was complemented by a virtual economic blockade against Argentina. Even so, on March 26, 1944, despite strong opposition within the GOU, Argentina broke relations with the Axis powers, still hoping for better ties with Washington.[28]

PERÓN TAKES POWER

During early 1944, Juan Perón rapidly rose to power within the military government. While the Americans viewed him as a fascist, Perón was a political pragmatist who stayed clear of pro-Nazi and pro-Allied factions within the armed forces. Designated director of a new Labor Department in October 1943, Perón was named war minister in June 1944, and he used the latter post to generate support among the officer corps. Because the War Ministry managed relations between the government and the armed forces, Perón supervised the assignment of matériel to different units and oversaw promotions. Through late 1944, Perón cast himself as a defender of Argentine interests against a rearmed Brazil and advocated a massive and quick rearming of the Argentine military.

The war minister also generated support among working Argentines by expanding military government programs in favor of tenants and workers. Through 1944, Perón took control of the country's trade union movement, purging communists from the ranks of organized labor and placing his supporters in positions of prominence within the union movement. He oversaw the creation of labor courts to mediate worker–management conflicts. And he introduced government-regulated and -mandated health care for workers, workplace accident benefits, and paid vacations. Union affiliations rose sharply through the end of the war, as did worker support for Perón.

When Cordell Hull stepped down in Washington as secretary of state in November 1944, some saw an opportunity for better bilateral relations. U.S. business leaders called for an economic rapprochement with the Argentines so that they might fully take advantage of postwar opportunities. The military wanted better ties with their Argentine counterparts and a revival of inter-American defense planning. Within the State Department, Under Secretary of State Nelson Rockefeller objected to Hull's hard line.

In early 1945 Perón spoke openly of the need for revived economic negotiations with the United States and lobbied for a postwar commercial treaty with the British. It was Argentina that called for a Pan-American Union meeting in 1945 to reexamine the possibility of inter-American cooperation. U.S. delegates reached the Chapultepec Conference in February 1945 concerned about shoring up support in Latin America for a new United Nations. But a number of Latin American governments warned that in return for such backing, they expected large-scale U.S. economic support after the war. They also called for Argentina's integration into the new body and pressured Washington to find a way to end its conflict with Buenos Aires. After preliminary discussions at Chapultepec, Argentina declared war on Germany at the end of March. The United States thereupon recognized the Argentine government, and Argentina was included as a founding member of the United Nations.[29]

The political and bureaucratic climate in Washington had changed. With Hull gone, Latin American specialists in the State Department, backed by Secretary of State Edward Stettinius, outlined a pragmatist position toward Argentina. To win Argentine backing for U.S. leadership in the hemisphere, the most effective policy would combine economic agreement with a more cooperative diplomacy. This dovetailed with a sentiment among some in the U.S. Senate that isolating Argentina simply encouraged the growth of communism. There were editorials in a number of U.S. newspapers calling for rapprochement with Argentina.

This warming conflicted with the activities of some lingering pro-Hull functionaries in the State Department. That persistence of anti-Argentine sentiment led to the appointment of Spruille Braden as ambassador to Argentina. Braden reached Buenos Aires in May 1945 and quickly set about making an unprecedented mark on Argentine politics and society—a mark that would have a lasting impact on bilateral relations. He pressed hard and publicly for the government to expel Nazi agents and to confiscate Nazi property. Perón countered that Argentina was continuing in its essential wartime role, sending foodstuffs to Europe. As a Perón–Braden antagonism grew through mid-1945, Rockefeller opposed Braden's hard line, as did the British government, which pressured Washington to recall him. But both

Rockefeller and Stettinius saw their power decline. Meanwhile, Braden had the backing of unbending Hull-era bureaucrats, political liberals, organized labor, and a national news media now convinced that Argentina was a Nazi outpost. *Time* magazine featured an illustration of a grinning Braden on its front cover holding a small, hand-held fogging machine. Behind him was a leafy branch in the shape of South America. In the area on the leaves where Argentina would be, tiny swastikas appeared like vermin.

Even though Argentina had never backed the Nazis during the war, this image of Argentina as pro-Nazi would continue to characterize how Americans thought of Argentines for decades. Thirty years later, in the aftermath of the 1976 coup d'état that ushered in Argentina's most brutal period of military rule, human rights advocates in the United States regularly (and wrongly) identified current human rights abuses with Argentina's "Nazi" past.[30]

At the end of World War II, Braden was named assistant secretary of state. Though no longer taunting Perón in Buenos Aires, in Washington he proved still more inclined to identify Perón as a Nazi. Braden played a major role in the development of a new, aggressive hard-line Argentina policy in Washington that would last through the end of the decade. He did all he could to thwart British–Argentine economic ties and won the classification of Argentina as an "ex-enemy." Under that designation, Argentina could receive no U.S. aid in the postwar period and would be excluded from taking part in new discussions on hemispheric defense. Again, the British found the American position on Argentina incomprehensible except as an irrational effort to denigrate the Argentines.

Meanwhile, in Argentina, Perón had problems of his own. In mid-1945, increasingly apprehensive over the personal power he wielded in government, the Argentine military removed him from power. But on October 17, a popular uprising led by Perón's partner Eva Duarte marked the start of Perón's campaign for the presidency in the 1946 election. Braden was determined to block Perón's ascent. In February 1946, only days before the Argentine election, he released the "Blue Book," a compilation of supposed Argentine links to the Nazis during the war. Intended to undermine Perón's campaign, the book had the opposite effect. Perón rightly labeled Braden's publication the grossest form of U.S. intervention in Argentine affairs, and he won the election in a landslide.

U.S. hostility during wartime had done more than usher in a nationalist government under Juan Perón. Years of U.S. hostility and bullying over Nazism and neutrality had created a popular base of anti-Americanism on which Perón was able to build his domestic agenda after 1945 in what historians Lila Caimari and Mariano Ben Plotkin call a "Peronization" of Argentine society.[31] Through the late 1940s, Perón's political language appealed to a revived anti-imperialism that, even when directed at Great Britain, drew on the hostility Argentines felt toward Washington. There was no mistaking the source of international oppression in 1949, for example, when a Peronist senator urged a doctrine of economic independence for the nation, where capital could no longer be a product of national or international oppression or enslavement.

After Perón's election in 1946, one of his first policy initiatives was to eliminate the external debt, which the government achieved by 1952. Perón's language in highlighting the foreign debt as a source of national weakness was replete with symbolism that emanated from the wartime conflict with the United States and a sense among many Argentines that the Americans were beating them down through economic bullying. While Perón's most celebrated nationalization of foreign capital was of British-owned railways, his language rarely stressed British dominance but rather an "anti-imperial struggle" that focused on the United States. In the first years of his government, as Perón began to transform May Day celebrations into a key cultural vehicle for his movement, recent U.S. hostility emerged as a target for the ire of Argentine workers. A May Day article in the 1952 Peronist organ *Democracia* admonished Argentines to remember that the enemy was not only Braden, but "all the Bradens" operating inside and outside the country. A year later, the same publication was even more explicit. It asked its readers, Who is our enemy? The answer was "the United States of America."[32]

CONCLUSION

When they thought of them at all, Americans tended to see Argentines very much as Spruille Braden and State Department intelligence had cast them: as irrational nationalists with Nazi sympathies. But ironically, despite tensions with the United States and despite Peronist politics, Argentines held on to their subtle and varied understanding of the United States. Despite much sympathy for the Peronist line and hostility to U.S. imperialism, Argentines continued to be attracted to the United States and to look to the United States as a trendsetter in many areas.

In the midst of the wartime crisis in relations, for example, Argentines never abandoned their passion for American consumer goods or Hollywood gossip. In 1941, the women's magazine *Para Tí* featured advertisements for Elizabeth Arden, Nivea, RCA Victor, Squibb, Brasso, Quaker Oats, and Helena Rubinstein. Another ad boasted that nine out of ten film stars used Lux soap. Betty Grable, whose photograph and signature appeared in the ad, commented, "I use it for my facial and my beauty bath."[33] In March 1944, thousands of Argentines leafing through the popular and widely read magazine *Leoplán* saw a photo of Joan Crawford happily combing daughter Christina's hair. An October 1944 issue made no mention of tensions between the United States and Argentina, but did feature an item on Ann Miller's world record for tap dancing speed and another one lasciviously captioned "Rita Hayworth's knees." In June 1946, only months after Perón's election, Argentines read cheery articles written especially for *Leoplán* about the Pulitzer Prize–winning author Louis Bromfield and canonical authors such as James Fenimore Cooper. They also saw cheesecake shots of studio starlets Leslie Brooks and Jane Carter and read the latest Hollywood updates on Jimmy Stewart and Ginger Rogers. In August, actress Evelyn Keyes was shown in a full-page photograph as a "naive vamp," while readers could ogle Leslie Brooks's legs, "the most beautiful in Hollywood." Despite five years of open hostility from the U.S. government and Perón's anti-imperialist response, most Argentines would not set aside what they liked about Americans.[34]

NOTES

1. These examples are taken from the *Leoplán* issues of April 13, 1938; April 10, 1940; December 3 and 31, 1941; October 1 and November 19, 1944; and April 3, 1946, and the September 30, 1941, issue of *Para Tí*.

2. Norman Armour to José Luis Cantilo, December 28, 1939, National Archives and Records Administration of the United States, RG 59 (hereafter cited as NARA), 611.3531/1445, no. 122; Cordell Hull to American Embassy, Buenos Aires, January 2, 1940, NARA, 611.3531/1441, no. 1; "Expónese hasta que extremo habría sido desventajoso al país el pacto con la unión," *La Nación*, January 14, 1940; David Rock, *Argentina, 1516–1987* (Berkeley: University of California Press, 1987), 241.

3. Randall B. Woods, *The Roosevelt Foreign-Policy Establishment and the Good Neighbor* (Lawrence: Regents Press of Kansas, 1979), 21–42; Andrés Cisneros and Carlos Escudé, *Historia general de las relaciones exteriores de la República Argentina*, part 2, vol. 10 (Buenos Aires: Nuevohacer, 1999), 290; Harold F. Peterson, *Argentina and the United States* (Albany: State University of New York Press, 1964), 410–12; Mario Rapoport, *Gran Bretaña, Estados Unidos y las clases dirigentes argentinas, 1940–1945* (Buenos Aires: Editorial Belgrano, 1981), 104–7; Tulio Halperín Donghi, *Argentina en el callejón* (Buenos Aires: Ariel, 1995), 130–31.

4. Joseph Tulchin, *Argentina and the United States: A Conflicted Relationship* (Boston: Twayne, 1990), 64.

5. Uki Goñi, *The Real Odessa: Smuggling the Nazis to Perón's Argentina* (London: Granta Books, 2002), 29.

6. Maria Luiza Tucci Carneiro, *O antisemitismo na era Vargas (1930–1945)* (São Paulo: Editora Brasiliense 1988); David Sheinin, "Argentina's Early Priorities in the European War: Compliance, Anti-Semitism, and Trade Concerns in the Response to the German Invasion of the Netherlands," *Canadian Journal of Latin American and Caribbean Studies,* Vol. 16, no. 31 (1991): 5–27.

7. Graciela Ben-Dror, *Católicos, nazis y judios: La Iglesia argentina en los tiempos del Tercer Reich* (Buenos Aires: Ediciones Lumiere, 2003); Leonardo Senkman,

"El nacionalismo y el campo liberal argentino ante el neutralismo, 1939–1943," *EIAL* 6, no. 1 (January–June 1995): 23–50.

8. Armour to secretary of state, June 17, 1940, NARA, 611.3531/1533, no. 229.

9. Tulchin, *Argentina and the United States*, 66–67.

10. Susana Pereira, *En tiempos de la república agropecuaria, 1930–1943* (Buenos Aires: Centro Editor de América Latina, 1983), 118–20; Tulchin, *Argentina and the United States*, 67; J. Edgar Hoover to Adolf A. Berle Jr., September 4, 1943, NARA, 835.00B/160; Espil to Cantilo, April 27, 1940, NARA, no. 226; Ministry of Foreign Relations, memorandum, May 6, 1940, NARA; Cantilo to Espil, May 7, 1940, Argentine Foreign Relations Ministry Archive (MRE), File 185, European War, no. 190.

11. Ministerio de Marina, "Cuestionario para el examen de la situación," n.d. [1941], MRE, File 192, European War.

12. Ministerio de Marina, "Defensa Continental Americana," December 2, 1941, MRE, File 192, European War.

13. Vicente Olivera, Argentine ambassador in Germany, to Argentine foreign minister, May 15, 1940, MRE, File 186, European War, no. 450; Cantilo to Argentine Embassy, Berlin, May 15 and 17, 1940, MRE, File 186, European War, nos. 249, 254; "Memorandum para la Dirección de Asuntos Políticos," January 24, 1942, MRE, File 186, European War.

14. Guido Di Tella and Manuel Zymelman, *Las etapas del desarrollo económico argentino* (Buenos Aires: EUDEBA, 1967), 472–85; Instituto de Economía Comercial e Industrial, *Libro rosado* (Buenos Aires: A. Riera & Cía., 1940), 17–25.

15. U.S. Department of State, Division of the American Republics, "The Pinedo Plan to Stimulate the Exports of New Articles from Argentina," November 29, 1940, NARA, 611.3515/6; Rapoport, *Gran Bretaña*, 77–80; Roberto Azaretto, *Federico Pinedo: Político y economista* (Buenos Aires: Emecé, 1998), 154–56; Tulchin, *Argentina and the United States*, 69–72; "Argentina to Seek U.S. Customs Union," *New York Times*, November 17, 1940.

16. Isidoro Ruiz Moreno, "Aide Memoire," MRE, File 192, European War; U.S. Department of State, Division of the American Republics, "Press Reception of the Argentine Trade Promotion Corporation," August 9, 1941, NARA, 611.3515/21.

17. Ronald C. Newton, *The "Nazi Menace" in Argentina, 1931–1947* (Stanford, CA: Stanford University Press, 1992), xiv; "Entrevista del Embajador de Alemania con el Señor Presidente de la Nación," May 31, 1940, MRE, File 186, European War; memorandum, May 20, 1940, MRE, File 186, European War; Edmund von Therman, German ambassador in Argentina, to Cantilo, June 10, 1940, MRE, File 186, European War, no. 86/40.

18. Domingo Di Núbila, *La poca de oro: Historia del cine argentino* (Buenos Aires: Ediciones del Jiguero, 1998), 264.

19. John King, "The Social and Cultural Context," in *The Garden of the Forking Paths: Argentine Cinema*, ed. John King and Nissa Torrents (London: British Film Institute, 1988), 6; Tim Barnard, "Popular Cinema and Populist Politics," in *Argentine Cinema*, ed. Tim Barnard (Toronto: Nightwood Editions, 1986), 14.

20. Agustin Mahieu, *Breve historia del cine nacional* (Buenos Aires: Alzamor Editores, 1993), 28.

21. Juan Antonio Heurtley and Andrés Chan, "El sonoro en la Argentina: Mitos

sobre el orígen y la crisis," in *Cine e imaginario social*, ed. Fortunato Mallimacci and Irene Marrone (Buenos Aires: Oficina de Publicaciones del CBC, Universidad de Buenos Aires, 1997), 20–23.

22. Waldo Frank, "Argentina—Unwilling Enemy," *Collier's*, September 26, 1942, 67–68.

23. Waldo Frank, *South American Journey* (New York: Duell, Sloan and Pearce, 1943).

24. Tulchin, *Argentina and the United States*, 84.

25. Cisneros and Escudé, *Historia general*, part 2, vol. 9, 75–77; Tulchin, *Argentina and the United States*, 87; Department of External Affairs (Canada), "Memorandum for the Prime Minister re: Mr. Hull's charges against Argentine good faith," October 4, 1943, National Archives of Canada, RG 25 (hereafter cited as NAC), vol. 2954, 3134-40c.

26. Kenneth D. Lehman, *Bolivia and the United States: A Limited Partnership* (Athens: University of Georgia Press, 1999), 82–83.

27. Rogelio García Lupo, *La Argentina en la selva mundial* (Buenos Aires: Ediciones Corregidor, 1973), 101; Daniel Lewis, "Internal and External Convergence: The Collapse of Argentine Grain Farming," in *Latin America in the 1940s: War and Postwar Transitions*, ed. David Rock (Berkeley: University of California Press, 1994), 218–19.

28. Daniel Rodríguez Lamas, *Rawson/Ramírez/Farrell* (Buenos Aires: Centro Editor de América Latina, 1983), 33–34; Miguel Angel Scenna, *Los militares* (Buenos Aires: Editorial Belgrano, 1980), 199; O. Edmund Smith, *Yankee Diplomacy: U.S. Intervention in Argentina* (Westport, CT: Greenwood Press, 1980), 92–93; Woods, *Roosevelt Foreign-Policy Establishment*, 147–49, 155; Department of External Affairs (Canada), "The United States, United Kingdom and Argentina," August 15, 1944, NAC, vol. 2856, 1607-40c (pt. 6).

29. Woods, *Roosevelt Foreign-Policy Establishment*, 184–87; Tulchin, *Argentina and the United States*, 90–91; Peterson, *Argentina and the United States*, 437–39; U.S. Department of State, Office of Intelligence Research, "Relationship of Inter-American Organization to a General International Organization for Peace and Security and to Such General Technical Agencies as May Be Continued or Established," March 21, 1944, NARA, Box 9, Lot Files; K. P. Kirkwood to secretary of state for external affairs, March 28, 1945, NAC, vol. 2955, no. 30, 3135-40c.

30. Tulchin, *Argentina and the United States*, 92; Leonardo Paso, *Del golpe de Estado de 1943 al de 1955/1* (Buenos Aires: Centro Editor de América Latina, 1987), 62–64; Ignacio Klich, "Perón, Braden y el antisemitismo: Opinión pública e imagen internacional," *Ciclos* 2, no. 2 (2000): 5–38.

31. Lila Caimari and Mariano Ben Plotkin, *Pueblo contra antipueblo: La politización de identidades no-políticas en la Argentina peronista, 1943–1955* (Buenos Aires: Instituto de Investigación en Ciencias Políticas, 1997), 20.

32. Cámara de Senadores de la Nación, *Diario de Sesiones, 1949* (Buenos Aires, 1949), vol. 1, p. 37; Noemí M. Girbal-Blacha, "Dichos y hechos del gobierno peronista (1946–55): Lo fíctico y lo simbólico en el análisis histórico," *Entrepasados* 6, no. 13 (1977): 66–68; Mariano Plotkin, *Mañana es San Perón: Propaganda, rituales políticos y educación en el régimen peronista, 1946–1955* (Buenos Aires: Ariel, 1993), 128, 139–40.

33. Advertisements from *Para Tí*, September 30, 1941.

34. "La colección de Ann Miller," *Leoplán* (October 4, 1944): 28; "Las rodillas de Rita Hayworth," *Leoplán* (October 4, 1944): 29; "Joan Crawford ama la actividad," *Leoplán* (March 1, 1944); Edward Green, "Campo abierto para Luis Bromfield," *Leoplán* (June 5, 1946): 8–10, 107; Alfonso S. Betancourt, "Fenimore Cooper: Novelista de la juventud," *Leoplán* (June 5, 1946): 14–15; "Ingenua . . . y vampiresa," *Leoplán* (August 21, 1946): 21; "Las piernas mas bellas de Hollywood," *Leoplán* (August 21, 1946): 20.

Select Bibliography

Archival sources are presented first, in alphabetical order by country, followed by *memorias* and yearbooks, general works (alphabetical by author), and finally country-specific books (also alphabetical by author).

ARCHIVAL SOURCES

Argentina

Archivo del Ministerio de Relaciones Exteriores, Buenos Aires. Relevant collections include the World War II series, Political Division, and Economics Division collections. Because there are no finding aids, archivist assistance is necessary.

Archivo General de la Nación, Buenos Aires. Details concerning the archive can be found at: www.mininterior.gov.ar/agn.

Papers of Enrique Ruiz Guiñazú (Buenos Aires). Privately held.

Papers of Isidoro Ruiz Moreno (Buenos Aires). Privately held by Prof. Isidoro J. Ruiz Moreno.

Brazil

Arquivo Histórico do Itamaraty, Itamaraty Palace, Rio de Janeiro. Permission for scholars to consult Brazil's official diplomatic correspondence with individual countries during World War II must be made by personal application to the Brazilian Ministry of Foreign Relations in Brasília.

Centro de Pesquisa e Documentação de História Contemporânea (CPDOC) in Botofogo, Rio de Janeiro. This repository holds the private Papers of Getúlio Vargas. Access is straightforward.

Canada

National Archives of Canada, Ottawa. Primarily Record Group 25. See also www.collectionscanada.ca.

Chile

Archivo del Departamento de Relaciones Exteriores, Santiago. A finding aid leads the researcher to specific files.

Costa Rica

Archivo Nacional, San José. Archivist assistance is necessary. The most important collection deals with the administration of German-owned properties. A few documents cover relations with the United States.

Dominican Republic

Archivo General de la Nación, Santo Domingo. Archival assistance is necessary to make the best use of the diplomatic records. There is very limited access to military records.

Ecuador

Archivo Histórico Ministerio de Relaciones Exteriores del Ecuador, Quito. Primary collections of interest include *Communicaciones Recibidas de las Cancilleríós Extranjeras: Estados Unidos, 1838–1949*; *Communicaciones Recibidas de las Misiones en Quito: País Estados Unidos, 1835–1941*; *Communicaciones Recibidas de las Misiones en Quito: Estados Unidos, 1942–1964*; and *Communicaciones Recibidas Misiones Diplomáticas: País Estados Unidos, 1937–1944*.

El Salvador

Archivo General de la Nación, San Salvador. Researchers will find only public records at the Ministerio de Relaciones Exteriores and Ministerio de Guerra.

Great Britain

The National Archives is the new name for the Public Record Office at Kew Gardens, London. See the Archives website at www.nationalarchives.gov.uk. The British Foreign Office records are a gold mine of information on Latin America and World War II because they contain not only official diplomatic correspondence but also observations on domestic political, commercial, social, and cultural affairs. British diplomats also often attached Latin American documents and clippings from newspapers, journals, and so forth in their dispatches to London. Foreign Office Records are organized in individual volumes according to individual countries under the general heading of F. O. (Foreign Office) 371.

Guatemala

Archivo General, Guatemala City. Archival assistance is needed to identify and retrieve specific files relating to World War II.

Honduras

Archivo Nacional de Honduras, Tegucigalpa. Very little material will be found here on World War II. Document collections are still housed and remain closed at the Ministerio de Relaciones Exteriores.

Mexico

Archivo General de la Nación, Mexico City. The AGN in Mexico City contains a wealth of information, but much of the material on the 1940s is not indexed. The AGN provides several basic collection guides to their materials for local use by researchers, including *Ramo de Presidentes, Lázaro Cárdenas (1934–1940), Manuel Avila Camacho (1940–1946), Dirección General de Información*, and *Departamento de Investigaciones Políticas y Sociales*.

Archivo Histórico de la Secretaría de Relaciones Exteriores, Mexico City. The Archive of the SRE provides a basic guide to materials for local use of researchers.

Nicaragua

Archivo Nacional de Nicaragua, Managua. Other than a smattering of Anastasio Somoza's letters, World War II documentation is missing.

Panama

Archivo Nacional, Panama City. Ministerio de la Presidencia, Panama City. Correspondence between Adolf Hitler and Arnulfo Arias. Documents are kept in unmarked folders. The National Archives in Panama City are not well organized. Many documents are not fully cataloged or indexed, and many are erroneously indexed. Any researcher who wishes to use the archives should follow a strategy of searching for as wide a range of years and documents as possible.

Ministerio de Relaciones Exteriores. Sitios de defensa, Tomos 1–17: 1942–1947. Contains the most complete accessible collection of documents on the subject of the base controversy during the period 1940–47.

Peru

Archivo Histórico del Ministerio de Relaciones Exteriores, Lima. Researchers need to obtain permission from the Foreign Affairs Ministry. The form to do so can be downloaded from the Ministry's web page (www.rree.gob.pe). A general catalog is also on line. Collections include correspondence between the ministry and its embassies and consulates around the world and between foreign embassies and consulates in Lima.

Archivo Histórico de Marina, Lima. Scholars may access this archive by writing to the archive at Av. Salaverry 2487, Lima 27. While rich materials are available through the 1920s, little is available for the 1930s and 1940s.

Centro de Estudios Histórico-Militares, Lima. Although it holds a substantial part of the Ministry of War and Marine records, archivist assistance is essential owing to a lack of finding aids. Scholars may use this archive by contacting the archive at Paseo Colón 150, Lima 1.

Puerto Rico

Archivo General de Puerto Rico. Archival assistance is needed to retrieve what little material is available on the World War II era. The U.S. National Archives houses the most complete records on Puerto Rico during the war.

Spain

Archivo del Ministerio de Asuntos Exteriores, Madrid. The Spanish Archives have country files covering each Latin American nation during World War II.

Archivo General de la Administracíon, Alcalá de Henares. The best material can be found in Caja 60, "15 D.N. Servicio Exterior, America-Latina, Correspondencia, Puerto Rico y Uruguay, 1937–1946."

United States

Library of Congress, General Collection, Washington, D.C. There are many Latin American government publications in the general collection from the 1940s.

National Archives and Records Administration of the United States, College Park, Maryland. The National Archives materials are well organized. Finding aids in the research room provide detailed information on contents of each file. Archivists are available to assist with the use of the aids and retrieval of materials. Some of the most important materials regarding World War II in Latin America are found in the following record groups and collections:

- RG 38, Chief of Naval Operations. This record group includes documents regarding U.S. naval wartime strategy and activities.
- RG 59, LOT file, Records of the Office of American Republic Affairs, General Records of the Department of State Department. There are separate files of diplomatic correspondence for each country.
- Records of the Office of American Republic Affairs; Office of American Republic Affairs, 1918–1947, vols. 1–3; and Division of Latin American Affairs. These include memorandums of discussions regarding the formulation and implementation of policy.
- RG 65, Records of the Federal Bureau of Investigation. This collection is important for understanding U.S. policy regarding Nazi espionage activities in Latin America. .
- RG 165, War Department, General and Specific Staffs. Contains material regarding U.S. Army and U.S. Army Air Force strategies during the war.
- RG 226, Records of the Office of Strategic Services. Contains intelligence analyses of internal affairs in each Latin American country.

- RG 229, Records of the Office of Inter-American Affairs. These are the records of Nelson Rockefeller's office and its activities in wartime Latin America.
- RG 242 is composed of captured Axis records.

Franklin D. Roosevelt Presidential Library, Hyde Park, New York. Researchers will want to begin by consulting www.fdrlibrary.marist.edu. Significant records are available in the President's Official File, the President's Personal File, and the Map Room File. Researchers should also examine the papers of Adolf Berle, Francis Corrigan, Harry Hopkins, Henry Morgenthau, Rexford Tugwell, and Sumner Welles.

Venezuela

Ministerio de Relaciones Exteriores de Venezuela. Relevant publications include *Anales diplomáticos de Venezuela*, vols. 6 and 7, and *Libro amarillo de los Estados Unidos de Venezuela*, vols. 1882–1968.

Memorias and Yearbooks

Most of the foreign ministries of the nations dealt with in this work publish a report on their activities each year. While these in-house publications generally put the best face on their own nation's activities, they can still be a valuable source of information.

GENERAL WORKS

Astilla, Carmelo Francisco Esmeralda. "The Martínez Era: Salvadoran–American Relations, 1931–1944." Ph.D. diss., Louisiana State University, 1976.

Bethell, Leslie, and Ian Roxborough, eds. *Latin America between World War and the Cold War, 1944–1948*. Cambridge: Cambridge University Press, 1992.

Blancpain, Jean-Pierre. *Les Allemands au Chile, 1816–1945*. Cologne, West Germany: Böhlau Verlag, 1974.

Child, John. "From 'Color' to 'Rainbow': U.S. Strategic Planning for Latin America, 1919–1945." *Journal of Interamerican Studies and World Affairs* (May 1979): 233–59.

Conn, Stetson, Ross Engelman, and Byron Fairchild. *The United States Army in World War II: Guarding the United States and Its Outposts*, Washington, DC: Office of the Chief of Military History, Department of the Army, 1964.

Conn, Stetson, and Byron Fairchild. *The United States Army in World War II: The Western Hemisphere; The Framework of Hemisphere Defense*. Washington, DC: Office of the Chief of Military History, Department of the Army, 1960.

Conniff, Michael. "Panama since 1903." In *The Cambridge History of Latin America*, ed. Leslie Bethell, 7:603–47. New York: Cambridge University Press, 1990.

Corbett, P. Scott. *Quiet Passages: The Exchange of Civilians between the United*

States and Japan during World War II. Kent, Ohio: Kent State University Press, 1987.

Cornwell, John. *Hitler's Pope: The Secret History of Pius XII.* New York: Viking, 1999.

Davies, R. E. G. *Airlines of Latin America since 1919.* Washington, DC: Smithsonian Institution Press, 1984.

Derby, Lauren H. "Magic, Money and Haitians: Raza and Society in the Haitian-Dominican Borderlands, 1900–1937." *Comparative Studies in Society and History* (July 1994): 488–526.

Dooley, Edwin R., Jr. "Wartime San Juan, Puerto Rico: The Forgotten American Homefront, 1941–1945." *Journal of Military History* 63, no. 4 (October 1999): 921–38.

Erb, Claude Curtis. "Nelson Rockefeller and United States–Latin American Relations, 1940–1945." Ph.D. diss., Clark University, 1982.

Espinosa, J. Manuel. *Inter-American Beginnings of U.S. Cultural Diplomacy, 1936–1948.* International Information and Cultural Series, no. 110. Washington, DC: Bureau of Education and Cultural Affairs, U.S. Department of State, 1976.

Fernandez, Ronald. *The Disenchanted Island: Puerto Rico and the United States in the Twentieth Century.* 2nd ed. Westport, CT: Praeger, 1996.

Frank, Waldo. *South American Journey.* New York: Duell, Sloan and Pearce, 1943.

Friedman, Max Paul. *Nazis and Good Neighbors: The United States Campaign against the Germans of Latin America in World War II.* Cambridge: Cambridge University Press, 2003.

Gallo, Max. *Spain under Franco.* New York: E. P. Dutton, 1974.

Gannon, Michael. *Operation Drumbeat: The Dramatic True Story of Germany's First U-Boat Attacks along the American Coast in World War II.* New York: Harper and Row, 1990.

Gellman, Irwin. *Good Neighbor Diplomacy.* Baltimore: Johns Hopkins University Press, 1979.

Hagedorn, Dan. "Lend Lease to Latin America, Part I: Army Aircraft." *Journal of the American Aviation Historical Society* (Summer 1989): 108–23.

Haglund, David G. *Latin America and the Transformation of U.S. Strategic Thought.* Albuquerque: University of New Mexico Press, 1984.

Hilton, Stanley E. "The United States, Brazil, and the Cold War, 1945–1960: End of the Special Relationship." *Journal of American History* 68 (1981): 599–624.

Holden, Robert H., and Eric Zolov. *Latin America and the United States: A Documentary History.* New York: Oxford University Press, 2000.

Humphreys, R. A. *Latin America and the Second World War.* Vol. 1, *1939–1942.* Vol. 2, *1942–1945.* London: University of London, Institute of Latin American Studies, 1981, 1982.

Kahn, David. *Hitler's Spies: German Military Intelligence in World War II.* 1st Da Capo ed. Cambridge, MA: Da Capo Press, 2000.

Lewy, Guenter. *The Catholic Church and Nazi Germany.* 1st Da Capo ed. Boulder, CO: Da Capo Press, 2000.

Mahan, Alfred Thayer. *The Influence of Sea Power upon History, 1660–1783.* 2nd ed. London: Methuen, 1965.

Masterson, Daniel M. "Caudillismo and Institutional Change: Manuel Odria and the Peruvian Armed Forces, 1948–1956." *Americas* 40, no. 4 (April 1984): 479–89.

Masterson, Daniel M., with Sayaka Funada-Classen. *The Japanese in Latin America.* Urbana: University of Illinois Press, 2004.

McCann, Frank. "The Brazilian Army and the Problem of Mission, 1939–1964." *Journal of Latin American Studies* 12 (1980): 107–26.

———. "Brazil, the United States, and World War II: A Commentary." *Diplomatic History* 3 (1979): 59–76.

Morales Carrión, Arturo. *Puerto Rico: A Political and Cultural History.* New York: W. W. Norton, 1983.

Morison, Samuel Eliot. *History of United States Naval Operations in World War II.* Vol. 1, *The Battle of the Atlantic, September 1939–May 1943.* Boston: Little, Brown, 1961.

Mount, Graeme. "Some Thoughts on Puerto Rican 'Loyalism' in the Nineteenth Century." *Canadian Journal of Latin Studies* 5, no. 9 (1980): 31–66.

Niblo, Stephen R. "British Propaganda in Mexico during the Second World War: The Development of Cultural Imperialism." *Latin American Perspectives* 10, no. 4 (1983): 114–26.

Porcile, Gabriel, "The Challenge of Cooperation: Argentina and Brazil, 1939–1955." *Journal of Latin American Studies* 27, no. 1 (February 1995): 129–55.

Rankin, Monica A. "¡Mexico la patria! Modernity, National Unity, and Propaganda during World War II." Ph.D. diss., University of Arizona, 2004.

Rodriguez, Avinola Pastora. "La prensa nacional frente a la intervención de México en la segunda guerra mundial." *Historia Mexicana* 29, no. 2 (1979): 252–300.

Rodriguez Asti, John. "La actuación de Marina de Guerra del Peru durante la segunda guerra mundial." In *Actas del VI Simposium de Historia Maritima y Naval de Iberoamerica,* 271–287. Lima: Instituto de Estudios Historico-Maritimos del Peru, 2003.

Roorda, Eric Paul. "The Cult of the Airplane among U.S. Military Men and Dominicans during the U.S. Occupation and the Trujillo Regime." In *Close Encounters of Empire: Writing the Cultural History of U.S.–Latin American Relations,* ed. Gilbert M. Joseph, Catherine C. LeGrand, and Ricardo D. Salvatore, 269–310 (Durham, NC: Duke University Press, 1998).

Rout, Leslie B., and John F. Bratzel. "FDR and World War II: The South American Map Case." *Woodrow Wilson Quarterly* 9, no. 1 (January 1985): 167–81.

Scheina, Robert L. "Major Boundary Disputes between the Wars: Ecuador and Peru." In *Latin America's Wars: The Age of the Professional Soldier,* 2:114–27 (Washington, DC: Brassey's, 2003).

Schoultz, Lars. *Beneath the United States: A History of U.S. Policy toward Latin America.* Cambridge, MA: Harvard University Press, 1998.

Senkman, Leonardo. "El nacionalismo y el campo liberal argentino ante el neutralismo, 1939–1943." *EIAL* 6, no. 1 (January–June 1995): 23–50.

Sheinin, David. "Argentina's Early Priorities in the European War: Compliance, Anti-Semitism, and Trade Concerns in the Response to the German Invasion of the Netherlands." *Canadian Journal of Latin American and Caribbean Studies* 16, no. 31 (1991): 5–27.

Torres Rivera, Alejandro. *Militarismo y descolonización: Puerto Rico ante el siglo 21.* San Juan: Congreso Nacional Hostosiano, 1999.

Uhlig, Frank, Jr. *How Navies Fight: The US Navy and Its Allies.* Annapolis, MD: Naval Institute Press, 1994.

Vilar, Pierre. *Spain: A Brief History.* Toronto: Pergamon Press, 1967.

Wood Clash, Thomas. "United States–Mexican Relations, 1940–1946: A Study of U.S. Interests and Policies." Ph.D. diss., State University of New York, 1972.

COUNTRY-SPECIFIC BOOKS

Argueta, Mario. *Los Alemanes en Honduras.* Tegucigalpa: Centro de Documentación de Honduras, 1992.

Atkins, G. Pope, and Larman C. Wilson. *The Dominican Republic and the United States: From Nationalism to Imperialism.* Athens: University of Georgia Press, 1998.

Baer, George W. *One Hundred Years of Sea Power: The US Navy, 1890–1990.* Stanford, CA: Stanford University Press, 1994.

Baptiste, Fitzroy. *War, Cooperation and Conflict: The European Possessions in the Caribbean, 1939–1945.* New York: Greenwood Press.

Barros Jarpa, Ernesto. "Historia para olvidar: Ruptura con el Eje, 1942–1943," in *Homenaje al Profesor Guillermo Feliú Cruz*, ed. Neville Blanc Renard. Santiago: Editorial Andrés Bello, 1973.

Barros van Buren, Mario. *Historia diplomática de Chile, 1541–1938.* Santiago: Andrés Bello, 1971.

Beluche Mora, Isidro A. *Acción comunal, surgimiento y estructuración del nacionalismo panameño.* Panama City: Editorial Condor, 1981.

Ben-Dror, Graciela. *Católicos, nazis y judios: La iglesia argentina en los tiempos del Tercer Reich.* Buenos Aires: Ediciones Lumiere, 2003.

Bushnell, David. *Eduardo Santos and the Good Neighbor, 1938–1942.* Gainesville: University of Florida Press, 1967.

Carr, Raymond. *Puerto Rico: A Colonial Experiment.* New York: New York University Press, 1984.

Castillero Pimentel, Ernesto. *Panamá y los Estados Unidos, 1903–1953: Significado y alcance de la neutralización de Panamá.* Panama City, 1953.

Castillero R., Ernesto J. *Historia de Panamá.* 6th ed. Panama City, 1959.

Cisneros, Andrés, and Carlos Escudé. *Historia general de las relaciones exteriores de la República Argentina*, part 2, vols. 9–10. Buenos Aires: Nuevohacer, 1999.

Clayton, Lawrence A. *Peru and the United States: The Condor and the Eagle*, Athens: University of Georgia Press, 1999.

Conniff, Michael L. *Black Labor on a White Canal: Panama, 1904–1981.* Pittsburgh, PA: University of Pittsburgh Press, 1985.

———. *Panama and the United States: The Forced Alliance.* Athens: University of Georgia Press, 1992.

Conte Porras, Jorge. *Arnulfo Arias Madrid.* Panama: J. Conte Porras, 1980.

———. *Procesos electorales y partidos políticos.* San José, Costa Rica: Litografía e Imprenta LIL, 2004.

———. *Réquiem por la revolución.* San José, Costa Rica: Litografía e Imprenta LIL, S.A., 1990.

Contreras, Ariel José. *México 1940: Industrialización y crisis política.* 7th ed. Mexico City: Siglo Veintiuno Editores, 1992.

Contreras, Carlos, and Marcos Cueto. *Historia del Peru contemporaneo: Desde las luchas por la independencia hasta el presente.* Lima: Red para el Desarollo de las Ciencias Sociales en el Peru, 1999.

Crassweller, Robert D. *Trujillo: The Life and Times of a Caribbean Dictator.* New York: MacMillan, 1966.

De La Pedraja Tomán, René. *Oil and Coffee: Latin American Merchant Shipping from the Imperial Era to the 1950s.* Westport, CT: Greenwood Press, 1998.

Dodd, Thomas J. *Tiburcio Carías: Portrait of a Honduran Political Leader.* Baton Rouge: Louisiana State University Press, 2005.

Escude, Carlos. *Gran Bretana, Estados Unidos y la declinación argentina, 1942–1949.* Buenos Aires: Belgrano, 1988.

Ewell, Judith. *Venezuela and the United States: From Monroe's Hemisphere to Petroleum's Empire.* Athens: University of Georgia Press, 1996.

Fluharty, Vernon Lee. *Dance of the Millions.* Pittsburgh, PA: University of Pittsburgh Press, 1957.

Frank, Gary. *Struggle for Hegemony: Argentina, Brazil, and the United States during the Second World War.* Coral Gables, FL: Center for Advanced International Studies, University of Miami, 1971.

Frye, Alton. *Nazi Germany and the American Hemisphere.* New Haven, CT: Yale University Press, 1967.

Gambini, Roberto. *O duplo jogo de Getúlio Vargas: Influência americana e alemã no Estado Nôvo.* São Paulo: Símbolo, 1977.

Gamboa, Carlos Calvo. *Costa Rica en la segunda guerra mundial, 1939–1945.* San José: Editorial EUNED, 1985.

Gardiner, C. Harvey. *Pawns in a Triangle of Hate: The Peruvian Japanese and the United States.* Seattle: University of Washington Press, 1981.

Goñi, Uki. *The Real Odessa: Smuggling the Nazis to Perón's Argentina.* London: Granta Books, 2002.

Grieb, Kenneth. *Guatemalan Caudillo: The Regime of Jorge Ubico.* Athens: Ohio University Press, 1979.

Hagadorn, Daniel P. *Central American and Caribbean Air Forces.* London: Air-Britain, 1993.

Hayes, Joy Elizabeth. *Radio Nation: Communication, Popular Culture, and Nationalism in Mexico, 1920–1950.* Tucson: University of Arizona Press, 2000.

Hilton, Stanley E. *Brazil and the Great Powers, 1930–1939: The Politics of Trade Rivalry.* Austin: University of Texas Press, 1975.

Hoare, Samuel. *Complacent Dictator.* New York: Alfred A. Knopf, 1947.

Ilq, Karl. *Das Deutschtum in Chile.* Vienna: Österreichische Landsmannschaft, 1982.

LaFeber, Walter. *The Panama Canal: The Crisis in Historical Perspective.* Expanded ed. New York: Oxford University Press, 1979.

Leonard, Thomas M. *Central America and the United States: The Search for Stability.* Athens: University of Georgia Press, 1991.

Leyva, Juan. *Política educativa y comunicación social: La radio en México, 1940–1946.* Mexico City: Universidad Nacional Autótoma de México, 1992.

Liss, Sheldon B. *Diplomacy and Dependency.* Salisbury, NC: Documentary Publications, 1978.

Loyola, Rafael, ed. *Entre la guerra y la estabilidad política: El México de los 40.* Mexico City: Grijalbo, 1986.

Major, John. *Prize Possession: The United States and the Panama Canal, 1903–1979.* Cambridge: Cambridge University Press, 1993.

Masterson, Daniel M. *Militarism and Politics in Latin America: Peru from Sanchez Cerro to Sendero Luminoso.* New York: Greenwood, 1991.

McCann, Frank D. *The Brazilian-American Alliance, 1937–1945.* Princeton, NJ: Princeton University Press, 1973.

Mikesh, Robert C. *Aichi M6A1 Serian: Japan's Submarine-Launched Panama Canal Bomber.* Boylston, MA: Monogram Aviation, 1975.

Moreno, Julio E. *Yankee Don't Go Home! Mexican Nationalism, American Business Culture, and the Shaping of Modern Mexico, 1920–1950.* Chapel Hill: University of North Carolina Press, 2003.

Mount, Graeme S. *Chile and the Nazis.* Montreal: Black Rose, 2001.

Moura, Gerson. *Autonomia na dependencia: A política externa brasileira de 1935 a 1942.* Rio de Janeiro: Nova Fronteira, 1980.

Newton, Ronald C. *El cuarto lado del triángulo: La "amenaza nazi" en la Argentina, 1931–1947.* Buenos Aires: Editorial Sudamericana, 1995.

———. *The "Nazi Menace" in Argentina, 1931–1947.* Stanford, CA: Stanford University Press, 1992.

Niblo, Stephen R. *Mexico in the 1940s: Modernity, Politics, and Corruption.* Wilmington, DE: SR Books, 1999.

———. *War, Diplomacy, and Development: The United States and Mexico, 1938–1954.* Wilmington, DE: SR Books, 1995.

Ogorzaly, Michael A. *Waldo Frank: Prophet of Hispanic Regeneration.* London: Associated University Presses, 1994.

Ortiz Garza, José Luis. *México en guerra.* Mexico City: Grupo Editorial Planeta, 1989.

Paguero, Valentina. *The Militarization of Culture in the Dominican Republic: From the Captains General to General Trujillo.* Gainesville: University Press of Florida, 2004.

Paz Salinas, María Emilia. *Strategy, Security, and Spies: Mexico and the U.S. as Allies in World War II.* University Park: Pennsylvania State University Press, 1997.

Pearcy, Thomas L. *We Answer Only to God: Politics and the Military in Panama, 1903–1947.* Albuquerque: University of New Mexico Press, 1998.

Pereira, Susana. *En tiempos de la república agropecuaria, 1930–1943.* Buenos Aires: Centro Editor de América Latina, 1983.

Peterson, Harold F. *Argentina and the United States.* Albany: State University of New York Press, 1964.

Pizzurno Gelós, Patricia, and Celestino Andrés Araúz. *Estudios sobre el Panamá republicano, 1903–1989.* Panama City: Manfer, 1996.

Rabe, Stephen. *The Road to OPEC: United States Relations with Venezuela, 1919–1976.* Austin: University of Texas Press, 1982.

Randall, Stephen J. *Colombia and the United States: Hegemony and Interdependence.* Athens: University of Georgia Press, 1992.

Rapoport, Mario. *Gran Bretaña, Estados Unidos y las clases dirigentes argentinas, 1940–1945.* Buenos Aires: Editorial Belgrano, 1981.

Ribes Tovar, Federico. *Historia cronológica de Puerto Rico.* Panama: Editorial Tres Amèricas, 1973.

Rock, David, ed. *Latin America in the 1940s: War and Postwar Transitions.* Berkeley: University of California Press, 1994.

Rodríguez Lamas, David. *Rawson/Ramírez/Farrell.* Buenos Aires: Centro Editor de América Latina, 1983.

Roorda, Eric Paul. *The Dictator Next Door: The Good Neighbor Policy and the Trujillo Regime in the Dominican Republic, 1930–1945.* Durham, NC: Duke University Press, 1998.

Ropp, Steve. *Panamanian Politics: From Guarded Nation to National Guard.* Stanford, CA: Hoover Institution Press, 1982.

Rout, Leslie B., and John F. Bratzel. *Shadow War: German Espionage and United States Counterespionage in Latin America during World War II.* Frederick, MD: University Publications of America, 1986.

St. John, Ronald Bruce. *The Foreign Policy of Peru.* Boulder: Lynne Rienner, 1992.

Sater, William F. *Chile and the United States.* Athens: University of Georgia Press, 1990.

Schoonover, Thomas D. *Germany in Central America: Competitive Imperialism, 1821–1929.* Tuscaloosa: University of Alabama Press, 1998.

Seitenfus, Ricardo Antônio Silva. *O Brasil de Getúlio Vargas e a formação dos blocos, 1930–1942.* São Paulo: Nacional, 1985.

Smith, Joseph. *A History of Brazil, 1500–2000.* New York: Pearson Education, 2002.

Soler, Ricaurte. *El pensamiento político en los siglos XIX y XX: Estudio introductoria y antología.* Panama City: Universidad de Panama, 1971.

Stepan, Alfred. *The Military in Politics: Changing Patterns in Brazil.* Princeton, NJ: Princeton University Press, 1971.

Tobar Donoso, Julio. *La invasion peruana y el Protocolo de Rio.* Quito: Banco Central del Ecuador, 1982.

Torres Ramirez, Blanca. *Historia de la revolución mexicana periodo 1940–1952: México en la segunda guerra mundial.* Mexico City: Colegio de México, 1979.

Tulchin, Joseph. *Argentina and the United States: A Conflicted Relationship.* Boston: Twayne, 1990.

Ureta, Eloy G. *Apuntes sobres una campana.* Madrid: Editorial Antorocha, 1953.

Vega, Bernardo. *Los Estados Unidos y Trujillo, año 1945.* Santo Domingo: Fundación Cultural Dominicana, 1982.

Wagenheim, Kal. *Puerto Rico: A Profile.* London: Pall Mall Press, 1970.

Walter, Knut. *The Regime of Anastasio Somoza, 1936–1956.* Chapel Hill: University of North Carolina Press, 1993.

Whitaker, Arthur P., ed. *Inter-American Affairs: An Annual Survey.* New York: Greenwood Press, 1969.

Wood, Bryce. *The Making of the Good Neighbor Policy.* New York : Columbia University Press, 1961.

————. *Nazismo, fascismo y falangismo en la República Dominicana*. Santo Domingo: Fundación Cultural Dominicana, 1985.

————. *Trujillo y las fuerzas armadas norteamericanas*. Santo Domingo: Fundación Cultural Dominicana, 1992.

————. *The United States and Latin America's Wars*. New York: Columbia University Press, 1966.

Woods, Randall B. *The Roosevelt Foreign-Policy Establishment and the Good Neighbor*. Lawrence: Regents Press of Kansas, 1979.

Zimbalist, Andrew, and John Weeks. *Panama at the Crossroads: Economic Development and Political Change in the Twentieth Century*. Berkeley: University of California Press, 1991.

Zook, David H., Jr. *Zarumilla-Marañón: The Ecuador–Peru Dispute*. New York: Bookman Associates, 1964.

Index

About the Contributors

John F. Bratzel is professor and graduate coordinator in the Center for Latin American and Caribbean Studies at Michigan State University. With the late Prof. Leslie B. Rout, Dr. Bratzel wrote *Shadow War: German Espionage and United States Counterespionage in Latin America during World War II*. He has also written many other articles and presented numerous papers. Currently, Bratzel is a member of the Executive Board of the Consortium for Latin American Studies Programs, is vice president and president-elect of the Popular Culture Association, and is the Latin American coordinator for the Less Commonly Taught Languages project, which facilitates offerings in numerous languages.

George M. Lauderbaugh, after earning his Ph.D. at the University of Alabama in 1997, joined the history faculty at Jacksonville State University in Alabama, where he teaches courses in Latin American, military, and United States history. His dissertation, "The United States and Ecuador: Conflict and Convergence, 1830–1946," is a case study of the diplomatic, cultural, and military dimensions of relations between the two nations. In addition to articles in the *Annals of the South Eastern Council on Latin America Studies* and *Proceedings of the Association of Third World Studies*, he has presented several papers in professional forums.

Andrew Lefebvre is a Ph.D. student at the University of Calgary specializing in relations between the United States and Latin America. His M.A. focus at Laurentian University in Sudbury, Ontario, was on relations between Spain and Puerto Rico from the outbreak of the Spanish Civil War in 1936 until the aftermath of Pearl Harbor. His varied published articles include studies on the smuggling of alcoholic beverages across the Canada-U.S. border during Prohibition and on the Puerto Rican press.

Thomas M. Leonard teaches Latin American studies at the University of North Florida, where he is distinguished professor and director of the International Studies Program. He has lectured at universities in Argentina, Bulgaria, China, Mexico, and Poland. Among his publications are *The United States and Central America: The Search for Stability* (1991), *Panama and the United States: Guide to Issues and Sources* (1993), *James K. Polk: Clear and Unquestionable Destiny* (2000), and the *Encyclopedia of U.S.–Cuban Relations* (2004). In addition three Fulbright awards, he has received grants from the National Endowment for the Humanities, U.S. Department of Education, and the Andrew Mellon and Ford foundations.

Daniel M. Masterson is professor of Latin American history at the U.S. Naval Academy, where he has taught for twenty-five years. His research specialties are modern Peru, civil–military relations, and immigration, with special reference to the Japanese diaspora in the Americas. His publications include *Militarism and Politics in Latin America: Peru from Sanchez Cerro to Sendero Luminoso* (1991) and its revised and updated Spanish edition, *Fuerza armada y sociedad en el Peru moderno* (2001), and *The Japanese in Latin America* (2004). Dr. Masterson served as a consultant to three U.S. ambassadors to Peru and is currently working on a biography of former Peruvian president Alberto Fujimori with Jorge Ortiz Sotelo.

Graeme S. Mount is professor of history at Laurentian University, Sudbury, Ontario, where he has taught since completing his Ph.D. in 1969. His books include *Presbyterian Missions to Trinidad and Puerto Rico* (1983), *An Introduction to Canadian–American Relations* (1984; 2nd ed., 1989), *Canada's Enemies: Spies and Spying in the Peaceable Kingdom* (1992), *The Caribbean Basin an International History* (1998), *Invisible and Inaudible in Washington: U.S.–Canadian Relations during the Cold War* (1999), *The Foreign Relations of Trinidad and Tobago* (2001), *Chile and the Nazis* (2002), and *The Diplomacy of War: The Case of Korea* (2003). He is currently working on a book on the presidency of Gerald R. Ford.

Jorge Ortiz Sotelo is a retired Peruvian Navy commander. Following his graduation from the Peruvian Catholic University, he undertook advanced studies in maritime and imperial British history at London University and subsequently earned his Ph.D. in maritime history from St. Andrews University, Scotland. Ortiz Sotelo took part in the peace negotiations between Peru and Ecuador and was executive director of the binational plan for the development of the border region. He is currently executive director of the Instituto Peruano de Economía y Política, general secretary of the Asociación de Historia Marítima y Naval Iberoamericana, and professor of strategy at the Peruvian Naval War Collage. He has published several books and articles on maritime and naval history, as well on international relations.

Orlando J. Pérez earned his Ph.D. in political science at the University of Pittsburgh and currently is associate professor at Central Michigan University, where he teaches courses in comparative politics, Latin American politics, and U.S.–Latin American relations. He has conducted field research in several countries of Latin America and has served as a consultant on public opinion surveys, democratization, civil–military relations, and corruption issues for the U.S. Agency for International Development and the UN Development Program. Dr. Pérez is the editor of *Post Invasion Panama: The Challenges of Democratization in the New World Order*, and he has written articles for the *Journal of Inter-American Studies and World Affairs*, *Hemisphere*, *Southeast Latin Americanist*, and *Political Science Quarterly* and has contributed numerous chapters to edited volumes.

Monica Rankin received her Ph.D. from the University of Arizona in 2004. She held a Fulbright García-Robles Fellowship for Mexico in 2001–02 and the Ramenofsky Fellowship for Doctoral Research in 2003. Her research focuses on the uses of propaganda in Mexico during World War II. She is currently a professor at Collin County Community College and a lecturer at the University of Texas at Dallas.

Eric Paul Roorda authored *The Dictator Next Door: The Good Neighbor Policy and the Trujillo Regime in the Dominican Republic, 1930–1945* (1998), which won the Herbert Hoover Book Award and the Stuart L. Bernath Book Prize of the Society for Historians of American Foreign Relations, and *Analuisa: Cuba, America and the Sea* (2005). Currently professor of history and political science at Bellarmine University, Roorda also serves as codirector of the Munson Institute of American Maritime Studies at Mystic Seaport, the Museum of America and the Sea, in Mystic, Connecticut.

David Sheinin is professor of history at Trent University in Peterborough, Ontario. His published works include *Searching for Authority: Pan Americanism, Politics, and Diplomacy in United States–Argentine Relations* (1998) and *Argentina and the United States: An Alliance Contained* (2006). His current research is focused on the nuclear sector in Argentina and Canadian–Latin American relations, among other topics.

Joseph Smith is a reader in American diplomatic history at the University of Exeter, England. He has written several books on U.S. foreign relations with Latin America, including *Unequal Giants* (1991), *The Spanish-American War* (1994), and *The United States and Latin America, 1776–2000* (2005). He has also published *A History of Brazil, 1500–2000* (2002) and has been the editor for several years of *History*, the journal of the Historical Association of Great Britain.